HAUNTED VICTORY

*Healing From Childhood Sexual Abuse
and the Decades of Addiction That Followed*

Gil Merrick

MC
PUBLISHING

MC PUBLISHING
An imprint of MC Publishing, LLC

AUTHOR'S NOTE: This is a work of nonfiction based on recollections going back to an early age. Where possible, I have corroborated my memories with journal entries, published interviews, news articles, and the historic record. Some names and identifying details have been changed to protect people's privacy.

Names: Merrick, Roderick Gilman, author.
Title: Haunted Victory: Healing From Childhood Sexual Abuse and the Decades of Addiction That Followed.
Description: First edition. | Delaware: MC Publishing
Hardcover ISBN   979-8-9902402-0-9
Paperback ISBN   979-8-9902402-1-6
eBook ISBN   979-8-9902402-2-3

Printed in the United States of America

To my parents

Contents

Prologue

I had no idea I was dying—that's how bad it had gotten.

After a lifetime career as a pathologist and ten years as my friend, Bonnie had watched my symptoms worsen over the past year. I could no longer walk unassisted—my gait was too unstable. My tremors had worsened, and I could not fill out a medical form. My short-term memory had long since been lost in a permanent brain fog. She intervened and sought help when she could see I was in trouble.

I was admitted for in-patient evaluation and treatment at the University of California San Diego's emergency care center in La Jolla. After four days, I was released and referred to a neurologist, orthopedic surgeon, psychiatrist, and hepatologist.

The first visit was to my hepatologist. After reviewing the lab results, he turned from his screen, looked me in the eye, and said, "Mr. Merrick, how much alcohol do you consume?"

I had been asked this question many times and I had my answer ready: "I've consumed alcohol every day for the past forty years. I always have a cocktail, or two, before dinner, and I usually have a glass, or two, of wine with dinner," I said, feeling proud I had not concealed my lifelong drinking habits.

"Your labs say otherwise. We have evaluated your blood alcohol levels. A number between 150 and 221 is suggestive of chronic and excessive alcohol consumption. Your number, Mr. Merrick, is 1261. You are an alcoholic, and if you don't stop drinking immediately, you will die." My mind went blank with the shock of his pronouncement, and it took a moment before I could focus on what came next.

"You have advanced cirrhosis, and your liver can no longer function properly. If you do not stop drinking, you will need a liver transplant. An organ is not made available to a patient until they have been sober for six months. Waiting periods can be up to a year after you go on the list, so you most likely would not receive a new liver in time to save you."

I was an alcoholic facing imminent death at sixty-three.

After the appointment, Bonnie dropped me off at my home in Carlsbad—the environment that had brought me to my final battle with drinking. The caregiver taking the next eight-hour shift was arriving to relieve her colleague. She was not there for me.

I had been living for the past eighteen months in the house belonging to my eighty-six-year-old friend Jane. Jane's husband of sixty years had passed away seven years previously and since then I had become her closest friend. After moving into her home, I had also become her full-time companion and oversaw her health care. She had lived a robust and healthy life and never had to deal with her own medical issues, but in the past year, Jane had suffered several falls, each more serious than the one before. Most recently, she had fallen in her living room and shattered the bones in her left shoulder. She had been bedridden and required around-the-clock care that I was not able, or willing, to provide; that's what all of Jane's money was for, I reasoned. Jane was extremely wealthy.

I went into Jane's darkened bedroom and let her know I had returned from the doctor. Although not heavily sedated, Jane was suffering from dementia and would not have been able to understand my diagnosis. I kissed her on the forehead and left the room as she faded in and out of consciousness—the pain of her broken bones torturing her frail body.

As I lay in bed that night, I panicked at the thought that I would never have another drink—ever. My fear intensified with every shriek and cry coming from Jane's bedroom as the caregiver tried to adjust Jane's position in bed. The screams continued for what seemed like an eternity—each one confirming I would have to deal with both of our situations without the help of alcohol. Jane's life was coming to an end, and my own was at risk.

One question ran through my head on an endless loop: *How did I get here, and where am I headed?* I was determined to survive and emerge victorious from the dungeon my home had become, but the challenges that lay ahead seemed insurmountable. It was my mission to prove they weren't.

Part 1

ENTER

Horses, an Olympic dream, and a pedophile

1
White Suburbia

By all appearances, the first twelve years of my life unfolded as one happy adventure after another. Truth be told, I seldom felt special, noticed, or celebrated. I was born an effeminate boy in a world that esteems masculinity. Bullied at home and school, I paid the price such boys often pay.

I grew up in the east suburbs of Cleveland and from the age of ten, my family lived in Shaker Heights. It was an idyllic environment where each house had a stay-at-home mother cheerfully preparing the evening meal while awaiting her husband—a businessman in a suit and tie, briefcase in hand. Just like June and Ward from *Leave It to Beaver*.

We had moved to Shaker Heights in 1968 so my father could be close to his office at Merrill Lynch in downtown Cleveland. At the end of each day, he would catch the yellow light rail train and relax on his ride to the Lee Road stop at the end of our street. From there, he would walk ten minutes to our three-story home on Chalfant Road. After sitting for a half-hour with my mother as she enjoyed a cocktail, he would join the family for a homemade dinner, spend a quiet evening in front of the TV, and get a sound night's sleep on a peaceful night in suburbia— white suburbia.

In the 1960s and 70s, Shaker Heights was a segregated city, designed that way. We fit well into the suburbs where most people were cut from the same cloth. It was a place where families belonged to the same country clubs, the kids went to the same private schools, and the fathers had often gone to the same Ivy League universities.

In my part of that world, everyone also drank. Family gatherings, or time spent with my parents' friends, were a great time for the kids to run off and amuse themselves while the adults enjoyed a cocktail hour that started when people arrived and didn't end until they left. No matter the occasion, there was always cocktail hour. By the age of fourteen, I had demonstrated my skills as a mixologist and bartended at most of these family events—a normal part of being a kid in my family.

I spent a lot of time on my own, and one afternoon, while indulging my early fascination for books, I was rummaging through the shelves in our den. As I leafed through one with the title *The Cleveland Blue Book*, I noticed the names and addresses of all the Merrick families living in Cleveland, as well as those of many of my parents' friends. I asked my mother why we had this small blue address book when everyone already had the *White Pages*—a book listing many more people in Cleveland than only the ones we knew.

My mother told me it was a social register, and at the age of eleven, I didn't understand what that meant. She explained it was a listing of "refined" families who preferred to socialize with others of the same "class." People like our housekeeper, or even many of our neighbors, would not be in *that* book; that's what the *White Pages* was for.

Without further explanation, I identified with a family that enjoyed all the privileges of being part of a White, Anglo-Saxon, Protestant community—middle-class WASPs in America's Midwest—unaware that any other version existed.

2

Discovering Equus

The real magic in my life appeared when I was eight.

July was always the highlight of my summers. My father would clear his work calendar for two weeks and we would drive to Sandbridge, Virginia to visit his sister and her husband. They lived year-round in a home they built on the Atlantic shore with only sand separating the cinder block building from the ocean. The house known as "The Pink Elephant" was Pepto Bismol pink.

The annual trip was a highlight for me; my older sister, Debbie; and my younger brother, Doug. The setting was a child's paradise. We stayed in a house that could accommodate fourteen overnight guests. We joined our many relatives from Norfolk and Virginia Beach and spent most evenings at the large dining table for family-style meals. Dinner always included local seafood, and the family favorite was the blue crabs the children caught before dinner. A group of us would head out—armed with our lengths of string and chicken necks—and lure in the little crustaceans from the inland ponds, scoop them up in our nets, and plunk them into our plastic buckets. We came home as proud hunters, toting dozens of sweet and tender, ready-to-boil crabs.

Sandbridge was also the setting for the most poignant experience of my childhood. At eight, I encountered my first horse. This life-changing event sparked a flame that fueled all my future dreams.

Two of my cousins kept a horse named Mrs. Ed at a nearby riding center. They invited me to come along one morning while they had riding lessons. They rode inside a fenced-in sand ring, after which the instructor asked if I would like to sit on a horse and go for a ride.

Every nerve in my body tingled as I walked toward the steed she had selected for me: Mr. Buttons—a tall, dark grey appaloosa. Only moments prior I had been admiring the horses from afar, not even daring to dream I might be invited to ride one. I stopped beside him and, as I awaited instructions, Mr. Buttons lowered his head about six inches, turning it slightly to the left to give me a good once-over, and our eyes met. In the blink of an eye, I felt a profound spiritual connection to him; it was as if our souls reached out and touched. The power of that connection was euphoric, and it revisits me every time I look a horse in the eye. It is the most spiritual and moving experience I know.

Being my first ride on a horse, the instructor had me bend my left knee while she grabbed my shin and boosted me onto the saddle. As Mr. Buttons strode off, I was transfixed by the sensation of his motion and the quiet power emanating from his body. It was a sensation I hoped would not end.

Those ten minutes inspired everything that transpired in my life over the next fifty years. When I dismounted, the instructor turned to my cousins and said, "Look at that—he's a natural!" I instantly knew I wanted to be around horses every day for the rest of my life.

All my senses had come alive. The heat radiating from the sand arena. The sound of hoofbeats. The sweet aromas of leather and sweat. The sight of those beautiful horses moving around the ring. But the sensation that grabbed hold and would never let go, was the feel of a horse's velvety nostril on my eight-year-old fingertip when I stroked Mr. Button's nose to say goodbye.

For the next three years, my interaction with horses was limited to when my father took me for rides through the Cleveland Metroparks. My father had spent his teenage years competing at horse shows and playing polo, so he knew horses well. He rode occasionally as an adult when we visited his friend with several horses stabled near the parks. We only went once a year and it always left me aching for more.

But fortunately, more was to come after I turned eleven. Red Raider was a camp thirty minutes east of Shaker Heights that offered a year-round riding program. Primarily a summer day camp, with horseback riding as one of its many activities, it stabled over seventy horses. When summers ended and the day campers went back to school, all those horses needed a job for the ensuing nine months. So, the camp sent an old yellow school bus into the suburbs to pick up kids after school and drive them out for riding lessons. They offered the same service on weekends.

Two of my cousins took riding lessons at Red Raider and I tagged along twice on a Saturday morning to watch. I wanted nothing more than to join them.

Our family spent weekends skiing at beautiful resorts in western New York, and we took long vacations at every school break. When I asked my parents if I could have riding lessons, they replied that as a family we were already engaged in a host of expensive activities, and they saw no need for me to take on another. Although we were well off, excessive drinking and some poor business decisions had bankrupted the family printing company. The privileges of being the owner's son had vanished, so my father was building a clientele in his new job as a stockbroker at Merrill Lynch.

After months of pleading with my parents to let me sign up for a ten-session program, I finally got them to concede, under the condition I paid half of the $40 fee. Mowing lawns and getting out of bed before sunrise to deliver newspapers provided the riches I needed to pay my $20, and at eleven, I began a lifetime of working to support my passion for horses.

These idyllic experiences encouraged me to look at the world with wide-eyed optimism and believe everything should always be wonderful and exciting.

3

I Am a Sissy

At the end of sixth grade, my idyllic life came to an abrupt halt when I went from Fernway Elementary School to Woodbury Junior High. Up to that point, a privileged and segregated suburban world was the only one I knew, but as I changed schools, I learned there was a different world awaiting me.

On the first day of attending my new school, I was confronted with a cavernous labyrinth of hallways where a new student could get lost. The noise and commotion coming from the large groups collected in the hallways—chattering and shouting as they waited for the morning bell to ring—was overwhelming and frightening. I had never seen so many people in one place who didn't look like me.

Woodbury was a fully integrated school. Bussing laws throughout the country were being hotly debated by both local and national politicians, but in 1970 all children in Shaker Heights over the age of twelve—as well as some from select areas of Cleveland's inner city—were offered equal educational opportunities and many were bussed in. Attending junior high meant I would experience what "real life" looked like, and for the first time, I would feel less special than my mother had led me to believe our family was.

Throughout elementary school and into my junior high years, I was always the smallest boy in the class. I was skinny and my face was effeminate. Built like those stick people we drew fingers on in math class when we learned how to count, I was told that I was "cute." With mousy-brown hair and a military-style buzz cut, bright-blue eyes framed in pinkish-white skin that exploded with freckles, I probably was cute. But I wanted to be "handsome." Puppies and monkeys were cute. The term seemed to connote something soft, diminutive, and somewhat comical—certainly not strength and masculinity. If the ideal was "tall, dark and handsome," I was "short, pale and cute."

During elementary school I had earned the nicknames Freckled-Face Strawberry (after a 1960s animated character who promoted a powdered drink mix like Kool-Aid) and Blinky, thanks to a nervous condition I had developed where my eyes blinked incessantly, over which I had no control. My petite build and waif-like appearance evoked relentless teasing, especially when it came to sports.

At eleven, my father insisted that I play for a Little League baseball team. I spent the summer far out in right field, praying no balls would come my way and prove my twig-like arms couldn't throw a ball any meaningful distance. I waited for my turn to step up to the plate, strike out, and hear the moaning and jeering of my teammates. I took all their teasing to heart and decided there was something wrong with me.

I became a "sissy" in the eyes of my classmates and, often, even in the eyes of my family. Debbie was three years older than I—at the age where picking on her younger brothers was a source of delight—and she delighted in calling me a sissy. Debbie's aggression included physical assaults; she knew how to throw a punch and fight dirty. Debbie could become angry at the slightest provocation from me—something as simple as calling her a name—and lash out with a punch to my gut that would knock the wind out of me and land me crumpled on the ground gasping for breath. My cries often went unheeded by our mother, who was nearby but uninterested in disturbing her own peace; she usually let us fight it out. I always lost and the matches ended in tears.

Debbie and I fought often. When my mother *did* intervene, it was to yell at us both and send us to our rooms, often with a swat of her hand on our backs or buttocks and orders to stay there until we were told to come out.

Debbie's taunts could be vicious. "Ooh, see what you did, you little sissy? How would you like it if I smacked your face so hard, I made you bleed? Or will you call for Mommy like a wimp?" A slug to the torso, or a kick to the leg, would follow and I would spend the rest of our "time out" crying in my room. I remember shoes being thrown at my head, doors being slammed in my face, and on numerous occasions being wrestled to the ground and sat upon. Out of anger and frustration, I would shout: "I wish you were dead!" When I told my mother I wished Debbie would disappear, she never reacted to my "childish" outbursts; she simply replied, "Just leave Debbie alone."

But even my mother, should she see me hesitate to take on a task requiring either a bit of courage or physical strength, would call me a sissy or weakling. The skinniest boy I had ever seen was a member of my Little League team named Mikey. If I didn't want to finish a meal, my mother would tease, "OK, Mikey.

Stay skinny then." Hearing the terms "skinny" and "sissy" from my classmates and my family had me questioning my masculinity. They sounded derogatory, and with every taunt, my belief deepened that something was wrong with me. I didn't fit in.

4

School Nightmares

While passing through the hallways or eating lunch in the cafeteria at Woodbury Junior High, I would hear the angry chants of students, laced with racial slurs, circled around two boys—or two girls—thrashing on the ground, punching and scratching, slapping faces and pulling hair. I was terrified this violence would be directed at me—a weak and vulnerable target, easy to intimidate and overpower. I had heard stories about a student being knifed in the parking lot and about another student being shot in the hall at the high school next door.

I needed a best friend and found him in Dave. Walking home from school one day, I asked about some names we were being called. I was pretty sure I knew what a "honky" was—I heard the term all the time—but I wondered if Dave knew what a "cracker ass" was. He wasn't certain, but he suspected it was some kind of slur for white kids, especially since it had a bad word in it. When I got home, I asked my mother. Her answer was: "Oh, it's another word for a white person." Those words somehow did not seem intimidating; it was the loud voices and physical violence that frightened me.

Fortunately, Dave helped me survive our new environment. He was taller than I and had a normal build for a boy our age. With handsome features, a quick sense of humor, and a confident demeanor, Dave could make the "cool" girls want to hang out with him. Trying to mimic his techniques, I set out to befriend the coolest Black girls in my classes. The combination of "cute" and "funny" served its purpose and soon those girls would walk with me through the halls, giggling and laughing, while enjoying the company of their adorable little white friend—a mascot of sorts. Because the Black boys were interested in catching these girls' attention, they left me alone while they flirted. Those girls became my protectors.

But the strategy was of no use in gym class, which had become its own special nightmare. In the fall, we went for cross country runs around the campus and I soon got used to coming back as one of the last in the group. We also played football, and for all the strength and prowess I brought to the game, I might as well have been the football. Winter included two of the ultimate horrors. The first was basketball, where I was inevitably last to be picked for a team, and my team was almost always the "Skins" in a game of "Skins vs. Shirts." Without a shirt, I looked like a walking skeleton, and I couldn't shoot a hoop to save my life. The other, even more debilitating horror was wrestling. Being thrown around on a mat like a rag doll by a boy who always outweighed me, proved humiliating—and it hurt. Pinned quickly, I could at least escape the court-side laughter and teasing.

After gym class, I faced what became a bigger and more disturbing emotional challenge: the locker room and showers. I was required to remove all my clothes in front of a group of boys and then march into a shower room—a large open area with a handful of shower heads mounted on the wall. There was no escape from the vulnerability of being naked and the inevitable contest that ensued as the boys compared their physiques and degrees of sexual development; the skinniest boys were always the target of the meanest taunts.

Actions by some of the physical education instructors also disturbed me. In one gym class, the instructor made all the boys stand shoulder to shoulder in a line-up so he could take attendance. He would walk to one end of the line, stand in front of the first boy, and ask: "Name?" Checking it off the list on his clipboard, next came: "Jock?"

Our uniform was a pair of navy-blue shorts and a white T-shirt. We were all required to wear a jock strap, and at his command, each boy would pull up the leg of his shorts, reach underneath, and pull down the strap running from the bottom of the cup and around the buttocks to the waistband. Once ensured the boy was in fact wearing a jock, the instructor moved on to the next boy and repeated the drill. As he made his way down the line, I noticed the bulge in his snug, grey sweatpants protruding more with each exposure of a boy's buttocks and jock strap. Dave, who was not in the same classes as I, had noticed the same thing.

A similar experience played out in the swimming pool. I found it odd that our instructor would have all the boys jump into the water and line up along the edge so he could take attendance. With the boys looking up from their place in the water, he would walk along the edge of the pool as he worked his way down the line, stopping in front of each boy, who had to look directly up the leg of his shorts to make eye contact. Dave was in a different class and also noticed the instructor did not wear any undergarment, so all we could see, with our upward gaze, was his naked manhood.

After swim class we joined the boys who had been in the gym and went to the shower room. Once finished showering, we exited through a small hallway leading past a bank of shelves stacked with fresh towels. We were old enough to grab our own towels, but the instructor found it necessary to sit on one of the deep shelves with a stack of folded towels on his lap. Each boy would walk up to receive a towel. The more physically mature boys with athletic builds were always required to stand for a minute and engage in conversation; lesser-endowed boys were silently handed a towel.

Dave and I were only twelve years old, but our instincts told us these instructors seemed to enjoy looking at naked boys with a little too much enthusiasm. Although the term "grooming" had not been coined, this was grooming. Two straight-acting men enjoying their own sexual perversions in a manner that made it seem like normal behavior to young boys. We never brought it up with our parents and assumed because it was our teachers—the responsible adults in charge of our education—nothing untoward was going on.

The locker room and shower experiences, combined with the humiliation of gym class, caused me to spend my nights dreading the thought of the next gym class. I was desperately searching for a way to escape. At the beginning of eighth grade, at fourteen, I found my escape.

One night at around 3 a.m. my left knee began to ache, and the pain increased throughout the night. After lying awake for hours, I went downstairs to tell my mother I didn't think I could go to school. As was typical in our house, no excuse was ever good enough, so I hobbled off. By mid-morning the pain became unbearable, and my knee had swollen to the size of a cantaloupe.

The school nurse saw there was a serious problem and phoned my mother, who took me to the emergency room at St. Luke's hospital, ten minutes from the school. I was admitted to the children's ward, where the doctors drained over 600 ml of fluid from my knee over the next twenty-four hours. They treated the swelling and pain aggressively with aspirin. After four days of observation, I learned I had a form of rheumatoid arthritis that had selectively attacked my knee. I was discharged with crutches, told to continue taking six aspirin, four times a day, and advised to give up any hopes of ever skiing or riding a horse again. I was also told I would be exempt from gym class for the rest of my school years: that part of my nightmare had come to an end.

5
My Parents

As tough as things were at school, things at home were no longer as carefree as an episode of *Leave It to Beaver*. My parents were not like June and Ward Cleaver.

My father was just shy of six feet with a lean build and a full head of medium-brown hair, neatly parted on the side. He dressed in conservative Brooks Brothers suits for the office, and in a more casual style for the country club or evenings out—a cross between Armani and Ralph Lauren. He was kind, always in a good mood, never argued with anyone or raised his voice, and had a fantastic sense of humor. If there was a mean bone in his body, I never saw it.

Growing up in a wealthy family, my father attended University School in Shaker Heights—a private all-boys preparatory school. He loved history and declared it as his major when he began Princeton University in the fall of 1943. The following year he was called to service in World War II, reporting to Fort Dix, New Jersey for his training as a surgical technician. Dispatched to West Germany, he treated critically wounded soldiers—many of them his buddies—returning from the front lines. The nurses, doctors, and medics worked long and exhausting hours caring for those men and witnessed some of the most horrific scenes of pain, suffering, and death imaginable.

In 1945, when he and the rest of the drafted veterans returned from Europe and Asia, PTSD (Post Traumatic Stress Disorder) was not recognized or treated. So, my father, like many others returning from war, reverted to self-medication.

My father's drug of choice was alcohol, and he battled alcoholism until 1966 when I turned nine. He received support from the Alcoholics Anonymous community and achieved sobriety for the rest of his life.

When I was fourteen, my father invited me to an AA meeting to hear his lead. This was when many pieces of our family puzzle came together for me. Before my brother was born, my sister and I always went to bed before 9 p.m. I hadn't noticed that with some exceptions on the weekends, my father was never home at night. During his talk, I learned he had gone to the same bar at Shaker Square every afternoon after work to drink with his buddies while our mother stayed home with us. This had always been after a day spent running the family company, when two-martini lunches were a ritual.

I also figured out what had been going on when my dad would take me on a Saturday afternoon to get a haircut. Our barber had a salon on the top floor of a shopping center, and after he buzzed my hair, we would go downstairs to a windowless upscale restaurant and bar called The Lion and Lamb, another of my father's favorite watering holes. The bartender would welcome my father by name and automatically pour his first drink. "So, Rod—what will the young man have, a Roy Roger?" The answer was always *yes,* and I would leap off my barstool and head to the end of the bar to steal maraschino cherries from an open jar. It was all a lot of fun and a special time for us to be together.

Given his regular absence, I stayed at home with my emotionally unavailable mother. Standing five-foot-five with perfect posture and a trim figure, my mother was always neatly put together, dressed in wrap-around plaid skirts and button-down cashmere sweaters. Her dark-brown hair was highlighted with streaks of blonde—back then they called it "frosted." Every outfit was accessorized with a conservative pin, necklace, or bracelet, and white or gold clip-on earrings. But behind this well-crafted appearance and consistently cheerful façade lay a deep depression she could never conquer.

My mother spent much of her time sleeping. She got up later in the mornings than the rest of us and often, while she slept, I would make my father breakfast. Her routine included an afternoon nap on the living room sofa, listening to soap operas on TV that served as white noise to help lull her off to sleep and offer some relief from whatever demons were tormenting her.

Most of what needed to get done around the house got done, but my mother's energy level was low, and she got through each day expending minimal effort. Any suggestion we made to do something outside of our normal routine was rejected. I told my friends that my mother was a *no* waiting to happen.

Many times, I would come home before dinner to find Mother on the couch, sipping her bourbon and water, and drawing on a cigarette while she waited for my father, sobbing quietly. I knew something was wrong, but I didn't know what. All I knew for sure was that I rarely looked forward to coming home.

6
Friends at Camp

I found a few bright spots through the clouds surrounding junior high. In the eighth grade, I learned I had an aptitude for mathematics and numbers. I excelled at algebra, and although most kids in those classes dreaded word problems, I loved them.

English class was as enjoyable as mathematics: learning correct grammar, writing essays and short stories, or even writing book reports. It all kept me engaged and excited. I was keen to study foreign languages and discovered a natural talent for them. I started speaking French in fourth grade. That set me on the path to becoming proficient in Spanish during my high school years, and fluent in German by the time I finished college. Little did I know that my flair for languages and my aptitude for numbers would play a significant role in my adult life and, ultimately, lead me down the path toward fulfilling my biggest dreams.

I excelled in other areas. Summer trips to the beach, swimming at The Mayfield Country Club where we were members, and having a pool at home, turned me into a strong swimmer. And having skied since the age of eight, I had also become an expert skier. Regardless of what kids at school might have thought, I knew I was an athlete. My classmates weren't there to witness my prowess and give me the respect they showed to the athletes at school. In their eyes, I was still a sissy.

But the sport where I excelled the most—and which they also didn't see— was riding horses. Although the kids at school taunted me for being unathletic, riding spirited, 1200-pound horses is challenging and dangerous. If my first ride on Mr. Buttons was the springboard that launched me into the life of an equestrian, it was the experiences at my riding camp, Red Raider, that gave me everything I needed to be fearless on and around them.

Because the camp sent buses into the suburbs to pick kids up from their schools and homes, I could take riding lessons during the spring and fall sessions.

My mother wouldn't give me a ride to school in inclement weather, let alone drive out to the country, wait two hours while I took my lessons, and drive another hour home, so for me the buses were invaluable.

Each day included a one-hour lesson on horseback in a ring with up to ten riders, followed by an hour in the stables learning the skills we needed on the ground: grooming and bathing horses, putting on and taking off saddles and bridles, cleaning riding gear, and administering basic veterinary care for the occasional cut or sore. In a classroom setting, we learned about the anatomy of the horse and how its digestive system works, lameness issues we might encounter, and the fundamental principles of correct riding. Passionate, dedicated, and hard-working teachers provided all-encompassing education in horsemanship. The four years spent at Red Raider were an escape from junior high and opened the door to three friendships that would last for many years.

Lori lived four blocks from my house, making it easy to spend time together when we weren't at camp. Lori was a tomboy with a rough-and-tumble demeanor that suited her big frame. Her chestnut hair was always in two long braids, and her uniform was untucked plaid shirts, denim pants, and Dr. Scholl's wood-soled sandals. She had a quick wit, was gregarious, and always lit up a room.

My other friend, Heather, grew up in Cleveland Heights, a bit north of Shaker Heights and equally affluent. Within our circle of friends, Heather stood out as the most focused, driven, and competitive. She was also the brightest. She brought a laser focus to everything she did, and when she set out to accomplish something, she did it; these proved to be character traits that would inspire me for decades to come.

7

My Special Friend

My third and closest friend was Mark. Mark's father was the camp's Property Manager and they lived in a small home on Red Raider's property. Thanks to his father's job, Mark was always there.

We couldn't have been more different if we tried. Mark's family was from the small rural town of Jackson, Ohio. It was about an hour's drive from West Virginia, where most of its residents worked in nearby factories or had minimum-wage jobs at local hospitality and leisure businesses. They moved to Red Raider before Mark started junior high. The joke among the kids at Red Raider was that being a "country" kid, he must have started chopping wood and lifting cows when he was four years old.

We were the same height, but Mark had an unusually muscular build for a boy our age. His biceps were well defined, even when his arms hung loosely at his sides, and the rest of his musculature was like that of a well-trained athlete. But he had never been to a gym or lifted weights; it seemed like he had been born into his physique. He was strong as an ox and limber, so he easily made his way onto the junior high wrestling team and pinned every kid in his ninety-five-pound weight class. He not only had the strength to excel at the sport, but he also had the aggression that helped fuel his wins.

I often found myself on the receiving end of that aggression. When I annoyed him, I would end up pinned to the ground, looking up at a clenched fist and his bulging bicep, cocked and ready to pound a blow to my freckled face. Fortunately, we were great friends and it always turned out to be only bluster. But he made it clear who the dominant male was. I couldn't have cared less. Spending time with Mark was a way to hang out with a "buddy" who made me feel like an equal and put to rest the doubts I had about being a real "guy." The kids at school could be especially cruel, and I took to heart their taunts of "sissy," "wimp," and "faggot." Being with Mark allowed me to assert my maleness while enjoying our adventures at camp.

It became customary for me to spend the night at Mark's house on Fridays and Saturdays. It made me feel special to wave goodbye to the other kids as they left on the bus for the suburbs while I had the privilege of staying overnight at camp and going on adventures with Mark—like gigging frogs at night.

Equipped with a burlap bag, two flashlights, a hunting knife, and what looked like one of Neptune's spears, we would set off for the fishing hole next to a large marsh. As we made our way toward the water, the only light came from the moon. There would be a thin mist hanging above the water, covering the cottontails and tamping down the pungent scent coming from the aptly named skunk cabbage. With a nonstop chorus of cicadas and the high-pitched chirping of tree frogs, the night was alive with sounds, including the deep-bass belching of the unsuspecting bullfrogs. Slinking through the marsh in the black of night, my job was to swing the beam of the flashlight left and right until a bullfrog's eyeballs reflected and announced its presence. Then, with the stealth of a serial killer, Mark would plunge his spear straight through the neck of the victim, causing it to emit a final, loud croak. After putting his booted foot on top of the frog's back, Mark would extract the gig and instruct me to pick up the not-quite-dead body and drop it into the burlap sack. I was a real "guy," and I loved that I could share it with my very masculine guy friend, Mark.

But even better than that was when we slipped out of the house after dinner and snuck up to the stables. We would quietly remove two bridles from the tack room and lead our favorite horses out the back door, where we couldn't be seen. Mark's horse was Smoke, a dappled-grey gelding barely bigger than a pony, and mine was Itty Bitty, a pinto gelding about the same size. Once outside, we traded their halters for bridles, grabbed hold of their manes, swung our legs over their backs, and slinked into the woods. Once out of earshot, we would quicken the pace and end up in large open pastures where we could gallop under the moonlit sky to our hearts' content. The rides themselves were thrilling, but knowing that no other kids had this unique opportunity made it even more special.

Mark and I enjoyed another activity that became special. At thirteen, a boy's hormones are coursing through his veins and his lower region experiences pleasurable sensations that seem to set things on a course of their own. With enough physical stimulation, things can quickly get exciting and erupt into a climax. Mark and I invented games to play to induce those climactic experiences. When alone in the woods or sleeping in the same bed in his small room upstairs, we would show our creative talents, and sometimes, we would practice our techniques on the other's mid-section. To us, it was just another game, and questions about our sexual orientation never came up.

Being at Red Raider with my friends meant everything to me. It became the center of my universe and my sanctuary. But things were about to change.

8
Disconnecting

Red Raider was my escape from the school bullies, Debbie's taunts, and the hushed home my mother insisted upon. I didn't understand my mother's need for peace and quiet, but by the age of fourteen, I was glad to get away from it all.

Late on a Sunday afternoon in early autumn, having spent the weekend at Red Raider, I returned home to the usual subdued atmosphere and the stench of cigarettes from a haze of smoke hovering beneath the living room ceiling. It always depressed me after a weekend at my special place with my friends. But that weekend's events had been far too exhilarating for my excitement to be squashed, so I bounded into the living room and sat on the cushioned radiator under the bay window next to the TV.

I looked across the small living room at my parents and launched into an excited and detailed telling of every event from my magical weekend. After ten minutes of my play-by-play, my mother had had all she could take. Her depression had become debilitating and what she craved most was tranquility as she sipped her evening cocktail and smoked her Chesterfield Kings. She interrupted me mid-sentence and shouted, "Enough already! Please stop with all the talk about that damned Red Raider!"

It hit me as if someone had slugged me in the chest. The five seconds it took for my mother to say those thirteen words devastated me. I felt as if she had pulled out the plug and sucked all the energy out of my soul. She had attacked everything in my life that made me happy. I never talked at home about the bullying at school and my fear of being hurt there, but I thought my parents might have enjoyed hearing about my adventures at camp—the place that made me feel like I belonged. The place where I thrived. My father said nothing.

I shut off the spigot of excited chatter, sulked out of the room, and crept upstairs to my bedroom, deflated. I sat on my bed for over an hour, staring out the window at nothing, and between small fits of crying, tried to revive the happy memories from the weekend.

The depression I experienced that Sunday afternoon resulted from years of feeling inadequate. My belief in my parents' indifference had been confirmed. That evening I decided that going forward, I would keep my excitement to myself and treat my life at Red Raider as a private experience. I disconnected from my family, determined to pursue my passion for horses on my own, without their support. Support I rarely felt I received.

In many of my friends' homes, every achievement seemed to be celebrated by their parents: a piece of artwork brought from school, scoring a point on a winning team, being picked for a role in a school play, or bringing home an "A" on a report card. Doing well was expected of us, and not a cause for recognition. Presenting a report card with grades other than an "A" brought about a discussion with my mother. To her, a "B" meant we just didn't try hard enough, and a "C" brought admonition about what was wrong.

After the outburst about Red Raider, my father sat the three of us down and explained the reason our mother seemed so sad and cried so often: she was sick and needed to go for treatment for her depression at the Hannah Pavilion, the center for psychiatric treatment located within University Hospitals in Cleveland. Electroconvulsive Therapy (ECT), often referred to as "shock treatments," was an accepted form of therapy for severe cases of depression. The procedure sends electric pulses to the brain to induce brief seizures lasting between thirty seconds and two minutes. I don't know how many treatments my mother received during her two weeks there, but when she returned home, she was not the same person we had said goodbye to when she had left for the hospital.

Most significantly impacted was her speech. She slurred her words as if she had suffered a stroke. Only after a few months could we understand what she was saying. It was frustrating for her and frightening for us. Her neurologist suggested her speech might improve with time. It never did. Almost no one outside of the family could understand her well.

When she came home, I was in the throes of dealing with my own traumas at school. Eighth grade had begun. By October, the fear, depression, and anxiety resulted in my own admission to the hospital to treat the arthritic flare-up in my knee.

My mother came to visit me every morning for about an hour, but she trusted I was getting appropriate care from the staff and left me in their charge. She was no doubt anxious to get back to the tranquility at home and shut down with an afternoon nap in front of the TV. I felt alone and abandoned.

After being discharged from the hospital, I spent the next weeks zipping around on crutches. Numb from all the aspirin and feeling no pain, I turned walking on crutches into a sport and amazed everyone with my speed and agility. By the end of the year, I decided to ignore my doctor's advice and continue with riding lessons.

I resumed normal activities but could still feel myself slipping deeper into a depression. Maybe it was knowing the weekends would end and the bus would transport me home—a place that had become more solemn on the heels of my mother's hospitalization. I was living in two worlds: one filled with happiness from being with horses and friends, and another where sadness permeated the air. Home was supposed to be a safe haven where I could recuperate after a day at school. Instead, I had to deal with my mother's sadness and my sister's aggressions while bracing myself for the next foray into the halls of Woodbury Junior High. Home was not my happy place.

9

The Pedagogue

In December of 1971, I thought my savior had arrived to make all things right in my world. Billie and Fox Smith, the founders and owners of Red Raider Camp, started every Saturday with morning announcements. About sixty sets of eyes and ears focused on them, intent on hearing every word that would set us up for the events of the weekend. They could have told us there was oxygen in the air and we would have been thrilled at the news.

But one day they announced something special. They introduced us to the new Director of Riding: Joe Brooks. He and his wife, Becky, had moved into a small house alongside a pasture behind the barns. Joe would oversee the riding programs for Beginner, Intermediate, and Semi-Advanced riders. Since I was at the intermediate level, I would take lessons with Joe. Becky was his assistant.

Joe brought with him a host of new training techniques that were unfamiliar to most riders in Ohio. This made him somewhat of an oracle. He knew how to train horses to perform at a level we had read about but had never seen.

Joe was also a graduate of a highly acclaimed Horsemaster course, where he had earned an accreditation qualifying him to present its stable management and riding curriculum in a lecture series at Red Raider. To us, he was one of a kind and a gift from heaven.

Over the course of the winter, while delivering his lectures to an audience that hung on his every word, Joe instilled in us the belief that if we followed his teaching, we each had the potential to become a superior horseman. He offered to be our "pedagogue"—our riding schoolmaster—and we accepted. I was determined to become Joe's top student. In my mind, Joe was the master, and I was the apprentice.

Joe was twenty-eight years old; I was fourteen. Standing about six feet tall with a lanky build, he had already developed a bit of a slouch. He had reddish-brown hair in the advanced stages of thinning; a shaggy beard and mustache that matched his hair; beady eyes set deeply behind his black-framed glasses; potted scar marks on his face left over from some serious teenage acne; crooked, discolored teeth; and a weak chin. He was an ugly man.

Becky was two years younger than Joe. She had thin red hair, always worn in two long braids, and a build that fluctuated between somewhat overweight and very heavy. Becky had a no-nonsense and often fiery demeanor. After years of working in stables, she was as strong as any man her size, and no one who knew her would risk provoking an outburst of her temper by igniting the short fuse attached to it. But to have access to Joe, we had to go through Becky, and getting on her good side was no easy task. She seemed jealous of the attention he gave all his students—clearly enjoying his time with them.

Although never a talented rider, Becky was a first-rate horsewoman and knew every aspect of horse and stable management inside and out. She commanded her barns like a military drill sergeant and did a fantastic job. Everyone respected her for it, but she didn't make herself loved.

Becky and Joe introduced us to horse activities none of us had experienced before. One of those was a riding discipline called "dressage." A French term meaning "to train"—and pronounced *dress-saj*—it is a form of riding performed in exhibitions and competitions. Dressage is competed at all levels, from beginner classes in local regions to High Performance events throughout the world. The highest level is called the Grand Prix. It has been part of the Olympic Games since 1912, and as well as being a sport, it is also an art—sometimes pursued solely for its mastery.

Joe lent me a book by one of the great riding masters of the 19th century: Gustav Steinbrecht. He was born in 1808 in Prussia and lived most of his life in Berlin. He died in 1885 but his book, *The Gymnasium of the Horse*, was published a year later by one of his students. Joe had lent me his copy and I came upon a passage that served as my primary source of inspiration:

> *Of all the fine arts, the equestrian art should be the most attractive to a young man. The art requires character traits that are not combined in everyone: inexhaustible patience, firm perseverance under stress, [and] courage paired with quiet alertness. Only a true, deep love for the horse can develop these character traits ... [if] he believes he is able to master it.*

That passage encapsulates every aspect of the art of dressage that appealed to me at that age. I was desperately searching for something in my life to inspire and motivate me; a search for happiness amid the depression and self-doubt I was struggling with every day. I felt a deep connection to horses, and I was looking for a way to join our souls through the art and beauty of dressage.

When dressage is executed properly, a bystander can hardly detect any movement on the part of the rider, whose aids are almost invisible. The horse and rider are dancing a ballet, and when set to music, it is like watching Olympic figure skating pairs execute their routines. The subtleties of the training methods and the use of disciplined gymnastic exercises over many years make it a challenging riding discipline. The same kind of athletic development is used to train Olympic gymnasts and is part of what inspired me to pursue the study of dressage for the rest of my life.

Joe also introduced us to the sport of "vaulting." Like a gymnast performing a routine on a pommel horse, a vaulter mounts a moving horse without a saddle and executes a series of movements. In its most advanced form, two or three riders will climb aboard the horse's back and perform acrobatics like a cheerleading squad might do. The real challenge for vaulters lies in overcoming the forces of a moving horse while maintaining their balance. The horse has been trained to stay at the end of a web line that is attached to its headpiece. The person holding the line cues the horse to go around in a fifty-foot circle without changing its tempo or speed—a challenging task.

Joe had formed a vaulting team and introduced us to all the beginner exercises. Due to my small size and light weight, I became proficient at it. Joe would be seated on the moving horse with me running alongside; he would reach down and take hold of my arms, swinging me up from the ground and settling me on the horse's back behind him. From there I would stand with my knees pressed into his back, extend my arms to the side, and then climb onto his shoulders. From this seated position I would stretch my arms above my head and then lean into a backbend. When we began giving exhibitions for local audiences, I performed under the moniker "The Flying Horseman." Joe made me feel special, and I got a thrill out of engaging in another sport I excelled at. My parents were never in the crowd.

My horizons as a budding horseman were expanding with Joe's introduction to new riding disciplines. I was getting special attention from the man everyone looked up to, and I believed Joe's mentorship and support would be the key to fulfilling my dream of becoming an extraordinary horseman. None of my challenges at school would go away, and my struggles at home would not lessen, but they no longer seemed to outweigh the joy and sense of belonging that Red Raider was providing. I thought Joe was the answer to all my problems and I proceeded innocently into his web of seduction.

10

Olympic Dream

When summer came to Red Raider, it transformed. From one day to the next, the center of activity shifted from the stables to a large grass field where each weekday a dozen buses and vans unloaded over two hundred day campers and staff. Everyone would assemble in front of the dining hall for morning announcements and the raising of the American flag. After singing a patriotic song and chanting loyalty to Red Raider, the groups were dispatched to their designated campsites in the woods, segregated by age and gender. From there they went off to enjoy daily activities, one of which was horseback riding.

For the dedicated equestrians who had been riding in lessons throughout the school year, the camp offered a ten-week program centered around horses. It was led by Joe. They assigned a horse to each rider for the summer, and besides having a morning and afternoon riding lesson, they were responsible for all aspects of caring for the horse and its equipment. It was total immersion into the world of full-time horsemanship.

My parents felt I rode enough during the school year that I didn't need a special summer activity. We went on family vacations and spent time at the country club, so they wouldn't split the cost of more riding lessons. I couldn't afford to be in Joe's program—delivering papers, cleaning gutters, mowing lawns, and shoveling snow barely covered the cost of my off-summer lessons— so I found another way to spend the summer with Joe and my friends. I joined the group of Apprentice Counselors and assisted full-time with the Junior Camp riding activities.

Although the buses returned to the suburbs at the end of each day, I had become accustomed to staying overnight at Mark's and soon became a fixture at camp. Red Raider was well established with a great reputation. As my father and the camp owner, Fox Smith, had been good friends since their Shaker Heights childhood, my parents had no concerns or objections about me spending so much time there.

The pull of Red Raider and living the life of a riding apprentice were far greater than spending my summer vacation with my family and so, that year, I decided not to go with them to Sandbridge. That gave me two weeks to stay at camp and enjoy evenings and weekends with Mark, the counselors and staff, and Joe and Becky.

Heather and I had bonded with a special friendship, and Joe saw us as inseparable. She was as dedicated to learning about the equestrian art as I was, and we shared the aspiration to become world-class riders. During those two weeks, Joe invited Heather and me to spend a night at his and Becky's home. He promised an evening of instruction in the history and theory of riding, as well as an introduction to a program of isometric stretching exercises he assured us would contribute to our success as top-level riders. Even though the prospect of being one-on-one with the master was intimidating, we accepted the invitation. I felt incredibly special—no other kids had been invited within the hallowed walls of the master's den.

With some trepidation, we walked to the back porch just before dinner and knocked. The door opened into the kitchen with a small breakfast nook, and the smell of fatty ground beef frying up on the stove hit us. Becky, a terrible cook, was treating us to Hamburger Helper. In fact, she prepared most dishes in a frying pan with about a half inch of Wesson oil, leaving the smell of grease permeating the air.

It was a small, one-floor house with three tiny bedrooms and a living room adjacent to the kitchen area. After dinner, Joe, Heather, and I shifted into the living room to begin our evening of learning. The house was at least ten years old and many resident staff members had lived there. The furniture and green shag carpeting were inexpensive and worn, but thanks to some crocheted blankets and quilts Becky had placed over the couch and chairs, the living room had a somewhat homey feel. But the fabrics and drapes harbored years of cigarette smoke that no amount of cleaning could remove. Joe's chain smoking added to the smell, and although Becky's two black terrier mutts were bathed regularly, the house still smelled of dogs. The lingering odor of cooking oil threw a cast over everything, and the smells were offensive. But enduring it seemed like a small price to pay for the privilege of receiving what Joe was about to share with us.

For a couple of hours, Heather and I sat on the sofa while Joe held court from his easy chair. Smoking one cigarette after another, alternating each long draw with a sip from the can of his favorite Rolling Rock beer, we listened intently to his lecture. He talked about the role riding masters from previous centuries had played in developing training principles we were following to that day. He explained what was required to master the art of dressage and gave us an in-depth analysis of what "perfection" meant. He described the inherent conflict in dedicating oneself to achieving a goal—perfection—that, by definition, is unattainable. And, most important, he convinced us that with enough time, dedication, hard work, and talent, we could both rise to the top of the sport and perhaps, one day, become Olympians.

Olympians!

I had dreamed for years of becoming an exceptional rider—but an Olympian!? It was 1972 and we had spent most of February in front of our televisions watching the Winter Olympics in Sapporo, Japan. The world was also getting ready for the ill-fated summer Olympics that would be held in Munich, West Germany in August.

Everything about the Olympics and what they stood for sang to my heart: being the best in the world; bringing glory to your country; taking part in the largest athletic event in the world; and being on the international stage—a winner! I already had a severe case of Olympic fever, and Joe had inspired me to pursue a new dream. He convinced us that if we became servants to his coaching and let him lead us down the path, he could help get us to the medal podium—if we were good enough. My Olympic dream was born. I fully committed myself to doing whatever it took to make the pedagogue proud.

11
The Seduction

Heather and I were hanging on Joe's every word, so he made his next move. Consistent with the need to perfect ourselves as world-class athletes, he directed us to include a daily program of isometric stretching in our lives. Those exercises would be an important adjunct to our riding lessons and imperative to our success. To provide an example of what that encompassed, he asked me to go to the bedroom I was assigned for the night and put on a pair of "workout shorts" he had placed on my bed—only the shorts, nothing else.

What I found on the bed was a pair of athletic support briefs the size of a Speedo, made from a stretchy white fabric that clung like a second skin. Ashamed of my skinny body, I changed into the briefs and hesitantly made my way back to the living room. Becky had retired to her bedroom across the hall from mine and spent the rest of the evening watching TV. That left Joe and Heather alone in the living room when I made my entrance.

Detecting the discomfort Heather and I were feeling, Joe began putting me through a series of floor exercises to demonstrate the program we would need to follow: standing straight and stretching both arms over my head—*hold*; bending at the waist with locked knees and touching my palms to the floor—*hold*; sitting on the floor with my arms stretched in front of me and touching my toes—*hold*; lifting my extended legs above my head and posing in a shoulder stand—*hold*; from the shoulder stand, dropping my feet down behind my head and touching my toes to the floor—*hold*; and from that shoulder-stand position, stretching both legs out to the side and making small circles with my feet—and *hold*.

He then had me lie flat on my back and left his chair to point out the three sets of muscles in our abdominal region. He explained how important it would be to isolate the flexion of each muscle group when we rode, especially our core—the base of support and control for all riding exercises. At fourteen years old, having spent an active childhood swimming, skiing, riding, and then vaulting, my whispy body was as supple and flexible as a Gumby toy and I found the exercises easy. I felt like I was a star and I loved it. The discomfort and embarrassment disappeared.

After completing our evening lecture and demonstration, Joe dismissed Heather to her room and said good night. While they were walking down the hallway, he asked me to stay behind for a few minutes so we could talk. Certain I was about to receive some special praise for my stellar demonstration, I eagerly waited for his return.

After making sure Heather and Becky had retired for the night, he reclaimed his place in his easy chair, lit a cigarette, and popped open another can of beer. Concerned the sound of our voices might disturb the others, Joe asked me to hop onto the chair and sit on his lap while we quietly had our talk.

It felt wrong. It was as if my junior high swimming instructor had removed the stack of towels from his lap and asked me to sit on it. But with my newly formed dream of standing on an Olympic podium, I put my hesitations to the side and accepted his invitation, hoping to learn more about how we were going to fulfill that dream. This confirmed my status of being his favorite student and I would not decline this very special invitation.

As I settled onto his lap, sitting sideways across both his legs, all I was aware of was the foul odor emanating from his body and the disgusting smell of his breath. After a day of drinking endless cups of coffee, chain smoking for over twelve hours, and putting several beers in his belly, the stench was revolting. He had spent a long day working under the hot sun in a dusty riding ring among a dozen sweaty horses, and he hadn't showered yet. The smell of cigarette smoke always triggered depressing associations with home. But in the instant all those sensations registered, I knew this special treatment required me to do what he wanted. It was all part of being the perfect student.

After a few minutes of listening to his words of praise and a firm declaration of his commitment to doing everything he could to help me, he asked some questions that seemed odd. The first was: "Do you know what a homosexual is?" Although I was familiar with the term, all I knew was what I had read in a copy of the recently released book, *Everything You Always Wanted to Know About Sex, But Were Afraid to Ask.* (A friend had stolen a copy from her parents' bedroom and passed it along to me.) I understood if two men had sex together, that made them homosexuals, but I didn't understand what was involved in those acts. I also knew there was a derogatory and negative stigma attached to the word; I was already familiar with being called a "faggot." But my abbreviated answer to Joe's question was: "Yes. It's what men who have sex together are called."

That prompted his next question: "Do you and Mark sometimes 'play' with each other?"—at which point he quickly touched the front of my briefs and let out a quiet, low-pitched giggle from deep in his stomach. An image went through my mind of my gym instructor reaching out and touching the front of my shorts. Almost frozen with anxiety, I whispered, "Yes. Just for fun. Like a game."

Joe then assured me that kind of game was perfectly normal for boys to play and speculated that Mark and I probably enjoyed it—as special friends. Unfortunately, I said we did. Joe was becoming sexually aroused and I knew I needed to get up and go to my room. Something *was* terribly wrong. This wasn't my best buddy Mark who was the same age as I; Joe was as old as my gym teachers. He was an adult I looked up to and respected, and this didn't fit in at all with that relationship.

Sensing my discomfort, Joe shifted the conversation to explaining the details of what would be required to train me as a world-class athlete. Desperate not to disappoint my teacher, I hid my apprehension. When I relaxed some, Joe explained that to effectively manage my physical training, he would need to know every inch of my body. He needed to see whether all my muscles were equilaterally developing, if my ligaments and tendons were strengthening over time, if my spine was properly aligned for perfect posture—both on and off the horse—and most importantly, if my core muscles were becoming strong and I could isolate and control each area of my mid-section. This would all be imperative to becoming an Olympic athlete and nothing short of perfection would suffice.

Joe listened to make sure the house was quiet and then instructed me to go to my room, turn off the light, get on the mattress he had placed on the floor, and wait for him to join me. As I lay on my stomach, I was acutely aware that Heather was sleeping on the other side of the wall and that Becky's room was across the hall.

Like a snake slithering through an opening, Joe slinked into the room, softly closing the door behind him. Wearing a pair of navy-blue sweatpants and a fresh white T-shirt, he knelt on the floor beside the mattress and asked me to turn onto my back. He gave me one more assurance that the exploration of my body he was about to conduct was no different than any other coach or trainer working through physical issues with their athletes.

The touching, light stroking and soft massage began on my neck and shoulders and progressed south from there. After exploring each of the muscle groups in my torso, he paused and moved his hands to my feet, ankles, and calves. When he began his slow ascent up my thighs, he interrupted the silence to tell me that because of the vitally important role the pelvis and hips played in effective riding, he would need to get very close to my tailbone. Not to worry, he whispered: if I should have a "reaction" due to the stimulation, it was normal and nothing to be embarrassed about.

With an overabundance of hormones and quite a few practice sessions with Mark, there was a reaction. But nothing compared to Joe's. As he maneuvered around my body, he occasionally pressed himself against my side and increased the pressure and range of his touches on my legs and hips. He acknowledged that a "problem" had developed and suggested he might know of a way to make it go away: and with one hand assigned to himself and the other to me, he did.

After Joe left, I lay awake for a long time trying to sort out my conflicted feelings. I knew something inappropriate had happened, but I also felt a deeper and more intimate connection to my mentor. I believed we had created an unbreakable bond—something I could count on and be assured I would never lose. That evening began a routine of abuse that would persist in various forms over the next seven years as I made my way to fulfilling my Olympic dream—all while feeding Joe's perversions.

12

Game On

I wrestled with my emotions toward Joe. I believed his recognition of my talent and his declared commitment to having me succeed as an Olympian were genuine. I understood what would be required of me as an athlete, and it made sense that my physical training was of paramount importance. But I couldn't help wondering if this new level of physical intimacy should somehow be stopped.

Toward the end of that summer, I was spending many nights at Mark's house. Seeing I was on the property evenings and weekends, Joe would set up special rides for me after everyone but the resident staff had gone home. As soon as the buses rolled down the hill, Joe would instruct me to keep on my leather chaps and walk up the hill to meet him at a designated spot behind the dining hall. He would take a large, dark-grey appaloosa gelding named Raccoon out of the barn, climb on a fence, mount the horse bareback, and ride away from the barn and up to the dining hall area.

After arriving behind the dining hall, well out of sight, Joe would grab my arm in the same way he did during our vaulting exhibitions, and like *The Flying Horseman*, lift me onto Raccoon's back—seating me in front of him—and off we'd go into the woods. Lest this be misconstrued as mere fun—I was in serious training for the Olympics—Joe said the purpose of riding together was so he could train me in the proper movement of the rider's hips, legs, and torso on a moving horse. For the training to be effective, he would need to have me press against his body so I could feel his muscles move. He would grab my hips, and with his fingers laced across my pubic area, pull me toward him as the horse walked on. Joe invented various ways to create stimulating physical contact, away from home and Becky's watchful eye.

* * *

Late one afternoon I was in Joe's home office while he worked on sewing together costumes for Mark and me to wear on the camp's upcoming "Indian

Day." Mark and I were to wear a loin cloth, and nothing else, except the baby oil he slathered on our bodies to help shield against the cold morning air. We were to ride Smoke and Itty Bitty—also dressed in feathers and makeup—and join other riders for our Wild West enactment. The buses would arrive that morning and park in a circle like a band of covered wagons as the Indians galloped around, whooping and hollering at the campers peering out the windows. Heather and Lori would play stellar roles as mounted squaws.

As he was fitting my loin cloth, Joe took a cigarette break and brought a shoe box from the closet. He took out a Polaroid picture showing a handsome boy, about sixteen years old, with an athletic build, wearing nothing but his underwear. Joe had taken the picture. He said the boy had been his top student at his previous stables and that he had also received special training from him. He assured me a similar physique would one day be mine.

The next day Mark came to the house for his fitting. Joe told him to take off his clothes and try on the garment. Although he was not shy, the request embarrassed Mark, but because Joe made it, he turned his back to us and did as instructed. Joe had Mark walk toward him so he could make final adjustments. In the process, Joe stroked his hand past Mark's front, causing Mark to jump backwards as if he had received an electric shock. He became angry and threatened to leave—declaring he had no interest in being some stupid circus actor—but Joe persuaded him to keep the loin cloth on, get dressed, go home, and bring it back to the barn the next day, after which Joe would make the final adjustments.

That scene added to my confusion. Mark had never been shy about his body or being touched when he was with me. And the previous week, a resident counselor named Phil had taken Mark and me out on a Saturday afternoon hike. While going through a pine forest on the way to our destination—a small lake across the street from camp—we were climbing a hill and Mark caught his toe on a tree root. Phil reached out to steady him and planted his hand on Mark's crotch, holding on for several seconds. Mark hadn't seemed to mind.

When we had gotten to the isolated lake, Phil told us the owners of the property were away and it was the perfect place for skinny dipping. So, we all took off our clothes and strolled into the lake. Once we were waist deep, Phil initiated a game of "duck your buddy under the water," which included a lot of mock-wrestling—a sport right up Mark's alley—and nobody had seemed to mind the touching: especially Phil, who had made no effort to hide his excitement. To me it had seemed like a few guys having some fun; what kid didn't like skinny dipping, even if there was physical contact? If the fun I was having with Mark was normal, then maybe there really was nothing wrong with what Joe was initiating. After all, wasn't it part of the very serious training program I was undertaking?

In the last days of summer, before camp ended and I returned to school, Joe devised a way to experience the kind of physical intimacy I suspect he had been craving but had to avoid because of Becky's presence. An international horse competition was being held on Labor Day weekend in Fort Riley, Kansas. The venue had been established as the home of the United States Cavalry School and was equipped to host a world-class horse show. He told me it would be a great opportunity to observe an international competition and that attending it would be important for my education.

After securing my parents' permission (they were already comfortable with me being away from home and considered Joe to be a responsible adult), we set off early Saturday morning for Kansas. Joe's light-blue, 1969 Chevy truck had a white aluminum cap mounted over the pickup bed he had equipped with one mattress and a cooler. We made the fourteen-hour drive from Red Raider to Fort Riley with only a few stops for food and fuel, and we talked the whole way about my Olympic dreams.

We arrived about ten miles from the showgrounds late in the evening and Joe found a secluded place to park under a grove of trees in a roadside rest area. We had already stopped for dinner, so once we arrived and Joe had downed a couple of beers, it was time to go to sleep. Accompanied by the deafening sound of cicadas, we climbed into the back of his pickup and crawled onto the bed. Before getting under the covers, Joe said, "Kid, your muscles must be tight after the long drive, and it's not good to go to sleep with tight muscles, so let me give you a massage." Joe had taken to calling me "Kid" right after I had spent the night at his house.

It was dark except for some light from the parking lot lamps coming through the vented side windows. To start the therapeutic procedure, Joe removed my clothes and produced a bottle of Johnson's Baby Oil. He massaged my body like a professional masseuse. But unlike a professional, Joe became aroused. With me on my back—legs extended, and ankles crossed—he climbed on top of me and inserted himself between my legs, moving his hips up and down until he was satisfied. It only took a minute. He asked if I wanted to try the same thing with him. He said it would be a good way for him to see if my abdominal muscles were developing properly—so I did. Through the course of the night, Joe awakened me three times to repeat the act, minus the massage.

We spent Sunday at the horse show and another night in the truck for more of the same. On Monday, we went to the show in the early morning, and after a couple of hours, headed for home. Exhausted after two days with no sleep, Joe invited me to lie down on the front seat with my head on his lap. For many hours, driving across the open fields of Kansas and Illinois, Joe stroked my hair and smoked his cigarettes, appearing content after his weekend with the Kid. It was game on.

13
New Year's in Nebraska

It looked like this new game was going to come to an abrupt halt.

After only a year at Red Raider, and offering no explanation, Joe announced he would be leaving to take a new position in Nebraska. Two weeks prior to moving there, Joe asked me to come to the house on a Sunday afternoon after riding lessons. Becky had left to run errands, so Joe and I were alone. Joe assured me he would continue to oversee my training and promised that sometime down the road we would get back together and begin the real journey to the Olympics; his move was a slight "pause."

To have a baseline for tracking my physical development, he wanted to take pictures of me. He had a Polaroid camera and a full box of film and told me to remove all my clothes and go through my regular stretching exercises—*pose, hold, snap; pose, hold, snap*—until all twelve photos had been taken. He put the developed pictures into his private shoe box and hid it in his closet—all before Becky got home.

Still embarrassed about my skinny body, I expressed my concern that there were photos of me: bone-white, naked, and in compromising poses. Joe told me the day would come—after enough diligent training—that I would appreciate having an athletic body and be proud to look at those photos and celebrate the progress I had made. That was something I had never imagined would be possible, so the day ended on a high note.

To ensure my dressage training would continue to advance in his absence, Joe had reached out to one of northeast Ohio's preeminent dressage trainers, Elizabeth Channing, to see if she would accept me as a student. Mrs. Channing was trained in England and adhered to the riding methods prescribed by the British Horse Society. She had a wealthy client with a passion for Lipizzan horses—the breed of white stallions known for their dressage talents.

The horses were stabled at a private farm in Aurora, about forty-five minutes from Shaker Heights. Mrs. Channing had permission to give select students lessons on his horses and accepted me into her program. I knew my dressage education would flourish under Mrs. Channing's tutelage and I was earning enough money with my odd jobs and paper route to afford a weekly lesson.

Later that year, around Thanksgiving, Joe phoned to say he wanted to buy me a ticket to fly out and spend the week after Christmas with Becky and him in Nebraska. There were horses there that I could ride, and he had also started a vaulting club and he wanted me to show its beginning vaulters the exercises I had learned. The invitation appealed to me: I wanted to see Joe and show off the expertise I had gained riding the Lipizzaner stallions, and I wanted to demonstrate my advanced skills as a vaulter to his new students. I was also missing Joe.

Becky and Joe's new home was on the stables' property. It was a two-bedroom ranch-style home with a full basement Joe had turned into an office and exercise room. He had procured an empty fifty-gallon drum, mounted it on two sawhorses, and padded it with carpet scraps so someone could sit on the barrel and straddle it like a horse. That was the centerpiece of the basement. The house had good central heating, and after a long day in the cold stables, Becky and Joe enjoyed returning to a very warm house. The heat exacerbated the familiar smells of cooking oil, stale cigarette smoke, and dogs. Stepping inside triggered the disturbing memories from being at their home at Red Raider.

My first day with Joe at the stables included two rides in the indoor riding arena, protected from the wind, but not the cold; the buildings were not heated. Joe had arranged for me to meet his two most aspiring students: Todd and Scott. They were about my age and were typical Nebraskan farm boys with wholesome features and athletic builds. After Joe had finished giving them their afternoon riding lessons, he suggested we all go up to the house and study the finer points of vaulting. Joe told them they had the privilege of learning from an advanced vaulter and that he could show them how some of the gymnastic exercises were done.

As stable manager, Becky was still in the barn finishing up for the day when we went to the house and headed to the basement. Joe was concerned we were bundled up in our winter clothes in the warm house. We might break a sweat as we went through the exercises, and risked catching a cold if we went back into the below-zero temperatures with damp clothes. So, the logical solution was for all of us to take off our clothes and exercise in our underwear. Since we had spent most of the day in the stables, Todd, Scott, and I all had on long johns and were at least partially clothed after we disrobed.

We each found a spot on the floor and went through a series of stretching exercises: standing straight and stretching both arms over our heads—*hold*, bending at the waist with locked knees and touching our palms to the floor—*hold*, and so on, as I had done that summer in front of Joe and Heather. For the next hour, Joe had us climb onto the carpeted barrel—sometimes individually, and sometimes together—and go through some moves vaulters execute on a horse. Many of the exercises involved two of us sitting on the barrel, one behind the other. They required us to grab ahold of the other's hips and thighs as we moved them from sitting behind us to sitting in front, or when assisting them in climbing onto our shoulders and performing backbends. Joe enjoyed every minute of choreographing our workout while he sat in his easy chair, smoking his cigarettes and sipping a can of Rolling Rock beer. Joe had mastered the art of deception, and neither Todd nor Scott thought anything was untoward, even with the excitement our close physical contact had aroused. We were all dressed and out of the house before Becky got home.

That night, thinking Becky had fallen asleep on the couch in front of the TV, Joe and I went into the kitchen and sat at the small dining table. He was already a few beers into the evening when he asked me to climb onto his lap. He said he had something very important he wanted to ask me.

Joe was wearing only his bathrobe and I had on sweatpants and a T-shirt. His arm was wrapped around my waist with his hand resting on my thigh when he asked his question: "Kid, you probably know that every hero has his clay feet—what do you think mine are?" The phrase "clay feet" was new to me, so I asked him to explain. He told me that even though I respected him and was dedicated to him as my coach and trainer, I would one day see that he, like anyone's hero, would show himself to have faults; heroes were, after all, only human. In view of his talents as a trainer, and his dedication to my ongoing success, I said I couldn't find any faults or identify his clay feet. After another sip of beer and a long drag on his cigarette, he stroked my thigh as he thanked me for my trust in him. He was fully aroused. With no warning, Becky appeared in the doorway between the living room and kitchen and came face to face with what was going on.

She stopped dead in her tracks and stared at us. After pausing for a moment, she said, "Oh, no, don't stop what you're doing on account of me." She swirled to the right, marched off into the hallway, and slammed her bedroom door. Joe needed to wait a couple of minutes to "relax," and then told me we had to wrap up for the night. After giving me a big, long hug, we went off to our rooms and I lay in my bed wondering how he was going to deal with Becky. Twenty minutes later, the snake slithered into my room and gave me my customary massage.

Becky knew what was going on, and now I was even more afraid of her and her wrath. I was also afraid my special relationship with Joe might end; he had Todd and Scott to give his attention to. But during regular visits to my room on each of the following nights, Joe assured me I had nothing to worry about.

14
The Pedophile Returns

In June of 1973, it was official: I had survived three years at Woodbury Junior High, and at fifteen, it was time to move on to Shaker Heights High. I had three months to work and save money while I waited for school to start.

One of the country's largest sellers of horse equipment and riding clothes was Schneider's Saddlery. They specialized in designing and manufacturing a line of handmade bridles, halters, and saddles branded as Billy Royal and made in their own workshop. As luck would have it, their showroom and workshop were in Beachwood, five miles from home. So, I rode my bike to Schneider's the Saturday before school ended and presented myself as an accomplished equestrian looking for a job.

The first person I talked to was a salesclerk working in the showroom. She told me they had no openings on the floor, but said if I could wait a few minutes, she would have Stanley Schneider come out to speak with me. Stanley oversaw designing all the custom show tack. He worked in partnership with the country's top trainers for Arabians, Morgans, Quarter Horses, and Gaited Horses, and they designed the tack that would catch the eye of the judges and spectators and assist riders in winning the top competitions in the country.

Stanley emerged from his office, offered a friendly smile, and asked if I would be interested in seeing their leather shop. Walking into the workshop was like stepping back in time. The room was filled with work benches covered in leather hides; knives of every shape and size; hand tools for etching and decorating; awls, needles, and beeswaxed threads for stitching; and saddle racks holding finely tooled western show saddles encrusted with pieces of filagree silver. Over a dozen craftsmen and women hovered over their work, concentrating on the details of their projects. A radio was playing country hits from Dave Dudley and Waylon Jennings—songs I had been listening to in the stables for years. The rich smell of leather and finishing dyes I had smelled in the showroom were magnified tenfold in this small workshop. I knew it was somewhere I wanted to be, but I wasn't sure why Stanley had brought me there.

After a detailed explanation about everything I was seeing, Stanley took me back to the showroom and asked if I would be interested in signing on as an apprentice leathersmith for the summer. He might as well have asked if I wanted my next breath. I emphatically said *yes*. He gave me the job and said I could start on the first Monday after my 16th birthday in early July. This was something I could never have dreamed of. I had no idea the leather shop even existed and that it was a mere bike ride away from home.

I advanced from "apprentice" to "journeyman" by the end of the summer and was able to do the work of an accomplished craftsman. Everything about the trade appealed to me. It required precision, concentration, dexterity, and a natural feel for the various types of leather. Sewing one section of a bridle could require more than a hundred stitches. It is the same skill Hermès artisans in France use to create their world-famous bags. It became a part-time job during the school year and provided the money I needed to continue riding with Mrs. Channing.

* * *

Later that year, I was walking along Lee Road on my way to a friend's house to pick up her gift of a used riding helmet. Looking ahead to the intersection of South Woodland Boulevard, I saw a familiar light-blue Chevy pickup truck with a white cap going west across Lee Road. *Could it be? No. Certainly Joe would have told me if they were going to be in Cleveland.* Two days later, I got a call from him. His father had died, and he and Becky had been driving through Cleveland on their way to his funeral. On their way back to Nebraska, Joe and Becky picked me up at home and we had dinner at a local Mr. Steak restaurant.

Joe told me he was concluding his contract with the stable in Nebraska and that he and Becky were planning to move back to the Cleveland area in two months. I was overjoyed that my Olympic coach was returning and we could continue my training.

He was bringing with him a horse he had purchased in Nebraska that he named Pedagogue (we would call him Paddy). Joe explained we would train Paddy to the highest possible level of dressage. He admitted Paddy had some limitations: his height, age, build, temperament, the way he moved—all the essential requirements for a successful dressage horse—but he had been affordable. We would remain true to the classical principles of dressage and fulfill Paddy's potential. It sounded like a great challenge, and I was excited to begin. Becky sat stone faced and silent throughout dinner.

Joe and Becky moved back to Ohio in January of 1974, settling into an apartment twenty minutes from my home on Chalfant Road. Over the next twelve months, Joe boarded Paddy at three different stables not far from Red Raider. None of them had indoor riding facilities, so we endured the rain, mud, cold, and snow that riding outdoors demanded. It was a huge letdown after the luxurious training facilities I had enjoyed with Mrs. Channing, but I believed the hardships were worth the sacrifice if it allowed me to train again with Joe.

Joe found a job as a data entry specialist at no other place than Schneider's Saddlery. He had conveniently secured a daytime job at the same place I was working, while still having evenings and weekends free to train his students.

I spent weekends at their apartment, diligently studying theories of dressage training from books Joe had introduced me to at Red Raider. And, of course, my physical training continued every Saturday and Sunday afternoon when we finished at the stables. As I lived close to their apartment, there was no need to spend the night, but Joe was clever and introduced a new training program that would substitute for the missed nights together.

With Becky in her bedroom watching TV, Joe would dress me in either Spandex unitards, ballet tights, nylon bodysuits, Speedos, or athletic support briefs, and put me through my workouts in the living room. He added ballet barre exercises to my repertoire, providing a new array of poses for him to observe. And he had purchased an electric massage device with two coiled, elasticized metal bands that strapped under the palm of his hand. He held the unit on top of his hand with the metal bands, which he could run over my clothed body—the vibrations passing through his hand to my muscles. When he was certain Becky would be out of the room for at least five minutes, he would have me lie on my back, moving the vibrator alternately between his mid-section and mine, and we would finish each session with a quiet sigh.

I was sixteen, ready to be in my senior year of high school, and looking forward to applying to colleges and beginning my life away from home. The future looked exciting, and I trusted everything would be better in 1975 when I graduated and started my new adventure at college. I was wrong about that.

15

Destruction

Tragedy often strikes when least expected.

In February of 1974, my brother, father, and I were skating at the community ice rink, when I noticed my father was taking frequent breaks from skating to stand on the side and catch his breath. He looked to be in a bit of pain, but after a few minutes it subsided, and he continued skating. I had also noticed him taking breaks walking home from work, and it was happening on our ski trips when traversing down a slope or loading our equipment in the car.

After several trips to the doctor, my father said he had been diagnosed with angina, causing pain in his chest due to reduced blood flow to the heart. No one told me it was a symptom of coronary heart disease. He told us that whenever he felt the pain, he would insert a tiny white pill called nitroglycerine under his tongue, and the pain would go away.

In October of 1974, after extensive testing at the University Hospitals, my father was also diagnosed with leukemia. That explained the large scabs he was treating on his legs—scabs he jokingly referred to as his "wounds." I learned later that the condition is called Leukemia Cutis and is a rare form of the disease often indicating it is in an advanced stage. However, my parents assured us that my father's medical conditions were being treated and he just needed to keep visiting the doctors and take care of his "wounds." We were not told his symptoms could become life-threatening.

But in March, late on a Sunday afternoon, I returned home from Joe and Becky's in time for our regular family dinner. Mother was on the couch, drinking her bourbon and water, and my brother and sister were upstairs watching TV. Normally, my father would have been in his chair smoking his pipe, so his absence signaled that something was wrong. My mother told me that my father had severe abdominal pain late that morning and by early afternoon he was spitting up blood. She rushed him to the hospital, where they admitted him for emergency surgery to treat a bleeding ulcer. After a difficult procedure, they transferred him to intensive care for twenty-four-hour monitoring.

I didn't know what went on in an ICU, and the fact that he wouldn't be home that night scared me. In our house, nothing ever changed: each day unfolded according to a regular schedule.

The next day after school, Mother suggested I drive myself to the hospital and visit him. Dad lay on the bed, alabaster white, gaunt, and with mussed-up hair dampened by sweat. I hardly recognized him. He was surrounded by an arc of machines with beeping digital displays, an array of tubes running from IV poles, and an oxygen mask the nurse removed as I entered the room. He was heavily sedated yet struggled to sit up to see who I was; he hadn't understood the nurse when she said it was his son. After a moment of looking intently at me, his face brightened, and it was clear he recognized me. Leaning forward with an outstretched arm, he attempted to speak. The beeping sounds accelerated; the nurse reached to re-attach the oxygen mask and asked me to leave. I left without a single word being exchanged between us.

I have no idea how I made it home. I went upstairs to where my mother had been resting to share the details of my visit. However, within seconds, I became nauseated and rushed to the bathroom, staying there until the vomiting and dry heaves stopped. After I recovered, I found my mother downstairs sipping her evening cocktail and trying hard not to cry.

The next morning, as I came down the stairs, I heard a man's voice that sounded like my father's. I bounded down the last steps and turned the corner into the living room. Instead of my father, I saw Uncle Fred—my father's brother. In an instant, I knew.

My mother sat slumped on the couch—destroyed. Uncle Fred told me my father had gone into cardiac arrest during the night and the doctors couldn't revive him. Speechless, I sat next to my mother and cried. Within minutes, Debbie and Doug came downstairs to learn our father was dead. We sat there: stunned, numb, scared, in disbelief.

16
The Grand Prix

Weeks before my father died, Joe proudly announced he was able to provide us with a once-in-a-lifetime opportunity. The days of our moving from stable to stable were ending; all our hard work and tenacity would pay off, as promised. He had received an offer to manage the operations of a private training facility in Aurora called Erlenhof Stables.

While finding a home for his students, Joe had phoned Erlenhof, hoping to speak with the owner and an old acquaintance, Ingeborg Swensen. However, what he got was her husband, Don, and his tale of woe. That winter, Ingeborg had left her farm in Aurora and moved back to Vienna to live with her long-time boyfriend, leaving Don, who had worked his entire life as a long-haul truck driver, to tend to the horses. The mortgage on the farm was in default and the IRS was demanding several years' back taxes.

Sensing an opportunity, Joe offered to move into the three-bedroom home and oversee the management of the farm and its horses. His small group of dedicated riding students could regularly exercise the horses and make them fit for sale. In due course, the farm would be foreclosed, and the IRS would seize all the property—including the horses—so it was important they were salable as riding horses; otherwise, they would be sent to the slaughterhouse and sold by the pound.

That summer, Joe and Becky moved into the upstairs of the house and Don relocated to the basement along with his five old and smelly Dalmatians: most of them covered with festering tumors and always in snarly moods. The home was not welcoming. Because of his work schedule, Don was only there on the weekends and spent a lot of time away with his girlfriend. That gave Joe complete control over all the activities at Erlenhof.

I worked again at Schneider's Saddlery, but that summer Joe was there as well. Each day after work I would hop into my Toyota rust-bucket, drive to Aurora, and join my friend Lori and several local riders for evening lessons on the farm's horses. My dressage skills had advanced with Mrs. Channing, so Joe was eager to see me apply those skills on a well-trained horse. There were two among Ingeborg's collection that had been trained to the highest levels of classical dressage.

One was a mature dark-brown European gelding named Alajos, and the other, an even older Lipizzaner stallion from The Spanish Riding School named Pluto Alga. Alajos had belonged to acclaimed trainer and International Equestrian Federation dressage judge, Natalie Lamping. He was beautifully trained and a delight to ride. Pluto Alga had spent his entire career in Vienna, performing for thousands of visitors in the magnificent riding hall at the Hofburg Imperial Palace.

For the next two years, I would learn to ride all the movements both those superbly trained horses knew so well. They were true school masters and allowed me to become an experienced Grand Prix rider at the age of eighteen—an age when most riders were still dreaming about being educated to that level.

We learned that the coach of the United States Equestrian Team dressage squad, Colonel Bengt Ljundquist of Sweden, was going to be giving a training clinic at Lake Erie College's Equestrian Center in the spring of 1976. Col. Ljundquist was a six-time Olympian: twice as a dressage rider for Sweden, and four times as a fencer. In 1974 he coached the U.S. Dressage Team to a bronze medal win at the Montreal Olympics. Heather had traveled there to watch the competitions and had shared all the glorious details with us. Her stories added to the excitement of the team coach coming to Lake Erie College, which was only forty-five minutes from Aurora. Joe contacted the clinic organizer and convinced them that although I was only eighteen, I was successfully riding a seasoned Grand Prix horse and would meet the Colonel's minimum competency requirements. I was accepted into the clinic.

Thanks to the fabulous job Natalie Lamping had done training Alajos, and as a testament to Joe's teaching skills, I was ready for the Colonel. On the day, the Colonel put us through a series of warm-up exercises to make sure Alajos and I were prepared for the advanced work that lay ahead. After the warm-up we took a short break. He asked me a few questions about my riding background and how I had come to be riding Alajos, and then put us back to work.

During the following thirty minutes, Alajos and I were asked to perform all the movements from a Grand Prix test, and we nailed them. At the end of the lesson, the Colonel gave me some general words of advice—ways to fine-tune my skills and improve my position on the horse—thanked me for riding with him, and wished me the best of luck in the future. Before the Colonel left, I asked the question burning in my mind: Did I have the talent to one day ride on an Olympic team? With a gentle smile he replied, "Young man, you are off to a very good start at a young age. Stick with it and work hard, and I'm sure you will continue to be quite successful."

That was good enough for me. I took it as affirmation of my goal.

Joe had delivered on his promise to lead his students to a top-notch facility with world-class horses, and he had demonstrated his ability to teach me at the Grand Prix level. After three years of confusing and unwanted physical intimacy, my belief that Joe would guide me to the Olympic podium anchored me further into his program of training—and abuse. I was paying a price for the victory I believed to be mine, unaware of its true cost and the destructive force its quest would become in my life.

17

Cutting Me Off

In the fall of 1974, it was time to select the colleges I wanted to apply to.

After looking at several colleges, Joe convinced me to take a drive with Becky and him to a small town about thirty minutes away called Hiram. Hiram College sits on a rural campus of about one square mile. With enrollment of 800 students and highly acclaimed academic standards, I knew I would receive a first-rate liberal arts education.

My application was accepted, with the proviso that I could pay for four years at this expensive, private college. Other than a small portfolio of stocks and the home on Chalfant Road, my mother had inherited no other assets. Money was tight. I would pay my tuition and living expenses through a combination of scholarships, grants, loans, and on-campus jobs in the student work program.

After being accepted at Hiram, I needed to declare a major for my liberal arts degree. On the heels of my Grand Prix debut with Colonel Ljundquist, Joe was talking about my future education in dressage. He said I should be looking outside of the local area to gain an even more advanced education—one he could not provide. For decades, the world's most successful international dressage competitors, horses, and trainers were from Germany. When I told Joe that Hiram offered a diploma in the German language, he urged me to declare that as my major. If I were fortunate enough to go to Germany one day for advanced training, Joe was certain nobody would want to teach me in English. He assured me speaking German would be more helpful to a career with horses than a business degree. Knowing I wanted to study business management, I declared a double major: Business Administration and German. Both would prove to serve me well in my pursuit of going to the Olympics.

* * *

Throughout the summer, the tension in Joe and Becky's relationship grew and Becky left to visit her family in Wyoming. With Don away during the week, Joe had the house to himself. For the first time in our relationship, Joe was able to invite me to sleep in his bed with him, which I did.

The house reeked of unbathed dogs, their stale urine, cigarette smoke, and unchanged bedsheets. The small rooms, paneled with dark wood, had few windows. Many of the lightbulbs were burned out. It was like a haunted house.

After we all had left Red Raider, Mark and his family moved to a suburban community in Ohio where Mark began his new life as a city kid. Given that he had always lived in small, rural communities, Mark didn't fit in with the middle-class suburban kids and he struggled to assimilate into his new school environment. He had been in trouble for breaking the rules around drug and alcohol use on school property. He was drinking regularly.

Knowing Mark was struggling, Joe invited him to come to Erlenhof for a long weekend and be with his friends in a welcoming environment. Mark had no interest in riding anymore, so we went to lunch at a local ice cream stand, hung out around the pool, and killed time in the stables. Saturday night, after all our friends had left for the day, Mark and I went into Joe's bedroom for an exercise session. Intoxicated, Mark gave in to Joe's requests: he put on an athletic support brief like mine and we both went through an entire exercise routine. Joe knew not to touch him, but he clearly enjoyed watching Mark's athletic body go through the moves.

When we finished our command performances, Mark headed to the guest room. As he was walking out, Joe put a hand on my shoulder. "Kid, don't you want to sleep here, with me?" It was a no-win decision on my part: Mark expected me to sleep in his room—I always did—and he had no idea why I would sleep with Joe.

I knew Joe wanted to spend every possible night sleeping with me, but I said good night to him. Joe showed his disappointment and gave me a look that said: "I'll give you one last chance to change your mind." I didn't. Mark went home the next afternoon and I stayed at the house as planned on Sunday night. Joe sat me down after my evening exercise session for a lecture.

He asked if I had ever heard the phrase "He travels fastest who travels alone." I hadn't, but I understood what it meant. Joe told me that with the changes coming up in my life as a college student, there would be many opportunities for new friends to distract me from my dressage training. As much as I would enjoy spending time with them, I would need to be diligent to protect my time and prioritize my choices about what I would do, and with whom I would do it. My schoolwork, employment, and dressage training would consume all my time. No time would be left for socializing or partying. He lamented that Mark was sliding down a slippery slope, and he wanted me to avoid that fate. I believed Joe when he said he was only trying to protect me and my promising future. I realize now he was committing a primary act of a predator: cutting the victim off from family and friends. The snake had teeth.

18

Violated

Even after four years of enduring Joe's sexual perversions, I did not recognize them as abusive. But during the summer of 1975, I came to know what sexual abuse was.

Although I worked at Schneider's during the day and as a busboy at night, I still spent time on the weekend at Erlenhof. Ted Pataki, a friend of Don's who lived down the street, came to the farm on Saturday mornings to help with the heavy lifting of cleaning the stalls. Ted was a big man. He was a few years older than I was, weighed over three hundred pounds, and had the sturdy build of an old-world farm worker. We all joked that if a horse didn't get out of Ted's way when he was trying to clean the stall, Ted would just pick the horse up and move it.

I joined the Saturday morning stall cleaning activities and was assigned the job of driving the tractor and manure spreader, following Ted as he removed the old bedding. When we finished the last stall, I would climb to the loft above the stalls and throw flakes of hay to the horses through small openings in the wood ceiling. Ted developed a peculiar habit after a few weeks working together. As I was starting my climb up the ladder, Ted would place his large, meaty hand between my legs and grab hold of my groin, pushing me up slowly until I reached the edge of the loft. The assist took much longer than necessary, and his grip was much tighter than called for. The first time it happened, I had a flashback to the walk Mark and I had taken in the pine forest with the camp counselor, Phil, and the skinny dipping and wrestling at the lake. That had been fun, so I wondered why I was not enjoying Ted's groping.

I put up with this for several weeks; I was too timid to tell him to stop. My inability to take action to protect myself only allowed the situation to worsen. One afternoon when we finished the barn work, our group took the rest of the day off to enjoy a swim in the backyard pool. Apparently, Ted knew all the same "duck your buddy under the water" games Phil had initiated, and I became Ted's new buddy. Given our size difference, Ted could have dunked me with one arm tied behind his back. But since it was just a friendly game, he found inventive ways to wrap his hulk around me and land his hand repeatedly on the front of my swimsuit.

Those games must have been what inspired Ted to invite me to join his younger brother, Ben, at their house on a Sunday afternoon. They had spent months working in their garage on a souped-up, cherry-red, 1965 Chevy they were planning to race at the local track. They told me I was the perfect size for driving a race car, and since I was so light, I would have an advantage over the other entries in the race. They asked if I wanted to learn how to drive a race car, and having just turned eighteen and always up for a challenge, I said *yes*. Under the pretense of needing to be measured for my flame-resistant driving coveralls, I followed them into their dank basement that smelled like a rodent may have died there recently.

There was a piece of maroon fabric on the floor meant to be tailored into a pair of coveralls for me. I couldn't imagine that either Ted or his brother, who was built exactly like Ted, could sew a garment, let alone measure for a proper fit. Something wasn't right. They told me that to ensure a correct fit, I would need to strip down to my underwear and lie down on the fabric. Unfortunately, I had done similar things with Joe, so doing it seemed familiar albeit uncomfortable. As soon as I was on the fabric, nothing was familiar.

The Pataki brothers began to slowly fold the fabric around my body, touching and pressing my hips and legs to "get an initial fit." Within seconds, Ted became aroused, stood up, and dropped his pants. He pulled the fabric off me and told me to get on my knees in front of him. I knew what was coming, and when the odor of his sweaty body hit me, I tried to pull back. Ben, standing behind me, grabbed my head and shoulders and pushed me toward Ted, forcing me to perform the act the show had been staged for.

Ted was a large man and I panicked with the sensation I would either choke, vomit, or suffocate. When Ted finished, he and Ben switched places and the rape was re-enacted. When the violence ended, they both pulled up their pants and suggested we all go out to the garage and look at the beautiful car they had been working on. Trying to hide my tears and control my shaking, I said I had a lesson with Joe, and left.

After that day, Ben and Ted acted like nothing had happened. I felt guilty about having allowed the situation to transpire: *How could I have been so naïve to believe I was going to be a race car driver?* I wrote it off as a poor decision on my part and said nothing to anyone. I had been sexually abused, but in my mind, I had been the victim of my own stupidity. It would not be the last time.

19
A Sophomore in Hamburg

My freshman year at college was filled with new experiences and the feeling of freedom that comes with moving away from home and living as an independent adult. The pain of losing my father was not lessened by the move to college, but I could suppress my depression from time to time by focusing on school.

I looked forward to all my studies, but I enjoyed German classes the most. My professor was Sigrid Anderson, originally from Germany and a gifted teacher. Thanks to my previous experience learning French and Spanish, I found learning German easy. My skills developed quickly, and in the spring, Prof. Anderson suggested I consider joining the sophomore study abroad program being offered that fall in Hamburg. The program required an extra tuition premium, the cost of air travel to and from Europe, and other expenses the students would incur while traveling with the group throughout Germany. If I took on extra jobs during the summer, I could scrape together the funds to go on the program, so I signed up.

Prof. Anderson was an enthusiastic dressage rider and had her own horses stabled in Hiram. Sharing the same passion, she suggested that while living in Hamburg—the city where she was raised—I should reach out to her friend, Rosemarie Springer, and see if I could visit her beautiful estate and horse breeding farm an hour north of the city. I was excited at the prospect, and Prof. Anderson wrote Frau Springer to make the introduction.

* * *

Twelve students arrived in Hamburg on a cold and misty September morning. Our host families greeted us, and for the next twelve weeks I lived the life of a typical German university student. We had classes throughout the week and gathered every Wednesday morning at the Hamburg Hauptbahnhof (central train station) and embarked on field trips to nearby cities. We learned about German history, art, and architecture, and visited cathedrals, museums, and city landmarks, including the Berlin Wall, Checkpoint Charlie, and East Berlin.

Three of my classmates and I had enjoyed our time together on those group outings and decided when we finished with our studies in November, we would go as a group of four and explore Europe for a few weeks. The plan was to travel in typical backpacker fashion: armed with a passport, a Eurorail pass, a youth hostel card, a tireless spirit for adventure, and some comfortable walking shoes.

However, the cost of the end-of-term excursion wasn't included in my original budget. I let my host parents know my plans and shared my concern about not having enough money for the trip. Our classes ended around 2 p.m. each weekday, and afterwards my days were free. They knew a man in nearby Bergesdorf who owned a small clockmaking factory and had two horses. They thought he might have an opening for a part-time worker in his shop.

One afternoon after classes, I hopped on a bus and headed out to meet the master clockmaker, Herr Berchthold. He was a spry man of about fifty, with salt-and-pepper hair, a twinkle in his eye, and the serious demeanor of a man who spent his life concentrating on all the intricate details that make clocks work with German precision. The hand-craftsmanship skills I had learned as a leathersmith transferred over to clock making, so Herr Berchthold offered me a job after school with a decent hourly wage—to be paid in cash—along with an invitation to join him in the evenings when he went to care for his horses. On the days I accompanied him, he drove me home in his brand-new white Porsche 911: his pride and joy.

Herr Berchthold boarded his horses at a friend's stable with easy access to beautifully manicured riding trails that wove through the forests outside of Hamburg's city center. On a bright Saturday morning we saddled up his horses and headed out to join a group of his friends for an all-day ride through the forest. After we returned and had taken care of our horses, Herr Berchthold told me we would meet with his friends at a local pub for a drink. I used the car ride to ask Herr Berchthold if he knew who Rosemarie Springer was. Trying not to embarrass the poorly informed American, he explained who the legendary Frau Springer was. I had no idea the answer to my innocent question was going to set the course for a major change in my life.

20
Meet the Grande Dame

Rosemarie Springer was the third wife of the German publishing magnate Axel Springer. He was founder of the international media conglomerate Axel Springer SE—Europe's largest publishing house, with control over the German newspaper market. Frau Springer had a lifetime passion for dressage and for breeding world-class sport horses. She established *Gestüt Halloh*, a hundred-acre estate and breeding farm about an hour north of Hamburg in a town called Großenaspe.

Axel had arranged for Germany's acclaimed *Reit Meister* (Riding Master), Willi Schultheis, to train Rosemarie over a twenty-five-year period, ending in 1973. During those years she won six German National Dressage Championships, took the Reserve Champion title three times, and earned a seventh-place finish in the 1960 Rome Olympics. I had seen her name in *The Chronicle of the Horse* and was well aware of Herr Schultheis's status in the world of international dressage, but I did not know about their long-term collaboration and the details of her many successes. She was known in German dressage circles as "The *Grande Dame* of Dressage."

Over drinks at the pub with his riding friends, Herr Berchthold told me he had been planning to breed one of his mares to a Trakhener stallion (Trakhener is a European breed of horse especially popular in the 1970s for dressage), and that Frau Springer owned one of those breeding stallions. He offered to phone her, tell her I was the American student Prof. Anderson had written to her about, and schedule a visit for us both. Two weeks later we hopped into his prized Porsche and sped along at top speed on the *Autobahn*, heading for *Gestüt Halloh* to meet the legendary *Grande Dame*.

From the moment we arrived at the gates of the estate, I was awestruck. Our drive down the quarter-mile, tree-lined way ended at a courtyard in front of two white brick stables with red tiled roofs. Across from them was the Springer home, reminiscent of a small Italian villa, surrounded by beautiful gardens. Behind the building complex were fenced-in lanes banked with lush bushes, leading back to open pastures where the mares and their foals were turned out to graze on the fresh grass. It was a beautiful and peaceful setting—a horseman's utopia.

Rosemarie Springer was every bit the *Grande Dame*. As she strode across the path from the house to the courtyard to greet us, I knew I was in the presence of someone special. She had her chin held high, an athletic physique befitting an Olympian, and perfect posture that made her look taller than her five feet eight frame. She extended her hand, and while lifting her chin ever so slightly higher, smiled broadly, and said, "*Guten Tag. Ich bin Rosemarie Springer. Willkommen an Gestüt Halloh.*" "Good day. I am Rosemarie Springer. Welcome to *Gestüt Halloh.*"

Frau Springer treated us to her European hospitality, offering a tour of the stables and a look at all the horses, followed by a British-style high tea. We sat in the sunroom, framed with French doors looking out onto her patio, gardens, and pastures. *Pinch me*, I thought as I took in the picture of her perfect poise, confidence, and geniality, highlighted by her impeccably coiffed blonde hair, lifted from her forehead and swept back in a slight wave. She spoke the most eloquent High German I had ever heard, and it was evident the lady sitting in front of me was from old money—and lots of it. After Frau Springer talked to Herr Berchthold about breeding his mare to her stallion, she hit me with the surprise of my life.

"Herr Merrick, if you should be free next summer and would like to come to Großenaspe, I could offer you a stay here. During the summer months my head trainer instructs several apprentice riders from the local schools. They each receive some time off during their summer course, and in their absence, I am certain he could use some help with all the young stallions we have to train. I could give you a place to stay here by the house, and in exchange for helping with the stable work in the mornings, caring for the horses, and riding the rather rambunctious stallions under my trainer's supervision, I could offer to give you a riding lesson each afternoon on one of my Grand Prix horses. They were trained by me under Herr Schultheis's direction, and I'm certain you could learn a lot by having lessons with me. I think you might enjoy that."

I understood German better than I spoke it at that point, and although all her perfectly enunciated words made complete sense to me, I looked over to Herr Berchthold to make sure I had understood what she had offered. With a wry smile and his twinkling eyes, he nodded and gestured for me to say yes. It was amazing how quickly my German improved. Uttering what was perhaps my first flawless delivery of spontaneous conversation, I thanked her, and assured her I felt privileged to accept her generous offer. I was certain life could not get any better, but it did.

She followed on with her next offer. "*Ja, gut.* If you have the entirety of your summer free, then perhaps when you have finished with your weeks at *Gestüt Halloh*, I could organize some additional education for you here in Germany. The German Riding School in Warendorf offers a two-week Amateur Riding Instructors Course in July that I could arrange for you to attend. Being an American, you could not receive a diploma for completing the course, but I think you would find the experience very useful for your future. And at the completion of that program, you could travel nearby to the town of Verden and participate in the Summer Dressage Course at the Hanoverian Riding and Driving School."

I didn't know that humans could still breathe when their hearts stopped, but I proved it to be true. When I revived from the shock of her offer, I slipped out of my dream-like trance long enough to accept the invitation and assure her I would have the entire summer free.

I am sure Herr Berchthold had a lot to say on our drive home, but given my euphoria, I had no idea what he said. My guess is, I nodded a lot and said, *"Jawohl."* I had taken my first step on what I knew would be a great adventure.

21
The Predator Closes In

I returned from Germany in a state of elation, only to discover Joe had encroached on the sanctuary of my college campus.

In my absence, the banks, the IRS, and the other institutions Erlenhof was in debt to, finalized their seizure of the farm's assets, including the home where Joe and Becky had been living. They searched for an apartment to rent and found one: an affordable two-floor townhouse in Hiram—a convenient five-minute walk from the dormitories where I would be living for the next three years. Joe had taken another step forward in his quest to dominate my life.

When I was not working as a waiter at nearby Hunter's Hollow Tavern or dispatching for the police department as part of my student job program, I would go to Becky and Joe's in the evening. We had fewer opportunities to ride after Erlenhof had closed, so Joe considered my physical training to be especially important for my development as an Olympic athlete. Many evenings Joe and I would walk to the college athletic facility, where I would run a mile around the track with him timing me, checking my pulse, and making sure all my muscles were stretched out and limber. No one was around in the evenings, and the overhang to the bleachers provided the privacy Joe needed to make his intimate assessments.

Joe maintained his evening ritual of drinking beer, smoking cigarettes, and giving me massages. But he had added something new to his ritual. Claiming he had allergies—or a persistent cold he could never quite shake—he alternated his swigs of beer with sips from a bottle of NyQuil. Over the course of an evening, he would drink the entire bottle—adding more alcohol, and now painkillers, to his six-pack of beer and his endless daily intake of caffeine and nicotine. At the time, NyQuil was made from ephedrine, doxylamine, acetaminophen, dextromethorphan, and 25 percent alcohol (50 proof), all delivered in a palatable licorice-flavored liquid. Joe was addicted to alcohol, caffeine, nicotine, and painkillers.

During my evening massages, Joe was ever alert to the sound of Becky walking from her bedroom and heading down the stairs to the kitchen. That allowed him plenty of warning so he could turn me over on my stomach if we needed to hide what we were doing. Becky was nobody's fool, and she was aware of what was going on. Despite witnessing Joe's indiscretions over the years, Becky chose not to intervene or hold him accountable. The abuse continued while I endured her looks of disapproval.

I hated being there and I saw no escape; Joe was living in my backyard. I still attributed .the success I was having with my dressage education to Joe's dedication and guidance, so I was not willing—or more aptly said, able—to consider breaking away from that existence. Joe was, in a sense, responsible for my invitation to Germany, and I felt I couldn't walk away now regardless of how much I wanted to leave. I was trapped.

22
Summer in the Big League

Six months after my studies in Hamburg, it was time to return to Großenaspe and begin my summer apprenticeship at *Gestüt Halloh*. The days unfolded as Frau Springer had promised. I joined the head trainer and his two apprentices in the stables every morning at six. We cleaned the stalls, fed the horses, prepared everything for the day's training, and then took a break for breakfast.

I spent the mornings riding the three- and four-year-old Trakhener stallions that were the progeny of Frau Springer's breeding program. Young stallions are strong and spirited. To an observer, riding them could look like a wrestling match, complete with sporadic leaps, bucks, and the occasional rear. The joke was, if I could survive the morning in the Colosseum with the young gladiators, I had earned my afternoon lesson with Frau Springer on one of her Grand Prix Ferraris.

I knew how to ride all the Grand Prix dressage movements, thanks to my time at Erlenhof and Joe's training. These lessons took my riding to a new level. They were an opportunity to polish my technique while being educated by an Olympian who had trained the horse I was riding. The horses were sensitive to my aids, and I floated around the arena on a horse that could almost read my mind. This higher level became my new benchmark for perfection.

On the last day of my stay, Frau Springer invited me to her garden room for afternoon tea. We sat alone in that beautiful room—the walls covered with mounted antlers of stags hunted on the property—and as the sunlight streamed in, I knew this was going to be the sad ending to an incredible experience.

Frau Springer thanked me for being an eager and hard-working student, as well as an enjoyable guest to have at the estate. Then came the biggest honor. It is a custom in Germany that young people address their seniors, especially those in elevated positions, as "Herr" or "Frau," along with their last name. There are two forms of the word "you" in German: *Sie* is the formal one used with Herr and Frau; *Du* is the informal one used with first names when addressing close friends and family. Poised in her chair like royalty, Frau Springer beamed a smile as she extended her hand to me and said, "*Ich bin Rosemarie. Ich freue mich auf Deinem nächsten Besuch. Hoffentlich kommst Du bald wieder zu uns.*" "I am Rosemarie. I look forward to your next visit. Hopefully *you* will come back to us soon." She had elevated our status to that of "good friends." If Cloud 10 is above Cloud 9, that is where I was sitting as I finished my tea and talked with Rosemarie about the adventures that lay ahead in Warendorf and Verden.

The next morning, I departed by train for Warendorf—the epicenter of German equestrian sport. It is home to *Die Deutsche Reitschule* (The German Riding School) as well as the German Olympic Equestrian Center. Every professional riding instructor and horse trainer in Germany is required by law to have a certificate earned at *Die Deutsche Reitschule*. Adults who want to teach at local riding clubs must earn an Amateur Riding Instructors certificate, which was the program I had been enrolled in. Only through Rosemarie's recommendation, and clout, was I accepted. I may have been the first American to attend.

At the conclusion of the two-week course, I traveled from Warendorf to the town of Verden, home of *Die Hannoversche Reit- und Farhschule*—the Hanoverian Riding and Driving School. Their ten-day Summer Dressage Program was a riding intensive, and participants received up to three lessons per day on the school's well-trained horses.

After completing the program in Verden, I had one more stop on my journey before returning to the States. It was in the town of Aachen to see the international dressage competition that attracted horses and riders from throughout the world. I had read about it each year in *The Chronicle of the Horse* and knew it was the world's finest dressage event, and the closest thing to competing at the Olympics.

I could not afford to buy a ticket for a seat in the stadium—it was the end of my trip and I had run out of money—but none of that mattered. I was there.

As the day's events ended, I knew I wanted to come back the following morning and watch one more day of competition, but I barely had enough money for the train fare back to Hamburg for my return flight to Cleveland. I didn't even have enough money to buy dinner. I decided that thanks to dry weather and warm temperatures, I could rough it out by hiding under the bleachers when the show closed up for the day and find a place to sleep on the lawn. My stomach would just have to suck it up and growl. A simple obstacle like being broke would not stop me from enjoying a once-in-a-lifetime experience in Aachen.

Fortunately, a young couple who lived nearby started up a conversation and learned about my evening plans. They invited me to join them for dinner at their home, be their overnight guest, and ride back with them in the morning to watch the show. They even offered to buy me a ticket, so I didn't have to stand all day.

I left the following evening on the train to Hamburg, armed with a bag full of sandwiches and the fruit given to me by my new friends. After two months in Germany, I returned home.

Upon my return, I was treated like an equestrian celebrity. None of my Cleveland friends or family had been to Europe, and as I had a collection of slides documenting every piece of my trip, many equestrian events invited me to share tales of my journey.

The trip to Germany shifted a few things for me. I felt special in my own right, both in Germany and on my return. I knew that the experience had taken me a step closer to fulfilling my dream of competing at the Olympics. I knew I needed to continue my education at a higher level than was available with Joe in Ohio. My time in Germany had taken my skills to a new level and the student had outgrown the master. I no longer needed, or wanted, the pedagogue. It was time to move on.

23

Goodbye to My Special Friend

Joining the Army turned out to be the wrong decision for Mark. He enlisted right after his visit to Erlenhof, and several months later he was admitted to a VA hospital for psychiatric evaluation. His aggressive behavior toward other soldiers was attributed to bipolar disorder, and after two months of treatment, he was honorably discharged. He was given prescriptions for psychotropic medications, but otherwise, no ongoing care plan.

In the fall of my senior year, I decided to visit Mark in southern Ohio to see how he was doing. His parents had moved back after Mark graduated from high school. I hadn't seen him in almost a year.

We spent the day hiking and swimming at Hocking Hills State Park, and it reminded me of our good times at Red Raider. On the way home, we stopped in a poor area of town to visit a friend of Mark's—Jim—who looked at least fifteen years older than Mark and lived alone. The well-worn La-Z-Boy in front of the TV was surrounded by videotapes in unmarked covers, and the empty beer cans strewn beside it suggested Jim spent much of his time there.

When we walked in, Jim greeted Mark with a close hug, and when we left, he swatted Mark's buttocks playfully. These intimate gestures seemed out of place to me. Something didn't feel right. *Did Mark have his own Joe?* It upset me to think that Jim might be preying on Mark, especially given his mental health vulnerability—and that Mark might get hurt.

However, I had no time to dwell on it, because as soon as we left Jim's house, Mark said he wanted to take a drive out of town and go to a bar he knew. It was a small, ramshackle wood building, sitting in the middle of an empty field. Inside, it was dark and smokey, smelling of stale beer and sweat—an Appalachian dive-bar that served as a hangout for the local factory workers.

After we finished a game of pool, Mark said he'd get us a couple of beers, and I headed for the restroom. When I joined Mark at the bar, I knew he was in trouble. He had already downed several shots of whisky—three, by the count of empty shot glasses in front of him—and was finishing the second of the two beers he had ordered. With that much alcohol on an empty stomach, he was drunk and incoherent. I knew I had to get him home.

When we got into the house, Mark's parents were asleep in front of the TV, so we slipped upstairs to his room and climbed into bed. To my surprise, Mark reached over and touched my leg, initiating a quick game before going to sleep. I was astonished he was coherent enough to recognize his urges, but we began to play. After a few minutes, Mark whispered, "Will you give me a blowjob?"

Our games had never included oral sex, and his request triggered memories of the vile rape by the Pataki brothers. I instantly said *no*. To my relief, Mark groaned, said *fine*, quickly and aggressively satisfied himself, and passed out.

The next morning, we got up shortly before noon, scarfed down a bowl of Cocoa Puffs, and then headed outside to say our goodbyes. We said we looked forward to seeing each other again soon, but as I drove out of their gravel lot, I knew we wouldn't. By asking for oral sex, Mark had taken our casual games to a level of intimacy I didn't want, and couldn't tolerate. I could not go on with our friendship, and I felt guilty that I was walking away from it.

That was the last time I saw my good buddy Mark.

24
Need to Escape

Walking away from Mark was the prelude to my next departure. The Fall of 1978 was the beginning of the end to the relationship with my predator.

Joe and I argued a lot—often about how I was spending my time on campus. Despite my obligations to school and work, he was frustrated I wasn't spending more time with him. He knew I was looking for excuses to distance myself and that I was spending time with my friends at college. Socializing was something new to me. I had devoted all my time over the previous six years to two things: my equestrian training and earning money to support my education and travels. I had never been to a party with kids my age, attended a rock concert, or even gone on a proper date with a girl. At college, I could finally have some fun and act more like the other students.

After the fall quarter began, Joe told me Becky would be taking her dogs and leaving for an extended stay with her family in Wyoming. Joe and Becky were separating in an attempt to save their marriage. I couldn't understand why they would want to save such an unhappy relationship.

Joe had the apartment to himself, so he altered our evening program to take advantage of our solitude. In Becky's absence, my exercise sessions concluded with me disrobed and anointed with baby oil. After my massage, Joe would mount me and pleasure himself like he had in the seclusion of his pickup truck, six years ago in Fort Riley. Joe would also remove all his clothing, and as he lay on top of me, insist I put my arms around his back. The combined effects of caffeine, alcohol, and painkillers had wrought havoc on his skin. As a result, he had developed several walnut-sized boils on his back, and I struggled to find a place for my hands where I could avoid touching them. The new intimacy of his naked body, along with the grotesque growths on his back and the revolting smell of his breath next to my face, almost caused me to pass out.

After a few of those sessions, Joe ventured into forbidden territory. While I was laying on my stomach for a massage, he attempted to slowly insert his index finger where it did not belong. My survival instincts kicked in and I violently clamped all my muscles. He immediately pulled back his hand and never made the attempt again. For the first time, I acted to protect myself from him.

I tolerated this new intimacy and abuse for a few months, and as my distaste for it grew, so did my hatred toward Joe. I needed to escape Joe's clutches and get away from his control. Graduation was coming up in May and it would be my ticket away from Hiram and everything this monster was inflicting upon me. I was counting the days.

25
Disco Is King

My release from Joe began unobtrusively one Thursday night in early May. I had returned to the dorm after working at Hunter's Hollow. A student I knew, Jonathan, found it odd I was wearing a tuxedo, and asked about my outfit. We struck up a conversation and Jonathan said he was about to drive to Cleveland for a night at the disco. I didn't really understand the concept of "going out to the disco." It was 1979 and disco was king—I had just been missing out on the fun—so when Jonathan asked me to go with him, I said *sure*.

After an hour's drive, we exited the freeway and made our way to an abandoned warehouse district on West 9th street. There were no streetlights, no retail storefronts, and no street traffic. The only people we could see were the few men who were walking, mostly in pairs, with a quick and intentional stride across the parking lot toward a windowless building across the street. The lot was oddly full for midnight on a Thursday. Something was going on inside that building. As we got closer to the front door, I could hear the steady beat of music pulsating through the walls. Two men had already reached the door and as they opened it, the volume tripled and all I could see was the flashing of lights at the end of a darkened hallway.

With each step, the music got louder, and it vibrated through my body: *boom, boom, boom*—the drum of the disco beat. At the end of the hallway, a man sat inside what looked like a closet with a half-door separating him from the entranceway. After collecting a cover charge for the two men ahead of us, Jonathan walked up, and a shrill greeting came from the man behind the counter: "Girlfriend! How the hell are ya? Come on in—Dean is playing tonight." We had just entered Cleveland's renowned gay disco: Traxx. Jonathan appeared to be a well-liked regular, so skipping the formality of paying a cover, we walked into the bar at the center of the club.

Men packed the room wall to wall and the music from the dance floor pulsed through every molecule in the building. Mixed in with the music was the roar of voices and the cacophony of excited laughter. The room smelled of alcohol, cigarettes, cologne, and marijuana. To the right of the bar, I could see two large doorways opening onto the dance floor. It was a cavernous room with a thirty-foot ceiling, speakers in every corner stacked from floor to ceiling, and multi-colored spotlights spinning and flashing to the beat of the music. The occasional blast from a strobe light ricocheted off multiple glitter balls, shooting diamond-tipped beams of light throughout the room.

My senses were overwhelmed, and I loved it. Jonathan could see I was enthralled and said, "Let me get you a drink and we'll head upstairs to see Dean. What are you drinking?"

That was a good question; I didn't really drink. Tapping into my memory from years of bartending at family gatherings, I looked for an obvious choice and landed on vodka, with a splash of cranberry juice to fit the festive atmosphere. The bartender filled what looked like a narrow water glass with ice, free poured at least three shots of vodka, and splashed a dollop of juice on top: my first real drink. After a few sips of what tasted like rocket fuel, Jonathan grabbed my arm and led me to a stairway leading to the DJ booth. Climbing the steps like we owned the place, we reached the top and walked straight over to the DJ: Dean Rufus. The dance floor was packed. Dean was working at full speed, alternating his hands between two turntables, and pumping his body to the beat of the music.

Jonathan introduced me and told him it was my first time at Traxx. With a mischievous grin, Dean shouted, "Oh, really? Wanna see the girls go crazy? Watch this!" I still hadn't figured out why the man in the hallway had addressed Jonathan as *girlfriend*, so I could only assume that by *the girls* he meant "everyone." And with the finesse of a true DJ-artist, Dean switched out the twelve-inch disc that had been spinning on the right turntable with another, and slowly faded in the introductory backbeat of Dan Hartman's hit "Relight My Fire." "Go crazy" was an understatement. The song was a fan favorite and as soon as Dean let it begin, dozens of men emerged from all corners of the club and flooded the dance floor. I was looking down at a sea of extremely fit, highly energized men—many shirtless or in some version of half-dress—dancing like no one was watching.

I saw men holding each other and pressing their bodies together as they danced, and it took me a while to process the sight of men kissing. I had no idea gay men kissed. In fact, I knew nothing about consensual gay sex. Leaving those mysteries to figure out later, I went downstairs with Jonathan, belted down another strong drink, and stood back to enjoy watching the next hour play out in front of us.

Jonathan knew a lot of people, and several offered to buy us drinks. After the first two vodkas, I was drunk, and I happily accepted more drinks. Thankfully, Jonathan had stopped with his second—he was our chauffeur—and at around 1:30 we headed back to Hiram.

My adrenaline was still pumping on the drive home and Jonathan could tell I was in a state of euphoria. Through a smirk he asked, "Do you want to go back with me on Sunday night? It's the biggest night of the week at Traxx."

"Yes."

I had just completed my indoctrination into the gay world and the culture of "partying." This unfamiliar lifestyle was intoxicating, and I was already craving more. It was the beginning of my headlong jump from the frying pan into the fire.

26
Let's Dance

Jonathan and I arrived at Traxx earlier on Sunday and there was a long line of people waiting to get in—this time with a sprinkling of women in sequined dresses, stiletto heels, and lots of colorful makeup. (I would learn later that most of them were men in drag.) Jonathan's celebrity didn't buy us any favors this time, and we had to wait in line and pay the cover. It was worth the wait and the money—the intensity of the club had increased by multiples since Thursday: the number of people; the heat generated by all those dancing bodies; the smells; and the charge of electricity in the air. While Jonathan socialized, I surveyed the room and sucked down my first drink.

Right after getting a second, my gaze went across the room to a small stairway leading from a lounge area into the main bar. Heading down the stairs was a man who appeared to be my age and height, with longish medium-blond hair, the face of a *Tiger Beat* teen idol, and a pair of tight-fitting cream-colored jeans. Our eyes locked and he walked over, joined by his friend and the woman they were with.

"Hi. I'm Dennis. This is Bill and his fiancé, Jenny. We're going downstairs to smoke a joint—want to come with?" With the pleasure receptors in my brain having taken over, I was on autopilot for *yes*. We descended into a dimly lit room with sofas and chairs set around tables of various sizes. The music from upstairs was still pounding, but the quieter atmosphere lent itself to having conversations and doing drugs. I had smoked marijuana occasionally in the dorms with friends, but I was a lightweight so was decently stoned after two hits from a pipe. Bill pulled out a neatly rolled joint, fired it up, and passed it to Dennis, who passed it to Jenny, who passed it to me. Terrified I might cough, I took a timid puff and handed it back to Bill. When it returned, I felt more confident and took a longer, deeper hit, and that did the job. I was flying high and after a few minutes of chit-chat, Dennis stood up, grabbed my hand, and said, "Let's dance."

Fueled by alcohol, adrenaline, and marijuana, I was up for anything. We stepped onto the dance floor as France Joli's voice began inviting everyone to "Come to Me"—a song with a slow start that accelerated into the throbbing rhythm a dance crowd craves. I don't think Dennis knew the two men dancing next to us, but when he saw them passing a small brown bottle to one another, he gave them a friendly nod and they graciously passed the bottle over to him. Dennis held it to his nostril, inhaled deeply, and handed it to me. Its acrid, medicinal smell reminded me of dirty socks, but I repeated what I saw everyone else doing, held the bottle to my nose, and inhaled. Immediately my head felt like it was heating up from the inside out and I felt weightless. My vision blurred as the room swirled around me and I became light-headed—not nauseous or dizzy, but euphoric. I had taken my first dose of amyl nitrate: "poppers," as they were called—a drug normally prescribed to someone like my father to counter the life-threatening effects of an angina attack.

Coming off this brief but intense high, Dennis clasped his hands around my lower back and as the rhythm of the song increased, pushed his waist against mine and swayed his hips to the music, enjoying the sensation through every inch of his body—as was I. As the song reached a crescendo, we separated, and I let loose to dance in a state of bliss. Winding down after a second song, Dennis motioned for us to leave the dance floor and return to the bar.

Drenched in sweat and our faces beet red, I looked around in search of Jonathan. What I saw stopped me in my tracks: standing in front of me was a new version of my Red Raider friend Lori, with the same look of shock on her face as mine. We hadn't seen each other in two years. It took a moment for each of us to comprehend that the other *was* who we thought they were, and then we let out a yell, pounced on each other, and embraced in a bear hug that should have broken our ribs.

I had lost contact with Lori. I was focused on school, work, and riding, and she had spent all her time attending cosmetology school. I could see she had graduated with flying colors: My tomboy friend had transformed into her own version of Elvira. Her hair, dyed the color of an eggplant, was cut into an asymmetrical bob. Her face was made up with heavy foundation and swipes of blue, black, and purple, on and around her eyes. The front of her dress was unbuttoned to a point way south of décolleté and revealed a new feature: two enormous breasts pushed together inside a black lace bustier, trying very hard to escape.

After our initial surprise, Lori suggested we have a drink. Dennis had already reconnected with Bill and Jenny, and I signaled I was heading to the bar with my friend. Before we had finished our drink, the beat of the music changed and the first sounds of Brainstorm's "Lovin' Is Really My Game" started pulsing from the speakers, and the entire bar erupted with screams of delight. About fifteen feet from where we were standing, a group of three men shouted to Lori, "Miss 'a Rahimy—it's our song!" One of the three bolted over, grabbed Lori by the hand, and swept her into the throng of dancing bodies. As she was being torn away, she turned and yelled, "I'll give you a call!" Lori went to dance, and I went to find Dennis and his friends. We finished our drinks, exchanged numbers, and Jonathan drove us home while I relived the night—thrill by thrill—the whole way back.

27

Confronting My Stalker

For months, I had been counting down the days to Hiram's commencement ceremony on June 10th. I was looking forward to my release from Joe's clutches and an end to the rigors of attending college and working three jobs. There was light at the end of the tunnel—I was about to become a free man and had already landed my first post-graduate job.

I was scheduled to leave for England on July 9th to receive training as a Financial Assistant for a German company named Demag with a subsidiary located in a suburb of Cleveland. I would have four weeks after graduation to wrap up my work obligations, prepare for my move to England, and, most importantly, get away from seven years of life with Joe.

With Becky still in Wyoming, Joe was alone at his apartment and growing desperate at the thought of losing me. I had put an end to evening exercise and massage sessions—with all I had to manage before graduation, and my new friendship with Dennis, it was easy to come up with excuses to stay away. But Joe had developed the habit of taking evening walks through town—walks that passed in front of my dorm. Joe was stalking me.

Despite my busy schedule, Dennis and I squeezed in some trips to the gay bars. Being with Dennis and his friends became an escape from the fear and anxiety surrounding my separation from Joe. Dennis provided me with an outlet to a new world: one filled with fun and excitement, fueled by alcohol and drugs, and one where I could abandon the disciplined behavior that had been the foundation of my life for so many years.

It was important within the gay community to pay special attention to appearances: in the form of fashion, grooming, and everything that contributed to one's persona. For those reasons, Dennis felt the name *Gil* didn't carry the right kind of cachet for a man who was going to be seen with him, so after learning my full name was Roderick Gilman, he decided *Rod* had a more sophisticated ring to it and changed my name for me.

I was not the only one who had undergone a name change. At her own admission, Lori was a "fag hag"—a straight woman who surrounded herself with gay men. Having created her new Elvira-like persona, her tomboy name no longer suited her. *Lori* had been laid to rest and she declared herself to be *Loren*; it was her given name, and *Lori* had become too "cute."

After reconnecting, Loren would occasionally take a break from her party life and venture out to the stables to spend time around Joe and the horses. Unfortunately, Loren had mentioned to Joe that she had run into me "downtown at a disco." Joe's antenna had shot up and he grilled her for information. She assumed Joe knew about my new lifestyle and gave him all the details. Pandora's box had been opened.

28
Let's Begin—It's Over

The day of my commencement ceremony arrived. It was held on the athletic field in front of the stadium bleachers where Joe and I had finished many evening training sessions. Over two hundred students in my graduating class had gathered inside the gymnasium to don our caps and gowns and line up for our procession outside.

The orchestra played Pomp and Circumstance as we left the gym and shuttled down the narrow hallway to the field. At the end of the corridor, we were to make a left turn. When I was about ten steps away, my eyes locked into the eyes of my stalker. Joe had positioned himself so I had to pass him. He had scoped out the venue and devised a plan to interject himself into the biggest celebration of my life.

Pierced by the intensity of his glare, I broke eye contact and swept past without saying a word. I refused to let Joe ruin my day, and I reveled in the ceremony the way any other graduating student would have. I hoped that I had seen the last of Joe, but there was one more episode to get through.

* * *

Dennis and Bill had secured a lease on a two-bedroom townhouse near where I would be working for Demag. As Dennis and I were in the throes of developing a meaningful relationship, and knowing I had four weeks before leaving for England, he suggested I move into the townhouse. The trip to England would only be for a few months and when I came back, we could live together as a happy couple. I was in love with the new lifestyle and the pleasures of drinking alcohol and smoking marijuana. I was in love with that more than I was in love with Dennis. In fact, I struggled with our physical intimacy, and I was reluctant to try anything more than fondling and touching. Memories from the assault by the Pataki brothers were still vivid and I was unable to even consider oral sex. Dennis, it seemed, was willing to be patient.

Joe, however, was not. He wanted me back.

The townhouse had one landline phone mounted on the kitchen wall. One evening, on the third ring, Bill picked up and said, "Hold on. He's right here." Loren had given Joe my number and he was infecting my newfound sanctuary. His desperate pleas for me to come to my senses and abandon my ruinous relationship turned into another heated altercation. Dennis knew it was Joe and could see I was upset.

He took the phone and said, "Now listen here. Your relationship with Rod is finished. He is moving on with his life, and if you ever try to interfere with our plans to spend time together, I will get my attorney, call the police, and do whatever it takes to keep you away from us. With any luck, you will go to jail, where you belong."

Thirty minutes later there was a knock at the door. We were having a couple of drinks as we got ready to go out for the night. Thankfully, we had already finished smoking a joint and had put away all the marijuana and its paraphernalia. It was the local police. They had received a call from a man named Joe Brooks who suspected illegal drug use in the home and was concerned about Gil Merrick's safety and well-being. Dennis had the sense to ask if they had a warrant to come into the house. The officer said he did not. After checking my identification and confirming I was safe and unharmed—and that there was no apparent drug use—he said the police department had fulfilled its obligation and could consider the call "handled."

Dennis was my hero. He had fended off my attacker and protected me. He had affirmed that I was loved and that someone other than Joe wanted to ensure my well-being. We kept to our plan of going to Traxx that night and I got both drunk and stoned, dancing the night away in a numbed state of bliss that, unbeknownst to me, was to become a familiar way of escaping from my traumatic life with Joe.

29

Coming Out

The police incident was Joe's last-ditch effort. My escape was complete. I was free to enjoy my new freedom and have fun with Dennis. That gave way to thinking about my new identity: one that no longer included being the pedagogue's protégé and a dedicated student of horsemanship. I was certain I was becoming something "else," but I couldn't sort through what that "else" was. After days of consideration, it hit me: I must be gay.

I had always enjoyed my special games with Mark and was attracted to his athletic body; I had tolerated Joe's attentions for seven years and had never walked away from them; I loved being with Dennis (although the physical intimacy was proving to be a challenge); I enjoyed looking at the trim and athletic bodies of handsome men; and I craved the fawning and sexually charged attention I was getting from strangers in the gay bars. I was turning twenty-two but looked much younger, I was lean and fit, and according to the gay lexicon, I was an alluring "twink"—a boyish, white, fashionable male. I *must* be gay, so I decided to "come out" and proudly declare my new identity to my family and friends. Dennis had proven to be the perfect role model for that and empowered me to start the process, beginning with my dearest friend, Heather.

Heather was house sitting for a family friend around the corner from her parents' house. I told her I wanted to talk, and we agreed I would spend the night where she was staying. As the evening progressed, I told her what she had already suspected. What came as a surprise to her were the details about the abuse Joe had subjected me to. Heather put the puzzle together and figured out why Joe, at first, had always peripherally included her in so many of our activities, but always came shy of showing her the same level of attention he did to me. Heather was simply the decoy to make me feel more secure and for Joe to have access to me.

Thanks to over nine years of friendship, coming out to Heather was both comfortable and comforting. Secrets I had been hiding about my relationship with Joe came into the open and brought about a new sense of freedom. It felt good.

Coming out to my mother evoked a different set of emotions. A couple of days after talking to Heather, I drove to Chalfant Road to visit with my mother. We were in the kitchen when I started telling her about the night I ran into Loren at Traxx and made a point of mentioning Traxx was a gay bar. My mother's first question was: "Do you think Lori is, you know, *that way* with other women?" I explained Loren's new persona, lifestyle, and unique role in the gay world as a "fag hag," after which she asked her next question: "Are *you* that way? Do you like other men?"

She couldn't have made it easier. All I needed to do was utter one word: *yes*. She made a quick inquiry whether I thought my "manhood" was perhaps too small (a concern my father had once shared about himself to her), hoping she might at least get an explanation to help her make sense of this disappointing and upsetting news. I assured her everything was fine in the size department, and then shared some details about my relationships with Mark, Dennis, and Joe.

She paused as she added sugar to her iced tea, and then said something that didn't register at the time: "Oh, your father and I thought something might be going on with Joe, but we knew you liked being with him and the horses, so we didn't say anything."

At the time, I was grateful my parents had let me pursue my equestrian dream. The profound disappointment I felt when I realized my parents had suspected I was being victimized by a pedophile, and had done nothing to protect me, did not set in until years later. But that disappointment would be minor compared to the incredibly high price I was going to pay over the coming four decades for having allowed the abuse to go on for seven years. Entering the gay world would only serve as a small deposit.

Part Two

HALT

Bad choices, addictions, and a struggle

30

Rape

There was a problem with my new gay identity: I still resisted full-on physical intimacy with Dennis. Before leaving for my training in England, he had been the epitome of patience. As planned, I moved back into the townhouse after three months in England and we resumed our relationship. That patience was about to run out.

One Friday night Dennis and I met after his shift as a front desk attendant in an establishment next door to Traxx: The West Ninth Street Club Baths. I arrived at eleven o'clock and we headed over to Traxx for drinks.

After several drinks and a shared joint, Dennis suggested we go back to the Baths. He greeted the attendant who had relieved him and asked for two towels and a key. We headed into the windowless maze of dimly lit rooms, sparsely populated with men meandering about with roving eyes. The only piece of dress allowed was a towel. The Club was a place to either watch men cruising in search of a trick, or to join the hunt and select a partner, or partners, for a casual sexual encounter. Guests had options. They could mingle in TV lounges; work out in a small room with a bench, dumbbells, and seating for onlookers; visit the steam room; or use a large open shower adjoined by a darkened observation deck.

After changing into our towels, Dennis showed me the lay of the land, after which he produced a bottle of baby oil and suggested we head to the showers and oil up our bodies for some fun. The pungent and familiar smell of the baby oil brought back memories of the hundreds of nights Joe had massaged me. As hard as I tried to participate in the fun, my mind could not escape the grip of the disturbing memories. We left the showers and headed to a private room (if you can call an eight-foot-square closet with a wooden bench built into a wall cubby, a "room"), where Dennis tried to enjoy some physical intimacy with me.

I was not on board for sexual activity in any form. I was an undesirable date. Frustrated, Dennis left me alone in the room and I fell into an intoxicated sleep. About an hour later I woke up and looked for Dennis. I found him sitting on a carpeted bank in a dark room, smoking a cigarette and looking through the flickering lights at a sex video playing on a TV. I realized he had found a willing partner and, satisfied, was ready to go home.

The next day, Saturday, Dennis went to work, and I spent the day running errands. When Dennis got home, Bill joined us in the kitchen and we began the night in our usual fashion, taking a hit of speed to energize us for the long night ahead. "Black Beauties" were the most popular form of speed: a mixture of amphetamines, like Adderall, but inducing an additional "high" along with a sustained increase in energy. We washed those down with our first vodka and tonic and mellowed out with a joint. With the songs from Supertramp's *Breakfast in America* wafting throughout the townhouse, we got ready for our night out. Jenny joined us, and we piled into Bill's car and headed to the freeway, destined for another big night on the town as Alicia Bridges sang out her apropos tune, "I Love the Nightlife."

Dennis and I enjoyed our usual drinks, many dances—accompanied by a few snorts of poppers—and after a few hours, we headed home. Bill and Jenny went straight to his room while Dennis and I stayed downstairs in the kitchen. He poured us another drink and then pulled out a small pill container. At this point, I was drunk and stoned, and my adrenaline was still pumping after the combination of speed and hours of rigorous dancing. I was also dehydrated. Dennis handed me a white pill about the size of an aspirin and told me if I took it with a glass of water, I could wind down and get a good night's sleep. I was on board. What I had unknowingly taken was a 150 mg dose of methaqualone, commonly known as a Quaalude: a central nervous system depressant with similar properties to barbiturates.

Before the effects kicked in, Dennis led me upstairs to our bedroom and undressed us. He told me to come with him to the bathroom and had me lie on the floor. He reached into the cabinet under the sink and pulled out two incompatible objects: a 5 ml plastic syringe without a needle, and a small bottle of whisky. What followed was an act that is familiar in the gay community but was foreign to me: administering a whisky enema. Aside from the normal flushing effects of an enema—normally given with water or mineral oil—the use of whisky ensured that its immediate absorption from the walls of the rectum would intensify the intoxicating and numbing effects of 80-proof alcohol.

When I could leave the bathroom and stumble into the bedroom, I was on the verge of passing out and losing all control of my muscles. This allowed Dennis to violate me with the physical act I had been resisting since the day we met. He raped me.

31
Can't Let Go

It was late Sunday morning when I regained consciousness, and I knew I had been injured. There was an intense stinging sensation between my legs, and I feared that the moisture I felt might be blood. It was. Dennis was still asleep as I packed my clothes. When he woke up, he seemed shocked I was leaving. In his mind, we had a "fun" night, and he couldn't understand why I was so upset. I packed quickly and we didn't engage in much conversation other than for Dennis to admonish me as I left with the comment: "Welcome to the gay-world, Rod. That's what happens to cock-teases."

Thirty minutes later, I showed up at my mother's house on Chalfant Road. Too embarrassed to explain why I was there, I said the new townhouse was too crowded for three people, and asked if I could stay in my old room until I found my own apartment. My mother was relieved and overjoyed. Hoping my time with Dennis had only been a "phase," she welcomed me with open arms. I was relieved to be back in a safe place, and glad to once again be called *Gil*.

The first order of business the next morning was to call the family doctor to set up an emergency visit. My injuries had not healed, and although mortified at the thought of presenting myself to a doctor I had been seeing since childhood, I needed medical attention. The doctor asked about the nature of my injuries (confirming what he already knew was the cause). He advised me to be "more careful" in the future and sent me on my way with a salve, some antibiotics, and a mild painkiller.

The physical injuries healed over the next few days, but they were minor compared to the emotional harm that was done. During the time I spent with Dennis, I thought we were building a committed, monogamous relationship. Instead, I realized Dennis had been having ongoing casual sex with tricks from the Baths and the bars, and I felt betrayed. And the rape? I rationalized something was wrong with me—I was inadequate in fulfilling Dennis's needs. I could not satisfy the needs of another man, and out of the frustration and disappointment I had caused, my partner forced a remedy to his problems. As a "cock-tease," I had deceived Dennis, luring him into believing I would provide something I could not. I felt I had failed: I had failed at being sufficiently gay.

* * *

To this day, I do not fully understand my actions in the aftermath of escaping from Joe's abuse and fleeing from Dennis, both within months of each other. Recognizing and understanding the effects of trauma is complicated, and what I proceeded to do was confirmation of that.

After I moved into my mother's house, I set up the rooms on the third floor as my new apartment. In need of a stereo, I phoned Dennis at the store where he worked as a salesman, saying I wanted to buy a new system. When I arrived at the showroom, he was all business, and neither of us mentioned our last encounter three weeks before. It was a high-end electronics store, so I asked if I could finance the purchase. We sat at a desk, filled out the form, and he returned to tell me the loan had been approved.

Despite the sexual abuse, I somehow needed Dennis to like me—I was still attracted to him and was missing all the positive attention and fawning I had enjoyed before the night of the rape. My overpowering need to be loved, combined with my feelings of guilt and inadequacy, overrode the rational thoughts that were screaming at me to stay away from Dennis.

My trip to his store was our last encounter, but when I think back to that time, I realize I had a powerful attraction to the lifestyle that was built into our relationship, and I found it painful to let go.

More perplexing, I deliberately inserted myself back into Joe's world. He was running a vaulting program and, perhaps, out of the same need I had felt with Dennis to make amends for the tumultuous way our relationship had ended, I volunteered to assist Joe with the training. I would arrive on the property, go to the arena where the horse and vaulters were waiting, participate in the training, and leave. I still wanted to receive approval from Joe—and each time, I heard the accolades that I craved: Joe told me I did a great job. That went on for two years.

Becky had stayed in Wyoming with her family, and Joe had already taken in a teenage boy who came from a dysfunctional home with an alcoholic father. Joe lived in an apartment on the farm's property, and I got to know the boy well. I never asked him questions, and I issued no warnings. I wanted to pretend nothing untoward had ever happened between Joe and me. What was wrong with me?

32

The Void

Black Beauties had become my new best friend.

With a full-time job at Demag, waiting tables on weekends at Hunter's Hollow, and now with evening classes for the MBA program at Cleveland State University, speed helped fuel my energy daily.

On the nights I didn't work, I partied with Loren at home or at her favorite singles bars. I loved having her back in my life. She had shared my mother's elation when she heard I had moved out of the townhouse with Dennis and Bill. "You are *not* gay," she said. "It was only a phase and you're over it." Or was I?

To fill the gap of sport in my life, I stepped up my physical training and joined a gym. The Athletic Club was ten minutes from my apartment with two floors of resistance equipment, cardio machines, free weights, a running track, and an indoor lap pool. I jumped into my new endeavor with both feet and became a "gym-rat."

I went to the gym on the way home from the office on nights when I didn't have class, and then again on weekends when I had more time and could work out, run laps, and swim. Every week I could feel myself getting stronger, and a look in the mirror told me that for the first time, my body was gaining some definition. I liked what I saw, and as my appreciation for my body grew, so did my desire to compare myself to other men in the gym—and in the locker room. What had been the scene of nightmares in junior high had become a place where I could show off my body and be proud of it. The pain of shame and inadequacy was gone.

I enjoyed looking at other men's bodies—as long as they had a build I aspired to have myself. Football, baseball, and basketball players caught none of my attention—the lean physiques of divers, dancers, and runners, did. It was not an attraction spurred by a desire to have sex with the men; I was attracted to their athletic physiques because they mirrored what I wanted to have for myself. It was the same way a straight woman might look at a Victoria's Secret model and be attracted to the display of her voluptuous body, longing to have that appeal herself but without a desire to have sex with the model. I was developing a physique like Mark's—one I had not only admired but could touch and explore with a mutual stimulation that made it exciting. I was still looking for that excitement.

Some men in the locker rooms and showers didn't hide their excitement in looking at my physique. The showers had individual stalls with plastic curtains for privacy, and it wasn't unusual for someone to find their way into my stall to assist with lathering up, and then engage in other touching activities. It reminded me of the times Mark and I would go swimming—either at the camp pool or across the street by the waterfall—and either slip into the woods to play our little game or end up at home to take a shower together. But these gym encounters were anonymous, and at the risk of being overheard, not a word was spoken. I suspect many of those men went home to wives and girlfriends.

My comfort with touching another man's body, or being touched by a man, had developed over ten years, and I was still enjoying it. There was no emotional investment, no commitment to follow up, and no apparent way I could get hurt. To me, it was just another game, and I was having fun. I loved the attention and the feeling that I was desirable; the part of being with Joe I had enjoyed; the part that kept me from realizing what he was doing was abusive. The shower encounters were exciting and forbidden, and each interaction provided a small dose of euphoria that filled a void in my life.

My frightening separation from Joe, followed by Dennis's rape, left me wounded and looking for a way to be nurtured and to heal. The positive attention I was getting at the gym, and the drugs and alcohol I used at home, were forms of treatment to help manage my pain and depression. My next-door neighbor was a middle-aged, stay-at-home invalid who treated the pain of lupus and her other ailments with marijuana and cocaine. To break her loneliness, she invited me over on a regular basis, and for the next three years, cocaine use became a regular form of recreation, especially on the nights she and I went out to local jazz clubs. Little did I know that in adopting these coping mechanisms, I was succumbing to my new disease of addiction.

* * *

Although I had moved away from my equestrian life, I still yearned for it. In the spring of 1983, I focused my time and energy on the one thing that could assure my return to riding: making lots of money and buying my own horses and farm. Purchasing a small farm where I could train for the Olympics, without the worry of having to move out, was an exciting vision to me. I could imagine the design of the stables, and sketched blueprints for the ideal layout—one that ensured maximum comfort for the horses, and maximum efficiency around its daily management. A haven for training that I owned.

I had four years of experience at a multinational corporation, my fluency in German was confirmed, and in a few months, I would have my master's degree. It was time to shift my career into high gear and move on to something that would exponentially increase my earnings and help me achieve my dreams. Within weeks, I received a job offer from another company as Financial Controller in their European office.

However, when I handed in my resignation, Demag was reluctant to let me go and offered me a position as Assistant to the Vice President of Finance for the company's parent company located in New York City: Mannesmann Capital Corporation. The position came with an attractive compensation package, and I would be a true New Yorker—living the dream in the Big Apple. I accepted their offer.

It was time to leave Ohio and escape from the scene of my traumas: seven years of sexual abuse by Joe; the rapes committed by Ted, Ben, and Dennis; and the sudden death of my father with the emotional destruction it brought upon our family.

I believed I was not so much running away from my life in Ohio, as I was running toward new opportunities to fulfill my dreams. I was certain I could guide myself through the next step on the journey, but I was woefully unaware of how ill-equipped I was.

33

The Big Apple

My great New York adventure began in early May. I moved into the Roosevelt Hotel—next door to Grand Central Station—until I found an apartment. After settling in on the first weekend, I got up Monday morning, selected my most professional three-piece suit, and took the first of what would be hundreds of daily walks through the city to the company's offices at 57th Street and Park Avenue. I was in heaven—a feeling confirmed every day when I looked out the window of my office on the 26th floor and savored the view of Midtown Manhattan from my perch above Park Avenue.

In short order, I had found my dream apartment: a 475-square-foot studio on the fourth floor of a recently built twenty-two-story luxury condo building. It was on East 86th Street between 2nd and 3rd Avenues in the Yorkville area— previously known as the "Heart of Germantown." Very apropos. There was a twenty-four-hour doorman and a beautifully landscaped rooftop terrace with unobstructed views looking east over the river and south over Midtown.

I discovered that the 92nd Street Y was only six blocks from my apartment and had one of the best athletic facilities and indoor pools in Manhattan. Staying true to my commitment as a gym-rat, I got a membership and worked out every evening. After an hour in the gym, I would don my Speedo for a half-hour of laps in the pool. A young, lean man with an attractive body could find plenty of other swimmers to take a post-swim shower with. After gaining the attention of a like-minded swimmer in the open shower room, we would slip away to one of the more private stalls. Showering together and doing something risky had a charge to it, and I loved receiving attention from men who showed their attraction to me.

I engaged in a more extreme version of risky public behavior on my weekend trips to Central Park. I would pull on my running tights, take a hit or two of pot, clip on my Sony Walkman, and strike off for the park, jogging along to familiar disco tunes. After completing my run around the Reservoir, I would head south for a stroll across the Great Lawn and take in the multitude of activities playing out in that large, open area. Then I would cross over the hill by Belvedere Castle and head into the much-less-frequented area embedded in the woods, just north of the lake, called the Ramble.

In 1983, this wooded area—whose trails traversed up and down small hills, around elevated rock structures, and into remote areas out of view by most park visitors—was a haven for gay cruising. There were plenty of secluded spots where two or more men could slip off the trails and have sex. But most men seemed to enjoy the voyeuristic and exhibitionist activities that culminated in an act of group self-gratification known as a "circle jerk"—the game Mark and I used to play, only with more players. As a voyeuristic participant, I did not have to touch or talk to anyone, and in the middle of the day, I felt safe. The hunt for like-minded voyeurs and the guarantee of a climactic ending was exciting, and excitement was what I craved—a way to fill the void created when I walked away from Dennis.

One Sunday afternoon, after finishing my jog around the Reservoir, I continued to walk along the bridle path that ran adjacent to the track. The Claremont Riding Academy was two blocks from Central Park and provided easy access for riders to the paths. Headed in the direction of the Great Lawn, I heard the hooves of two horses coming up behind me, so I stepped to the side to let them by. When the horses were about five feet away, the riders stopped to discuss which direction they wanted to proceed.

The aroma of the horses' sweat and the leathery scent of the riding gear reached my nose and triggered an immediate longing to be with a horse. I made eye contact with the bay gelding who was standing in front of me. Our gazes stayed connected for less than a minute, but during those fleeting moments, I experienced the familiar feeling of having my soul connect with that of a horse. In an instant, that feeling was snuffed out by a wave of sadness and the familiar ache of depression.

As I walked away, I recalled my first ride on Mr. Buttons. Images of Mark and me sneaking away at night, climbing bareback onto Smoke and Itty Bitty, and galloping across open fields under the stars, popped into my head. Memories from the stables in Germany returned. The exuberant feeling of rides on the Lipizzaner stallions revisited me.

Overwhelmed by sadness, I aborted my afternoon excursion in the park and headed home to begin my regular shut-down routine with drinks and marijuana. But this time there would be no dinner and no TV. It was only 2 p.m. and I wasn't hungry—only upset. It was the first day I had ever shut down in the afternoon and started drinking before "cocktail hour." I knew there was something wrong about that—and going for the vodka bottle disturbed me—but I shoved those feelings to the side and proceeded to get drunk. I was in bed by 7:30.

* * *

I spent more evenings alone in New York than I had in Cleveland after I left Dennis. As soon as I got home each evening, I would mix my first Smirnoff and tonic, bring out my collection of menus, order dinner, and hunker in for a night of TV and drinks.

That first sip of vodka released the right amount of dopamine to tell my brain I was feeling better. *Maybe the pain will begin to ease—so take another sip.* It worked. Since two sips worked, I thought the entire drink would be a well-earned reward for a good day's effort, and offer relief from my sadness. But as the alcohol numbed my brain, it acted as a depressant, and the sadness increased. I was certain another drink would fix it. *The first one worked wonders, so the second one should be even better.* But it wasn't—it made things worse. *Maybe another then? Where is that feeling of euphoria this drinking session started with?* I wanted to know when my brain would go "*click*," and when I would finally feel at peace—getting some sort of escape from the disturbing memories running through my head. Almost every night wrapped up with two or three hits of pot and an intense stretch-out session. I would be in bed by 10 p.m.—living the NYC dream.

One of my favorite pieces of literature is the play by Tennessee Williams, *Cat on a Hot Tin Roof.* It was made into a movie in 1958 and stars Paul Newman, who ironically was a neighborhood friend of my father's. This exchange between an aging football player, Brick, and his wealthy father, Big Daddy—the patriarch of the family's large estate in Mississippi—encapsulates the yearning I felt for something to turn off whatever was going on inside my head that made me feel so depressed and unsettled.

> Brick: Somethin' hasn't happened yet.
> Big Daddy: What's that?
> Brick: A click in my head.
> Big Daddy: Did you say "click"?
> Brick: Yes, sir, the click in my head that makes me feel peaceful.

Big Daddy: Boy, sometimes you worry me.
Brick: It's like a switch, clickin' off in my head. Turns the hot light off and the cool one on, and all of a sudden there's peace.
Big Daddy: Boy, you're, you're a real alcoholic!
Brick: That is the truth. Yes, sir, I am an alcoholic.

At the age of twenty-seven, my journey toward knowing I was addicted to alcohol was in its early stages; Brick was ahead of me on that count. But like Brick, I had already begun searching in earnest for that daily "click." I didn't realize the only thing keeping me from finding that peace was the alcohol itself, the Great Deceiver. I experienced no peace. Only night after night of *sip, sip, sip.*

34

On My Own

From time to time, I would take a one-hour flight from New York to Cleveland to visit family and friends.

I spent time with Loren, whose life was unraveling. She spent many nights drinking in swanky hotel bars and hooking up with men from out of town. Her other nights ended at home, drinking a half-gallon of Gallo chardonnay in front of the TV until the early hours of the morning. Loren's eating had also become an addiction, causing her to gain weight at an alarming rate. Having added plastic surgery and painkillers to her list of addictions and disorders, I could tell that my happy-go-lucky, bawdy childhood friend was becoming a tortured soul trying to exorcise her demons.

Every visit to Cleveland also afforded me time to get together with Heather. Heather's position as a paralegal had advanced and she developed proprietary skills that no one could replicate. Seeing an opportunity, she started her own business and marketed those skills to other law firms. She was on her way to building an incredibly successful company.

Each visit with Heather showed me how she was putting all the pieces together to accomplish her goals: owning her own business and generating the wealth she would need to support her ambitions to be part of the Olympic movement.

When I compared Heather's situation to mine, I felt I was on the wrong path to achieving my own goals and was certain I had to make a change. I spent several months wracking my brain to figure out what unique skills I had that I could build a business around and generate the cash I needed to own a horse farm. I finally came up with an answer.

I had worked for six years at one of Germany's largest manufacturing conglomerates; I understood the various strategies Mannesmann had used when entering each of its U.S. markets; I was accustomed to working with executives at the highest level of corporate management; I could travel back and forth between Europe and the U.S.; and I spoke fluent German. By pulling those attributes together, I could serve as a consultant to European companies wanting to expand into the U.S. markets. Since large, well-established companies already had sufficient in-house resources for those services, my target clients would be the many medium-sized, family-owned businesses that made up the backbone of the German economy.

I incorporated my company under the name Questus. I engaged Headquarters Companies, located at 100 Park Avenue (a prestigious address in the heart of Manhattan that Europeans would recognize), to provide virtual headquarters. I selected Frankfurt for my European base where I would establish the same office presence.

I gave notice to Mannesmann, terminated my studio lease on 86th Street, sold my furniture, packed my bags, and prepared to leave for Frankfurt. Everything was set and ready to go. *What could go wrong?*

35
Off and Running

What *could* go wrong? Had I known the situation I would find myself in three years later, in 1988, I never would have left New York.

To begin with, I was embarking on this new adventure with only $15,000 to cover future expenses and I was still obligated to make quarterly payments on my outstanding student loans; money would be tight.

I was also naïve—to the point of being stupid—about many things. Believing my new company would be a rousing success in short order, I felt entitled to begin my venture in style—as if I were already a successful business owner. So, I booked a one-way ticket to Frankfurt on a TWA flight from JFK—in business class—costing at least four times as much as an economy class ticket and eating up a significant chunk of my limited capital.

I also thought it would be a good idea to bring along an ample supply of marijuana since resources in Frankfurt would be unknown. That was my addiction driving the decision-making process: getting alcohol would not be a problem, but finding pot was going to prove impossible. So I wrapped up two ounces of the green buds in Saran wrap, bored a hole into a jar of Jif peanut butter, inserted the stowaway substance into the middle of the jar, covered it back up with the peanut butter, smoothed the top, shut the jar, and placed it in my suitcase, along with a jar of Smucker's grape jelly: what American wouldn't be traveling overseas with the makings of their beloved PB&J? I assured myself this irresponsible act was worth the risk.

Consistent with my reckless frame of mind and bad decision-making, I tucked a small joint into my briefcase for the journey. Upon discovering I had the entire upper deck of the Boeing 747 to myself—and given that smoking was still allowed on international flights—after dinner was served and I had enjoyed several drinks, I smoked the joint. I should be writing this from a prison cell, but I was not caught for either smoking a forbidden substance over international waters or transporting illegal drugs, and my new life in Frankfurt began according to plan.

I arrived on the morning of May 1st—a national holiday in Germany—and settled into my hotel room by the Old Opera House in the middle of the city. The next morning, I was ready to put the pieces of my new business together.

I established a business presence for Questus in the heart of Frankfurt's business district, then went to the local Chamber of Commerce and purchased a directory of German companies and a booklet that outlined the dates and cities for every trade show and business conference for the coming year. The next challenge was accommodation.

A friend from work had given me the number for her nephew in Frankfurt, and as luck would have it, he was wrapping up his studies in Frankfurt and about to move to Berlin in pursuit of his medical degree. He had a long-term lease on his apartment in Sachsenhausen—across from the river Main that runs through the center of Frankfurt, and only minutes from the business district. He did not want to lose the lease while he was away at school, so he offered me an inexpensive sublease and I jumped at the opportunity. He provided me with a furnished apartment, in an ideal location, at a price I could afford (for a short while) and gave me something that would prove to be a highlight of my life: an introduction to one of his close friends, Alexandra.

We met Alexandra at a local café, and in my eyes, she was flawless. She had a youthful face with doe-like eyes, a pixyish look with a broad toothy smile, medium-brown hair that she wore in a pageboy cut, and a lean and athletic build. She exuded the cosmopolitan confidence I admire so much in European women, and she was chic in every sense of the word.

Within days of meeting Alexandra, we began to date, and I shared my business plan, which included attending industry trade fairs in major European cities. Alexandra gave me sound advice about which ones might be the best prospects for meeting potential clients. Even though my venture was loaded with risks, she had confidence that if any American could make the plan work, it would be me. So, I began my hunt for clients by attending trade fairs in Hanover and Munich.

While at the trade fair in Munich, I remembered an invitation I had received from Uwe, an acquaintance I had met when I first arrived in Frankfurt. Uwe had invited me to visit him should I ever be in Munich, so I called him. As it turned out, Uwe and his wife, Vicky, were leaving Munich by train on the day I was arriving—heading north to their home in Denmark—but said he would be happy to get together for a drink at the train station before they left.

When we had met in Frankfurt, I had given Uwe a quick overview of what my company, Questus, was all about. It turned out that after our meeting, Uwe had teased out the details of a business idea he wanted to share with me. His own company, Quintessa Embroideries, was losing sales in Europe to competitor firms doing business out of India, Pakistan, and mainland China, where the labor costs were considerably less than they were at his workshop in Hong Kong. To lower Quintessa's manufacturing costs, Uwe had inquired about shifting their manufacturing operations into a contract workshop in what was then called Canton—now Guangzhou. Those mainland workshops were massive hand-labor facilities set up to handle large volumes of work. Uwe had been told that if he wanted Quintessa to move its production work into the Canton workshops, he would need to give assurances that the annual volumes would meet their minimums. At the time, they did not.

Uwe made me an offer. I would travel with him to Hong Kong and visit Quintessa's workshops and get an overview of their operations. We would then go to Canton, meet the local factory managers, and confirm, by virtue of my presence, that Quintessa had an agent in New York—Questus—who would sell its embroideries into the high-volume fashion houses in New York City. Uwe was certain that between my indisputable "American" looks (making me a certifiable *gwailou*—a derogatory Cantonese term for "white Westerners") and an established business presence on Park Avenue, I would be a credible testament to Quintessa's pending business expansion and the ensuing increases to production volumes.

As the departure of his train was being announced, Uwe asked me to join them in their carriage before the train left. They wanted to open the small black case they had been carrying with them and show me their collection of embroidery samples. With only minutes to spare, I boarded the train and went with them to their sleeper compartment, whereupon Vicky laid the case on the bed and snapped open its two brass clasps.

The leather case was the size of a large medical bag and as it opened, my eyes fell upon what looked like a pirate's treasure: beads, pearls, sequins, gemstones, and crystals of all colors—hand-stitched onto organza fabric in a variety of motifs and designs. It was a collection of their finest embroidery samples, assembled over years of doing business with Europe's top fashion houses. The display looked like an offering that visitors hailing from a foreign land might present to royalty upon their arrival at a palace. I was mesmerized. The platform attendant blew his whistle and announced the train's departure. Uwe instructed me to present myself at their home in Munich on August 1st and we would put together the details of our plan. I jumped off the train as it was rolling out of the station and left in a daze.

I lay awake all night visualizing life in the New York fashion industry as if watching a film on the ceiling. Most exciting of all, I imagined the financial rewards that could come with that life. It looked like my plan for Questus was going to work. I was on my way to owning a successful business and one day purchasing the horse farm I had been dreaming about for fifteen years.

36

Peace

As soon as I returned to my apartment in Sachsenhausen, I phoned Alexandra and told her I had exciting news. We got together the next evening at her apartment for a quiet dinner in; she too had exciting news to share. Alexandra was an only child, and her parents were living in the family home near Hamburg where she had grown up; a home that would one day pass on to her. She had a successful career as an account executive with Ogilvy and Mather and they had offered her a promotion to a new position in Hamburg, so she decided to make the move and enjoy being closer to her parents.

Although we had only been dating for a short time, I was developing feelings for her I had never had before. I couldn't stop looking at her when we were together, and I couldn't stop thinking about her when we were apart. Her quick wit and intellectual humor made me smile. She made me feel appreciated and cared about, and what I wanted more than anything was to take her in my arms and kiss her. I was falling in love, but because of the upcoming changes in our lives, I felt I should wait and not complicate things.

My August meeting with Uwe and Vicky at their home in Munich was a success, and we agreed to proceed with a two-week trip to Hong Kong and China to establish business connections. When I returned from Asia, I visited Alexandra in Hamburg. She had found a one-bedroom apartment on a quiet side street near the city center that ran inland from the banks of the Außen-Alster—a small lake in the middle of Hamburg.

On the day I arrived, we had dinner at a local restaurant and then stopped by a trendy nightclub. The club was on the ground floor of a converted house across from the lake, facing a tree-lined walkway that hugged its shores. After enjoying a couple of cocktails, we agreed it was the perfect night for a walk. We went across the street and stood at the water's edge, looking out at the city lights shimmering on the lake.

A light breeze drifted across the water, and it was playing with the fringe of

Alexandra's hair when our eyes locked, one of us said something funny, and we both giggled. I acted upon the impulse I had been suppressing for months: I took her into my arms, and we enjoyed a long, passionate kiss. We did not need words to convey our feelings after parting lips, so we relished the moment and took in the peacefulness of the setting. Then we struck off, hand in hand, and enjoyed our quiet walk along the Außen-Alster.

That night with Alexandra was the first time I was intimate with a woman. I was almost overwhelmed, not only by the physical passion but also by the strength of the emotions it created. I never knew how it felt to love someone fully. It was healthy, refreshing, and deeply moving. A whole new world opened up to me. Alexandra had given me the biggest gift of my life.

After several relaxing and nurturing days together, I said goodbye—promising to return in a few days—and continued by train to my intended destination: Uwe and Vicky's home in Denmark. Uwe declared the trip to China a success and briefed me on how the sales process worked in the European fashion houses. He also cautioned that I might meet with a different set of protocols and procedures when I began exploring the New York market. Feeling adequately briefed and in possession of the magical sample bag—my portable treasure chest—I took my leave. I was eager to see Alexandra and spend another blissful week together in Hamburg.

But first, considering that I would devote my time to establishing Quintessa in New York, I no longer needed the apartment or office services in Frankfurt. So, I returned to the city, closed shop, and headed back to Hamburg to join Alexandra in what was to be my new home, living together as a couple.

In the short time I was away, Alexandra had rearranged her bedroom closet and dressers to accommodate my belongings. She had two rows of shoebox-sized containers neatly arranged on the closet shelves to store my socks and underwear, a section in the closet cleared to hang my shirts and suits, empty drawers for my other clothing, and a small table she had moved into the bathroom where I could arrange my toiletries and shaving gear: simple acts of kindness and a display of love. I was being nurtured by someone who genuinely cared for me, with no quid pro quo—only a desire to make my life better. Although grateful, I was in disbelief that someone would perform such unselfish and loving acts—for me.

As a result, for the first time in over six years, I did not feel the need to numb myself with alcohol at the end of the day. Alexandra and I enjoyed sharing a bottle of wine at night or a couple of cocktails when we went out in the evening, but the feeling of desperation to finally make it to 5 p.m. and begin drinking, was no longer there. I didn't feel I needed to find that elusive *click*. Being with Alexandra was its own version of peace, and I was hooked.

37

Thank You, Mr. de la Renta

I returned to New York, ready to jump into the arena and do battle in the rough and tumble fashion industry. A battle I believed I'd win.

On day one, I knew I needed to be on 7th Avenue and that the higher the address number on the buildings, the higher the level of dress house inside. When I came across the 550 building on the west side of 7th Avenue, just south of Times Square, it looked like the garment district ended there and I had reached the top of the pyramid. I went into the lobby to see what companies were listed on the directory.

There they all were: Oscar de la Renta, Bill Blass, Donna Karan, Ralph Lauren, Geoffrey Beene, Carolyne Roehm—designers whose labels were well known to me. I had found a one-stop shop. After a bit of pushing and shuffling, I found myself ensconced inside the elevator, almost asphyxiated by the overpowering smell of Christian Dior's *Poison* and Yves St. Laurent's *Opium*. I was on my way to one of the two floors Oscar de la Renta called home.

The elevator door opened into an elegant reception area that reflected the world-class taste and sophistication of the renowned designer who worked behind its walls. I knew there was a team back there, busily creating some of the most beautiful gowns and clothing to be had on Seventh Avenue, for some of the wealthiest and most famous women in the world. I walked up to the reception desk and told the attractive young woman that I had come from Europe with a dazzling collection of embroideries I was certain Mr. de la Renta's design team would be interested in seeing. To my surprise, she made a quick phone call, and minutes later a tall and elegant woman emerged and asked me to follow her back to the design room.

Without sitting down, I gave an overview of Quintessa and its well-established place in the European world of women's fashion. But my words were superfluous for, as soon as I laid my treasure chest open, my host's eyes fell upon the bounty presented before her. After a quick fingering-through of the designs, she excused herself and returned with what appeared to be two assistants.

All three helped themselves to a tour of the collection, and after about five minutes, my eye caught the image of a very tall man entering the room. It was Oscar de la Renta. He was every bit the soft-spoken gentleman I knew from newspapers and magazines to be his repute. He studied the embroideries, with his eye falling to several black pieces reminiscent of Russian brocades, and asked if I knew Jack Goldman. I told him I did not. Mr. de la Renta explained that when in Europe, he worked exclusively with the famed Parisian embroidery house of Lesage, but that in New York his go-to embroiderer was Jack Goldman. He suggested I meet Mr. Goldman, who was located on 40th Street, around the corner from 550.

The design team had finished their work on the upcoming collection but said if I returned in February, they would be working on their next collection and would be interested in taking another look. I spent the rest of my day riding the elevator from floor to floor to see if I could replicate my good fortune. The gods were smiling upon me, and I did. I ended the day having met with Bill Blass, Carolyne Roehm, and Donna Karan.

I found a temporary apartment rental and then returned to Europe to debrief Uwe and Vicky. I enjoyed time with Alexandra and even took a trip to Großenaspe to introduce her to Rosemarie Springer. Several weeks later, I returned to New York and followed up with the designers.

A few identified samples that caught their eye and handed over fabric swatches to confirm their color direction, along with sketches to clarify their ideas for Quintessa's designers. The only catch was that those designers were eight thousand miles and twelve time zones away in Hong Kong. I got the sense these designers were expecting to see samples in a matter of days, not in weeks, as was customary in Europe. And my sense was correct. After a couple of days, my phone started ringing and the voicemails left on my answering machine were becoming agitated and impatient: they wanted their samples.

When I met with a designer named Nahid, I was up-front and explained the long turnaround times required for Quintessa samples. She kindly, but bluntly, told me that without the ability to provide samples within a couple of days, I could not compete in the market; it did not work that way. She seemed to have a soft spot in her heart for me and offered to help.

First, she asked the same question Mr. de la Renta had asked: did I know Jack Goldman? Nahid worked with him most seasons. When I said I did not, she offered to phone him, tell him we were meeting, and say I had a unique and beautiful embroidery collection from Europe. Nahid thought Mr. Goldman might help produce my samples right there in his loft on 40th Street. That was the day I met Jack Goldman.

38

We're In Business

Two-fifty West 40th Street was a two-minute walk from the dozens of other design houses that made up the New York City Garment District. Jack Goldman Embroideries was located on the fifth floor of that building in a loft about twenty-five feet wide and sixty feet deep. The building was over eighty years old and badly in need of a facelift. This was not like 550 7th Avenue; there were no glitzy showrooms to impress out-of-town buyers or wealthy clients. The actual work of garment manufacturing got done here—lots of it—with no frills.

The greeting I received was a quick bellow: "Who da hell are you?" Jack Goldman squinted as he peered through the thick lenses of his black-framed glasses, behind which I could see dark-brown eyes sunken into puffy eyelids with bags the size of small cushions—everything hinting at an older man who got very little sleep. His curly dark-grey hair was short-cropped, and the same color hairs were creeping out of his nostrils and ears. He cocked his head as he put the pieces together and said, "Oh. You must be da *goyim* the I-ranian lady just called about, sayin' you got some nice stuff from ... Europe or somewhere?"

So, in a manner appropriate for commencing a meeting in a corporate boardroom, I stiffly walked up to extend my hand and said, "It's a pleasure to meet you, Mr. Goldman. I've heard so many wonderful things about you and your beautiful work."

His reply was friendly and delivered with a smirk, "Waaat? Is my fadda here? My name is Jack."

After explaining how this *goyim* came to be standing in his loft with a mysterious black bag, I opened the treasure chest. His response was the one I had hoped for, and his face lit up like a kid's in a candy store as he dove in to riffle through its sparkling offerings. I told him about my problem, and he agreed: I had a *big* problem.

Jack was in his late seventies, tired, and ready to retire and enjoy more time with his wife and large family in Brooklyn, so he proposed a solution. If "my people in Europe" wanted to buy his collection of embroidery samples— representing the evolution of fashion over four decades—and purchase the equipment and machinery that had served his business so well over those decades, it was all for sale. Since I was new to the business, he said he could stay on in a part-time capacity for "a year or so" to mentor me, if he received a small monthly retainer, time off whenever he wanted it, and payment of his daily car service to and from Brooklyn. He set the price at a firm $75,000 with the monthly retainer to be negotiated "with my people."

The next day I got up early to phone Uwe in Munich. I explained the conundrum I faced in New York and shared the details about my meeting with Jack, including his offer to sell his company's assets to Quintessa. Uwe spoke seven languages—many of them fluently—and regardless of which one he may have selected to give his reply, it would have come across as clearly as the one he gave me in English: *No!* After a few tense exchanges, we reached an impasse, and his final *no* was the dealbreaker. It was time to part company.

I stayed at my apartment that morning and over several cups of coffee contemplated my next plan of action. After the third cup, an idea came to me. Loren's father, Tom, was a successful business owner who had made his money in the world of design, both as a florist and as a much sought-after interior designer. Being part of the New York fashion industry seemed like it might be something he would want to invest in.

Tom was enamored with the idea of being part of the fashion industry and jumped on board. We agreed to be 50/50 partners in the new venture. Tom would put up 100 percent of the $75,000 purchase price, plus $25,000 to cover initial operating costs. I would receive a small salary, and after the business had generated enough profit to pay back his up-front investment, we would split future profits 50/50. He needed a couple of weeks to put the money together, after which he would come to New York, establish a bank account, meet the famous Jack Goldman, and transact the sale of his assets. Tom and I had become business partners, and I was sure I was on my way to owning a horse farm.

39

Goodbye

I phoned Alexandra to share my news and she offered to take some time off to visit me. It turned out I shouldn't have been as excited as I felt.

My temporary apartment was not an ideal place for a romantic get-together, so Alexandra found a hotel in my area. She flew in on a Friday afternoon and we rode into the city from JFK as excited as two kids on their way to an amusement park. I had made dinner reservations at a Scandinavian restaurant on E. 55th Street called Aquavit. The restaurant was a dozen blocks from the Roosevelt Hotel, where she was staying. After a long dinner, we took a quiet walk along Park Avenue with perfect spring weather. Our night together was pure bliss: all the intimacy and passion from our nights in Hamburg was revived, and once again I felt like I was one with my partner. On that night, all was well in my world.

We enjoyed breakfast in her room and then headed out for my guided tour of Central Park. I knew every inch of the park and was thrilled to be able to share everything with Alexandra as we strolled along the roads—everything except the Ramble. I felt mixed emotions during the twenty minutes it took to walk by the area. The dominant one was embarrassment, but I also had a profound feeling of guilt. *What if Alexandra were to ever learn about my past—about my attraction to lean, athletic men and my desire to touch and to be touched? How could I spend my life with a woman that I kept secrets from?* At some point, I would need to tell her about my past, and that point would have to come before we made a serious commitment to one another—like marriage.

When we returned to the hotel, tired from hours of walking, and looking forward to a brief rest before dinner, Alexandra started a conversation that solved the problem of how I should reveal my past to her.

Before coming to New York, she had given a lot of thought to where our relationship was headed. We had declared our love for each other, and since we were sharing our bodies, the relationship was no longer casual. Getting married would be the appropriate next step. She had already spoken to senior management at Ogilvy & Mather, and they were willing to relocate her to their headquarters in New York. Alexandra and I could make our home together in New York while I built up the new business, but when the first of the children was five years old and ready for school, we would need to find someone else to run the day-to-day business. At that point, we would move back to Hamburg where the children could attend the far superior German schools. She would then give up her career and we would take ownership of her family home and live there with her parents until they died. Then it would be ours to raise the children in.

That is part of what endears me so much to the German people: they are direct with their communication. Alexandra's expectations were clear. I had also given thought to our future and was certain I wanted to spend my life with her, so marriage was also in my plans. *But kids?* That threw me off guard. Not because I knew I did—or did not—want to have them, but because I had never given it any thought. I had focused my attention on business and business only; making enough money to afford a farm and a life with horses. Once I established those things, I could pursue my dream of making it onto an Olympic team. My hopes of Alexandra being my partner in that didn't involve a family.

Alexandra picked up on my discomfort and asked me flat out: "You *were* planning on getting married and having children right away—weren't you?" I had to be honest and say I was only halfway there; I could not commit to a timeframe for having children. Right away, Alexandra let me know she could not continue our relationship. She wanted a husband and children, and she was ready to get started. So, without any drama or argument, we agreed it would be best to move on in our own directions.

We did not stay together that night, and I went back to my apartment heartbroken. Every part of our relationship had been healthy, honest, and fulfilling. She made me feel I was cared for, that I mattered, and that I was worthy of being loved. In one day, that was all gone. Returning to my empty apartment and aching again with feelings of emptiness and failure, I sought out the comfort of alcohol—and despite my efforts, failed to experience that elusive *click*. There was to be no peace that night.

Alexandra changed her flight and returned to Hamburg two days later. I took her to the airport, where we both suffered through a tearful goodbye, with each of us thanking the other for everything we had shared and all the good times we had enjoyed. We promised to remain friends and stay in touch—which we did. Alexandra married a successful lawyer in Hamburg before the end of the year, sent me pictures of their wedding, and one year later sent me the announcement of the birth of their beautiful baby boy. The enclosed pictures made me weep with joy—Alexandra was fulfilling her dream. If anyone deserved to be happy, it was she.

* * *

Within days of dropping Alexandra off at the airport, I relapsed into my familiar routines: evenings at the Y, drinks and dinner at home, and weekend walks through the park, including regular strolls through the Ramble. I filled the void our breakup had created by satisfying my need to be looked at and admired while engaging in risky, anonymous sexual encounters, and I invited vodka back into my life—finishing every day with the robotic routine of drinking. Most nights included a hit or two from my pipe and in short order, all my addictions had taken back control, and I was slipping into a depression that had taken only a brief hiatus.

40
Bankrupt

Summer was approaching and disaster was on the horizon. Production orders for the upcoming fall/winter season should have been coming in. Fashion week had come and gone, so the buyers should have placed their first orders from our samples. Something wasn't right.

On a Saturday morning in August, I went to the third floor of Saks Fifth Avenue, where women's evening wear was sold; I found the answer to my questions. There were mannequins on display throughout the floor, and many of them sported dresses with embroideries that had been designed by us but manufactured by someone else.

After talking with several designers, I learned that a competitor from India had visited the design houses where we delivered samples and offered to produce the pieces for a fraction of the price we had quoted. Our work was being stolen right out from under our noses and we could do nothing about it. An Indian industrial conglomerate with deep pockets funded the company—they could drive us out of business.

I explained the situation to Jack and Tom, and they agreed: we were engaged in a battle we could not win. It was time to sell our assets, cut our losses, pack up our tent, and go home with our tails between our legs.

Without steady orders, I had not paid the payroll taxes over the past two months—a desperate move that no business owner should ever make—so the late penalties and fines were compounding rapidly. By the time all the company's financial obligations had been met, Tom had invested $200,000. As an equal partner, fifty percent of that loss was owed by me. I was in debt to Tom for $100,000, and I had just lost my job.

In the face of our financial downfall and a mountain of personal credit card debt, I consulted with our lawyer, and in addition to dissolving our corporation, I asked him to file for personal bankruptcy. Sitting in a room with twenty other bankrupt individuals and presenting myself in front of a judge was the most humiliating day of my adult life. For someone who had lived every day in pursuit of being acknowledged for his success, who held a master's degree in finance, and who had always strived to get to the top of whatever game he pursued, I was well and truly at the bottom. Personal bankruptcy did not absolve me from the student debt I still carried, and I had every intention of paying back Tom the entire amount I owed him. Regardless of being awarded my plea, I walked out of the courthouse a financially and emotionally broken man.

By the end of that year, I was grappling with the biggest challenges I had ever faced: a failed business, personal bankruptcy, and no place to call home: I was being evicted from my apartment. I needed to figure out how I was going to manage my life going forward.

Not only had my business failed, but I had also quit a job with Mannesmann that would have led to a lifetime career as a senior manager—because I naïvely believed I could be more successful on my own. And to top it all, I had failed in my relationship with Alexandra.

I had let optimism and hope replace common sense and intellect. In the absence of common sense, I chose to do things that could harm me. In the years following my graduation from Hiram, I repeatedly chose to participate in high-risk activities—a proven symptom of chronic post-traumatic stress.

I had been using illegal drugs and often had driven while under the influence of both marijuana and alcohol. I had been initiating sexual encounters in public places such as athletic facilities and the Ramble in Central Park—a venue that was notorious for acts of sexual violence when the AIDS epidemic was in full force. I had transported illegal drugs across international borders. And to secure some quick business during the company's slow periods, I had made a half-dozen trips to Port-au-Prince, Haiti to access its cheap labor for embroidering bridal laces. The U.S. Department of State had issued warnings to Americans to stay away from the country due to political violence and the heightened risk of kidnappings. I knew that and went anyway.

But I did not understand why I had done those things. *Was it exciting to do something risky and forbidden? Did that create a high for me? Did I subconsciously want to be caught, and if so, was it for the attention I would receive, or was it because I might be imprisoned and taken away from my troubled environment? Maybe I would be physically harmed and receive the punishment I felt I deserved as an unworthy person?* Those were heady questions, and I did not have any answers to them.

The only thing that had been consistent during the ten years after Hiram was the daily presence of my Great Deceiver—alcohol—and I realized that all my friendships had had a pervasive connection to my addictions. First, with the drugs and alcohol I had shared with Dennis and his friends, and all my partying with Loren and my neighbor after that. Even Mark and Joe had been dealing with their own addictions when I was with them. It was unsettling to realize what an overwhelming influence drugs and alcohol had had on my life—not only over the past ten years but also while growing up in a family with a culture steeped in alcoholism.

Addiction and depression seemed to be linked to every component of my life since the day I had my last ride on a horse. Somehow my dream to be an Olympian and a master of equitation—training out of a farm I would build and own—was still burning somewhere deep inside of me. But I realized I was losing touch with that dream every time the fog of alcohol took over my brain—yet I continued my ritual of *sip, sip, sip.*

41

The Turnaround

Bankrupt and homeless, it was time to rebuild. I phoned my friend Dan, who lived across the Hudson River in Hoboken, to ask if I could stay with him for a while. We had become friends over the past year while attending a series of seminars called the Team, Management and Leadership Program (TMLP); something I felt would help as I managed the challenges facing our company.

As soon as I moved in, I began my job search. My first effort was to contact German fashion houses and inquire about openings in their finance or administrative departments. The hope was that my language skills and management background would dovetail with my experience in the garment industry and qualify me for an executive-level position. Knowing that getting a foot in the door of a company like Hugo Boss, Jill Sander, or Escada would involve many attempts and dead-ends, I also looked for more immediate work.

I learned about a temp agency in Manhattan that had quality clients and regular work, so I took their skills assessment test and joined their pool of temporary office workers. Fourteen years after working as a temp during summer break from college, I would once again be earning an hourly wage sitting at a keyboard. But the private coaching I had sought from a seminar leader with the TMLP echoed in my head: "From this point forward—no matter what situation you are in—when you must choose what to do, the *only* thing you do is the thing that makes you money. Don't do anything else. Do that thing, bank the money, and do the next thing that makes money. Nothing else."

My first assignment was so much fun it hardly seemed like a job. *Sesame Street* was produced by the Children's Television Workshop. My job was to sit in front of a Wang word processor and watch *Sesame Street* videos. Listening through headphones, I transcribed every word, moan, groan, or utterance from the characters. The international licensing department translated my transcripts into more than a dozen languages for overseas distribution.

My second assignment was at a law firm in the North Tower of the World

Trade Center. They specialized in maritime law, and I transcribed dictation from lawyers who were feverishly starting work on the Exxon Valdez oil spill. The oil tanker had been traveling from the Prince William Sound in Alaska to Long Beach, California, and over three days in March of 1989 had spilled 10.8 million gallons of crude oil into the waters.

After two months of steady work, I had developed a routine with the temp agency. Every morning between 7:30 and 8:30 someone would phone and confirm my assignment for the day. One Monday morning after Labor Day, 8:30 came and went without a call. By 9:30 it seemed there was no work, so I decided to enjoy the beautiful weather and treat myself to a day at Brighton Beach near Coney Island. I packed a duffle bag with my beach gear and readied myself for the long train ride out to Brooklyn; my brain had switched into vacation mode. I had worked consistently since I began temping, and although I had had no luck with the executive job search, I had been pursuing it diligently.

As I was stepping out of the apartment, the phone on the table by the door rang. The agency said they had received a late call from a publishing house on 42nd Street; their receptionist had called in sick and they needed a temp. Since I was already dressed for the beach and on my way out, I felt entitled to at least one day off and said I was not available. While placing the receiver back on the phone cradle, I heard my seminar leader's voice again. Walking away from a day's pay and going to the beach seemed like a bad idea. As soon as the phone touched the cradle, I picked it up and dialed the agency. I reached the same woman who had phoned and told her I was available.

The publishing house offices were quiet, and I had very little to do. About halfway through the day, an account executive who had been sitting two desks behind me got up to go to the break room. He stopped at my desk and began a conversation.

"Things are pretty quiet around here today. Not sure why they had you come in. Sorry."

"That's OK. I was happy to help the temp agency. They've been good to me."

"I'm just curious—it doesn't seem like temping is what you really do for a living. Am I right?"

"You're right. I'm between jobs and earning some extra cash while I search for a new one."

"That's what I thought. What kind of a job are you looking for?"

I gave him a quick review of my background and told him about my search.

As soon as I finished, his eyes lit up and he said, "We publish a national magazine for the salon industry. A major advertiser is a German company called Goldwell Cosmetics. They sell hair coloring, shampoos, and all the other products used in salons, and they have offices outside of Baltimore. Their Director of Finance is moving back to Germany to send his kids to school, and I believe they are looking for his replacement. Let me give him a call."

After lunch, I got the good news. Detlef Adler was in fact moving his family back to Germany and they had not found his replacement. My new friend handed me a card with Mr. Adler's number and suggested I call him. Within minutes I was speaking to Mr. Adler and giving him a summary of my background. He asked a few questions, confirmed I was a viable candidate, and asked how soon I could come to Baltimore for an interview. Thanks to Amtrak's Acela train service, I arrived the next day.

The interview lasted three hours. Since Goldwell was in the cosmetics industry—an integral part of the fashion world—Mr. Adler believed that my background in the embroidery business, combined with my financial management experience at Mannesmann (a company as well known to him as General Electric would have been to an American), qualified me as his potential replacement.

Mr. Adler's boss from Germany happened to be in Chicago on vacation and I was told to fly there to meet for a final interview. It was the end of September, and Chicago was being treated to some beautiful late-summer weather. I met Herr Steinhauser in the center of Grant Park and after exchanging cordialities, he suggested we walk through the city and along the waterside. He jumped into casual conversation about the differences between Germany and America, the politics in both countries, current events in the Middle East, different types of cuisine and places in the world we had tried them, travel tips for surviving long-haul flights, and pretty much any other topics that popped into his head. We spoke German the entire time and he confessed that after a week's vacation, it was a refreshing break from his struggles with English. After several hours he suggested we go to dinner at a French restaurant where he had reservations, and we sat down to eat shortly after 6 p.m.

After drinks, an appetizer, a salad course, our entree, and dessert, Herr Steinhauser was ready to move on to a cheese platter and port. It was 9 p.m. and we hadn't talked at all about my career with Goldwell. Just as I was ready to hijack the conversation and try to get him on track, he described a childhood friend he had recently seen as being *biederlich*—a term typifying a romanticized simplicity and soft youthfulness. I smiled knowingly when he used the term and Herr Steinhauser dropped his cheese knife, gaped his mouth, and said, "Herr Merrick—do you know what the term *biederlich* means?" I had studied German literature from the Biedermeier period, so when I gave him my description, he laughed. "Well, that does it! You certainly are a Renaissance man and I definitely want you on my team."

Having had no prior conversation about the job in Baltimore, I said, "That is fantastic. Thank you. But we have not discussed either the position or my qualifications. Do you believe I'm qualified for the job?"

Keeping the smile his laughter had created, he said, "Herr Merrick—I am not offering you Herr Adler's position." I froze until he continued. "I want you to join my team at Goldwell's headquarters in Germany. I am creating an international controlling department so our Japanese owners can better understand our finances. We have subsidiary companies throughout the world, and they need to be monitored. I have two people in my department, and I want you to join that team and work with me."

Two weeks later, I packed my bags and thanked Dan for providing me with a healthy space to recalibrate my life while I pulled back on my drinking. On October 16th, I headed from Hoboken to Darmstadt, my new home in Germany. This time, Goldwell bought my ticket—for the business class cabin. It looked like I had earned my way into the front of the plane while on my way to becoming an International Financial Controller. The rebuilding had begun.

42
Sydney Via Darmstadt

How could I have known that studying German literature as part of my liberal arts education would land me a job with a multinational cosmetics company?

Hans Erich Dotter founded Goldwell Cosmetics in 1948, focusing exclusively on hairdressers as business partners. The company remained true to his vision and expanded from Germany into sixteen countries. In 1989, the Kao Company—the Japanese equivalent of Proctor and Gamble—bought 75 percent of Goldwell Cosmetics. After the acquisition, they noticed some subsidiaries were profitable, and many were not. They wanted to understand why.

Herr Steinhauser was the Director of Finance and was putting together an International Controlling department that could answer their immediate questions and then monitor future performance. Because English was my native language, I was assigned to the subsidiaries in England, the U.S., Canada, Australia, New Zealand, and Hong Kong. My French capabilities won me the assignment of France, and although only passable, my Spanish got me Spain.

For twelve months, I would visit Goldwell's subsidiaries in London, Madrid, Paris, Hong Kong, Los Angeles, Toronto, and Sydney. After visiting each subsidiary, I presented a report, in person, to Goldwell's CEO and board of directors. After a trip to southeast Asia, I reported that the losses in Australia were increasing and explained where the problems were. The biggest were with the financial management. Our global auditing firm, KPMG, did its own review of my findings and agreed the problem was with senior management.

The board's solution was for me to fire the Managing Director and Financial Controller and replace them with executives we selected. To make that happen, they asked if I would relocate to Sydney and take over as Director of Finance and Administration. My second order of business would be to recruit a new Managing Director.

As Director of Finance and Administration, I would be responsible for operations in Perth, Melbourne, Adelaide, and Brisbane, as well as Hobart in

Tasmania. Headquarters were in Sydney—which would be my home—and I would also have oversight of operations in New Zealand. The losses were mounting quickly, and the board wanted the problems addressed immediately, so two weeks later, I moved to Sydney.

I had landed my first senior-level executive position, with over one hundred staff to manage and financial responsibility for a twenty-five-million-dollar company. I had no idea at the time how that move would help me fulfill my Olympic dreams—but it did. Thank goodness I didn't go to the beach that day in Hoboken.

43

Pure Magic

My life changed forever after arriving in Sydney. Without knowing it, my path was veering toward the Olympics.

I jumped into my new job with vigor. After two weeks I had completed my first order of business: firing the Managing Director and Financial Controller. The next month we recruited the previous Managing Director for L'Oréal in Australia. We were off and running with a plate full of new projects and the requisite amount of management experience and enthusiasm to make them work.

Late one afternoon, a sales rep peeked into my office and asked if I had a minute. "I understand you are an accomplished equestrian. Have you found anywhere to ride yet? I know a man named Paul Jacobs who boards two horses at the Moore Park stables in Sydney and only has time to ride one of them. He may be interested in leasing the second one out so it can be exercised and taken care of."

With my focus on regular sixty-hour work weeks, I had not thought about riding.

"No, I haven't. But I'd be interested in meeting him. Who knows, it might turn out to be a great opportunity to get back in the saddle."

I met Paul the next week and it turned out to be more than a great opportunity—it was the opportunity that changed my life.

Moore Park is in the heart of Sydney, part of a nine-hundred-acre cluster that makes up the Centennial Parklands. It is home to beautiful lakes and abundant species of birds and wildlife, and it is the site for the annual Royal Easter Show. Paul's horses were boarded at one of several stabling and riding facilities in the park, next door to Lachlan Murdoch's barn. Paul's soul mate was a chestnut mare named Shenoah. She was extremely sensitive and challenging to train, leaving little time for his other horse, a jet-black gelding named Jasper.

Paul went to the stables every morning at six, rode his horses, and showered on-site before heading to his office job. He said if I wanted to join him in the mornings, I could pay for Jasper's board, and in exchange, ride him every day.

After riding Jasper for several weeks, I experimented with some advanced dressage movements. To my delight, I discovered Jasper had been extremely well trained and I wondered if Paul had done the training.

When we both took a riding break, I asked, "I don't know if you saw what I was doing, but Jasper really knows his stuff. Did you do the training?"

"Well, I've done my best with the time I've had, but when things have gotten too busy to ride both horses, I've sent Jasper out to a farm near Windsor to be trained by a guy named Miguel. I reckon he's a pretty good trainer. So, with his help, I've been able to keep moving Jasper along."

Windsor was about an hour's drive northwest of the city and on the edge of the spectacular Blue Mountains. I asked some more questions and learned that the trainer, Miguel Tavora, was from Portugal but had made Windsor his home. Paul did not know more than that. He restated that Miguel was "pretty good" and suggested we drive out on a Saturday to meet him.

Paul phoned Mr. Tavora and arranged a visit to his farm to watch his morning training sessions. The farm sat on twenty-five acres and the small house, riding arena, and stables were set back from the road at the end of a long dirt driveway. We parked near the house and quietly made our way to the arena. No one was in sight as we approached, and the only sounds were the calls of the kookaburras in the trees and the voice of Luciano Pavarotti singing "Nessun dorma" from a CD player inside. Paul signaled with his hand for me to stop before entering. He peered through an opening and saw that Mr. Tavora was in the middle of a training session. Paul waited for him to take a break, asked for permission to enter, and we settled in to watch the riding. Mr. Tavora did not look away from his horse or speak to us while he enjoyed a relaxing walk around the arena. As Pavarotti's voice melded into an aria from Verdi's *La Traviata*, Mr. Tavora picked up the slack in his reins and put his horse back to work.

Within minutes I was transported to another world. A light mist had begun to move through the covered arena—drifting across from the open sides and lingering long enough to make the image of horse and rider appear to be in the clouds. The exercises they were performing made them look as if they were floating through those clouds.

The first movement was the "passage": a requirement of Grand Prix riding where the horse executes a slow-motion trot—alternately lifting each diagonal pair of legs and hesitating for a split second at the apex of the stride—and then moving a small distance forward as the next diagonal pair springs off the ground. After moving slowly about the arena with this elastic and suspended gait, Mr. Tavora gradually brought the horse to execute the same style of movement, but without moving forward. It was a trot in place called the "piaffe"—a hallmark of Grand Prix riding.

I had seen some of the top riders in the world training these exercises in Germany and had ridden several Grand Prix horses trained by Olympians and riders from The Spanish Riding School in Vienna. But this was riding at a new level. The quiet approach of the rider, the picture of complete harmony with his horse, the elasticity, suppleness, and brilliance of its movement, and the pure beauty of their partnership, were beyond anything I had seen—it was what the riding masters from past centuries had been writing about. What I was seeing for the first time was a man who had mastered the art of equitation.

Words from an inspiring quote I had read when I was fourteen came to mind. German riding master Gustav Steinbrecht had written: "Only a few have an idea of how much time, patience, and effort is required to give a horse such a complete education. … Only a true, deep love for the horse can develop these character traits to the height that alone will lead to the goal." Miguel Tavora was one of the few.

We watched two more horses go through their paces, and Mr. Tavora exchanged nothing more than brief pleasantries between rides. He focused on the work at hand and did not interrupt the tranquility of the morning or divert his attention. When he finished with the first horse, he pressed a button mounted on the wall. Within minutes a blonde woman of about forty entered the arena (I later learned it was his wife, Diane), handed Mr. Tavora the next horse, and took the other down to the stables for a well-deserved shower. He mounted the fresh horse and spent the next hour creating the same magic that had just swept me away. He was a master. I wanted to learn from him.

When the training sessions were complete, Paul explained to Miguel that I was riding Jasper full-time and asked if we might be able to return with both of his horses for lessons. We set up an appointment for three weeks later. I wondered what it would take to be the master's protégé.

44

So, This Is Mastery

Major Miguel de Lancastre e Tavora had been born in Portugal, son of the ninth Marquis and Marchioness of Abrantes: he was an aristocrat. At the age of eight, he began riding with legendary Maestro Nuno Oliveira. Major Tavora had trained with him until he turned eighteen and joined the Portuguese Military Academy, commanding soldiers in the Colonial Wars in Mozambique and Angola. During his military career, he completed the Course of Masters at the Portuguese Military and Civilian Riding Academy of Mafra and was later appointed as its Chief Instructor and Director of the Equestrian Division.

In 1974 the military, along with civilian revolutionaries, overthrew the Portuguese government, and the following ten years were filled with political unrest. Miguel decided to leave Portugal—aristocratic families from the old guard were being persecuted. Through Nuno Oliveira's contacts, Major Tavora relocated to Sydney.

I learned this from an article I found in a magazine at a local saddlery. Inspired by how this master had achieved his status, I spent the following three weeks upping my game and training Jasper with new rigor, applying all the principles of good riding I had learned over the past twenty years. I hoped to begin my journey to attain a level of mastery I had always dreamed of.

On the appointed Saturday morning, Paul loaded Shenoah and Jasper into his trailer and drove us to Major Tavora's farm. The Major instructed me to warm up my horse while he sat at the end of the arena and observed. After fifteen minutes of what I thought was a flawless "performance," he told me to stop. Major Tavora left his chair and stood beside me, ready to give his initial evaluation. I was beaming inside and eager to receive my accolades.

In his heavily accented English, he said, "Very pretty. So very pretty. You sit all nice and straight on your horse and do not move nothing. Have you been riding in Germany?"

"Yes," I said, not knowing why his tone was stern and borderline condescending.

"Of course. You sit all straight and rigid and do not move—you do nothing. You are useless to your horse. You know how to ride, but you do not know how to train. You must learn to be effective, to correct your horse when he is wrong, to make him better. That is what a trainer does. You are not a trainer; you are a rider. You have talent, OK. You could do. But if you study with me, I teach you how to train, using my system—the classical system. Oh—and you call me Miguel. I am not one of the stuffy German trainers you know so well."

For the remaining forty minutes, he put Jasper and me through a series of exercises that demonstrated his gymnastic approach to training: using one exercise to prepare for the next; increasing the difficulty with each progression but going back to the previous one if the new one was too difficult for the horse. Miguel was showing me a new approach to riding. I would no longer be acknowledged only for my ability to ride a trained horse. I would learn how to train a horse to do the movements of the Grand Prix based on classical principles. I had found my master and could once again assume the mantle of apprentice— a role I thrived in.

I spent every weekend at Miguel's watching him train horses in the morning and teach students in the afternoon. When he was away from Windsor teaching clinics in Canberra, Adelaide, or Melbourne, I traveled to watch them. He allowed me to ride his Grand Prix schoolmaster—a competition horse he had retired a few years back. Those rides allowed me to feel what a horse, classically trained by him, was like. I committed to becoming Miguel's protégé and set going to the Olympics with him as my coach as my new goal. I was finally able to answer the question I had posed in Darmstadt: *How will my move to Australia help me be on an Olympic team?* I knew I had put a big part of that puzzle together.

* * *

While watching Miguel teach on a Saturday afternoon, I observed something that made a profound impact on my life. A middle-aged woman led her horse into the arena and was the picture of composure. She and her horse were turned out impeccably, and she walked toward Miguel, highly focused and with an air of serenity. She had an incredibly effective training session—devoting 100 percent of her attention to her horse and following every word of Miguel's instruction to a tee. Their hour together had been rewarding for horse, rider, and trainer.

The next student was also a middle-aged woman, but her training session was very different. She and her horse were disheveled and looked as if preparation for the lesson had been hurried. She distractedly mounted her horse and had forgotten to prepare the saddle properly. Her lesson went poorly. Flustered, she had trouble concentrating and easily became frustrated. As a result, she was abrupt with her aids, which distressed her horse, and she occasionally gave up trying to do what Miguel asked. When she left, neither horse, rider, nor trainer felt rewarded.

I wondered why these riders had such different experiences. I thought about it for days. Then it hit me. The first rider was in control of her life—before, during, and after the ride. The second rider was out of control. I thought about my own life and realized I was effective when I was riding a horse because I was able to focus—to live in the moment—and not bring all the upsets in my life and their stress into the arena. Our effectiveness as riders was directly proportionate to our effectiveness in managing our lives away from horses.

And from that insight, a course was born.

I devoted the next five months to creating a two-day seminar that applied all the management skills I had learned in the business world, to managing life as an equestrian. I called it Mastery in the Art of Equitation and then put the curriculum and course manual on the shelf until the time was right to present it.

More inspired than ever about the pursuit of mastery, I asked Miguel how to ensure a thorough education with him. He explained I needed to buy a young, untrained horse, move it to his farm, and ride with him every morning before I went to the office. He agreed to meet me in the arena at 6:30, and day by day, walk me through the process of training a horse to Grand Prix. We found a three-year-old dark bay Trakehner gelding named Kalif that I purchased and boarded at Miguel's. The real learning journey was about to begin.

45

I'm Out

Goldwell sold to over 8,000 unhappy salon owners. We sent a survey to several hundred salons and got consistent feedback from them all: they loved Goldwell's products but hated its service.

Our head of customer service came to me one day with a brochure. It was for a seminar in Sydney called The Art of Giving Quality Service, offered by Mary Gober, founder of Mary Gober International—a global training company. Mary's credentials were impressive, and the time was right to address our problems.

Two weeks later I was inviting Mary Gober into the conference room to discuss a consulting engagement. Mary was about my height, with a lean build, wearing a tailored navy blazer and a skirt that I guessed were both by Chanel. Her posture, confident stride, and radiant smile forecasted the professionalism she would exude throughout our meeting; Mary was a cut above the rest, and I would enjoy working with her. After an initial discussion, I smiled and said, "I know you are going to do great things for our company. When can we start!?"

We held the training two weeks later at a local conference center and it was a rousing success. A year later—as sales continued to grow, and customer retention rates increased—we surveyed the salon owners again. We had achieved our goal of being ranked #1 for customer service in the industry. Another cause for celebration.

I was grateful for the contribution Mary had made to the success of our business and I enjoyed working with her tremendously. I could tell we would become friends and continue to work together, but what I didn't know was the important contribution she was going to make to my personal life.

* * *

After creating my Mastery Course, and then watching Mary transform our company, I realized I had a passion for training and development. I was motivated to build strong teams and I had an insatiable hunger to learn more. I attended a six-month Leadership Intensive with the coach who had designed the Team, Management and Leadership Program. The program required multiple trips to his training center in Minneapolis.

That began in June of 1992, and after my first session, I initiated a project to advance my leadership role in the cosmetics industry. I committed to designing and running a national program for salon owners called *WIN—Women in the Nineties*. I would conduct seminars to teach management skills that helped women accelerate their success. The 1990s were all about female empowerment, and the mission seemed timely. I convinced myself it would be a value-added service Goldwell could offer as part of its commitment to salon owners. It sounded good on paper, and my first few presentations to salon owners about the concept were well received. But there was a problem.

I was going off track and losing sight of my responsibilities as the Director of Finance and Administration. I was playing in the sales and marketing arenas. My proposed project had no place on my list of accountabilities and was taking things in a different direction than the sales and marketing teams were headed. I was out of line and a major disruption to the company's plans. I was unable to rein in my exuberance—I was like a horse with blinders on. My reporting Financial Controller was managing all the finances and operations himself, and his loyalty to me was enabling me to run off course. I had to be stopped.

After a year of training Kalif with Miguel, it was time to pay the price for allowing my distractions at Goldwell to derail me. Our Managing Director had had enough of my misguided energy and the disruption it was causing. When I arrived at the office after a morning's training session, his secretary said he wanted to see me right away. The look on his face told me I was about to receive bad news. He had received a fax from headquarters advising him my position was being eliminated and the Financial Controller would take over my responsibilities. I had been fired.

My optimism and enthusiasm had derailed me—something I was familiar with. I failed to see the problems I was causing because I had stopped reading the signs. I was embarrassed and ashamed—another failure. But this time it was worse: *How am I going to continue training Kalif and learning from Miguel if I have to return to the U.S.?*

The problem seemed insurmountable, and once again, I was crushing my dreams. But this time it depressed me more. I had found my mentor and he had taken me under his wing. I was certain this was the path to my own mastery—I could taste it. I went home that afternoon to ponder how to tell Miguel, especially because I did not have a solution to the problem. In my distress, I stopped at the liquor store and spent the rest of the day embracing the familiar ritual of *sip, sip, sip.* After a few years of moderate drinking, I had fallen back in with the Great Deceiver.

46

New Job—New Horse

The distance between Sydney and Cleveland is 9,500 miles, and for the next six months, it was to become my regular commute.

As my severance package from Goldwell included a half year's salary, I was going to be financially OK for a while. My work visa allowed me to stay in Australia for six months before I had to renew it regularly as a tourist visa, so I stayed a few months in the house I was renting and continued to train Kalif in the mornings. Miguel did not seem to care why I had lost my job but was curious about what I was going to do for income. So was I.

After two months of adjusting to my new situation, I went to Cleveland to seek out a source of income. Heather's business had tripled in size after being awarded a large contract from a global company defending itself in a class action suit with thousands of plaintiffs. With the rapid expansion, Heather asked me to help with internal organization and workflow management while they adjusted to their increased case volume. Both the challenge of the assignment and the opportunity to work with Heather excited me. Throughout the years, even with oceans between us, we had remained close friends.

After a few months of consulting with Heather's company, she asked if I could sign on full-time as General Manager and oversee the operations and finances while she fulfilled her role as CEO and focused on business development.

Heather's passion for horses and dressage had grown over the years and she understood why I wanted to continue training with Miguel. I accepted the full-time position, with the understanding I could take three weeks' leave every quarter to train with Miguel. We kept that arrangement in place for three years, until 1997.

* * *

Since I was earning a salary that more than covered my living expenses, I bought a horse I could train during the nine months of the year I was in Cleveland. He was a seven-year-old thoroughbred gelding named Dancer whose body was the color of a copper penny, accented by a silky black mane and tail. He had been bred to race but proved to be too slow, so he had spent four years lazing around in a pasture. Because he was untrained, he was affordable, and because he had not raced for long, he had suffered no injuries to his legs and had no bad habits. He was athletic, built to perform dressage, and a sweetheart.

I boarded Dancer at a private farm in Hunting Valley whose owner was an avid dressage rider. With only ten stalls in her immaculately kept barn, an indoor riding arena, plus an Olympic-size outdoor ring nestled among the pastures, it was a tranquil environment and perfect for training an inexperienced and energetic thoroughbred.

I had developed a morning routine that enabled me to create a bond and spiritual connection with Dancer that I had always known was possible but had never experienced. Every day for two years—with the regularity of Big Ben and the dependability of Old Faithful—I awoke at 5 a.m. and put myself through a forty-five-minute yoga routine that prepared my mind and body for the training session that would begin at precisely 6:30.

After a quiet ten-minute drive through the small village of Gates Mills, past the Chagrin Valley Hunt Club, and along a winding stretch of the Chagrin River, I would arrive at the top of the valley and park in front of the stables just as the sun was rising. Liz was the stable manager and lived with her family in a small house adjacent to the barn. She was busy getting her day started inside, so I was the only person in the stables at that early hour. Whether in the heat of the summer or the cold of winter, the same smells and sounds greeted me when I slid open the side door. The scents of the oak-paneled stalls—filled the night before with fresh wood shavings—melded with the grassy aroma of the hay the horses had been fed before closing the barn for the night. The horses were bathed every day, so the clean smell of shampoo and liniments blended with the unmistakable scent of "horse" that is familiar to anyone who spends their life around stables; it is intoxicating.

The only sounds were the slow munching of hay, a few birds in the nearby pines, and the occasional rustling of a horse getting up from its last sleep and shaking off the shavings that had collected on its face and neck. Horses have excellent memories; they recognize people and learn their routines, and Dancer knew mine well. I was greeted with a soft nicker while his eyes followed my approach to the front of his gated stall. His ears pricked forward in anticipation of my customary greeting: "Hey, big fella. Did you have a good night?" He always answered with a slow release of breath that fluttered through his soft nostrils, evoking the image of butterflies tumbling out and dissolving into the fresh morning air.

I would throw a large handful of hay into the corner of his stall so he could quietly eat while I brushed off the dust and shavings and gave him a final polish with a soft cloth before putting on his saddle and bridle. The process of grooming and tacking unfolded like a ceremony—the same actions, in the same order, every time—unhurriedly and gently. Horses crave routines so they don't fret about what might happen next. They can relax and enjoy the stimulation that comes from being brushed and toweled off, especially if they trust that the upcoming training session will be enjoyable.

Horses are athletes and respond to training in the same way human athletes do. After a night in their stall, their joints are stiff, and their muscles can be tight. They may have slept in an odd position and woken up with a kink in a joint or a knot in a muscle. If the previous day's training session was especially demanding, they might even have muscle soreness or tension that can only be relieved through a proper warm-up.

Miguel had taught me to always warm a horse up with the same exercises. Not to teach the horse anything new; they were designed to get the horse's heart to pump more blood through the lungs and warm up its muscles as it began the cardiovascular workout. It also allowed the rider to warm up while paying attention to every step the horse took and registering how it felt compared to the previous day. If Dancer seemed tired, I would pull back on the intensity of the following training exercises so he wouldn't be overworked. But if he came out fresh—as was usually the case on a brisk morning—I would make sure the exercises after the warm-up required Dancer to use up the energy he seemed to have in abundance.

With each day of training, Dancer's muscles strengthened, which allowed him to suspend himself in the air between strides after pushing off his hind legs and propelling himself forward. With strength came balance, and his gaits became more rhythmical, allowing him to maintain a steady pace and move as if synchronized to a metronome. The undulating flow of his body—with me anchored to the saddle—felt like riding the swell of a big wave. We had such a close connection that it seemed as if we could read each other's mind—my cues and signals being transmitted almost telepathically. Accompanied by Pavarotti's voice floating from the overhead speakers, the rhythm, harmony, and synchronization of our movement was musical; we were creating our own art.

Dancer was bred to race, and thoroughbreds are known as "hot bloods." When he occasionally heard a noise that startled him or saw something move that he didn't recognize, he might bolt or jump to the side. Nevertheless, I always relaxed into the saddle and simply went with the flow. After a few bouncy strides, Dancer would give me his full attention and we would go back to work as if nothing had happened. I trusted him and he trusted me.

Although I had enjoyed long stretches of training with horses like Pluto Alga and Alajos, we had never become partners. They were schoolmasters whom I had stewardship of, but my role was minimized compared to someone who trains a young horse from scratch. The emotional connection was different: they didn't need to trust me like Dancer did; they already knew what to do.

Because of my travel, Miguel's wife rode Kalif more than I did, so I wasn't his exclusive partner. And although I had ridden Jasper every day for over a year in Australia, he did not belong to me and I knew our time together would be short, so we never truly bonded. I had ridden over a hundred different horses in my life, but I had never enjoyed the kind of relationship I had developed with Dancer, progressing his training day by day and deepening our emotional bond after every session.

Dancer's routine finished with me handing him off to Liz, who had arrived at the stables and fed the horses while readying things for the day. She would treat him to a long walk to cool down, followed by a shower, breakfast, and then most of the day grazing in a pasture. I would head home to shave and shower and then drive to the office in downtown Cleveland, reliving each moment from the morning and planning the next day's training session. It was everything I had always hoped for—both as a corporate manager and as a horseman—enjoying the best of both worlds. My life felt perfect.

47

The Journey Begins

In May of 1997, Heather's company had to downsize. So did my life.

A key client had been providing almost 80 percent of the work. When the client announced a decision to change their litigation strategy, all work on their cases came to an abrupt halt. Although Heather had been focused on bringing new clients on board and was on the cusp of landing their contracts, they were still several months from closing.

I decided it was time to move on. As much as I had enjoyed working with Heather over the three years, I wanted to focus on bringing Miguel to the U.S. to conduct training clinics. I wanted to become his business manager. I needed more time and flexibility for that, so I resigned as General Manager.

Kalif had reached the peak of his training with Miguel and was not progressing toward the Grand Prix level as hoped. He had some physical limitations we could not spot when we had bought him and unfortunately, he had not grown into the athlete we expected. Miguel found Kalif a new home, and I no longer had a horse to train in Australia.

Since Dancer was coming along so well in his development, I suggested to Miguel that I organize for him to come to Ohio and conduct week-long training clinics with the area's top riders. I could continue working with Miguel and he would have a substantial source of income. We talked through the details and agreed to have him come in August.

I began showing videos I had made of Miguel's riding to seven of northeast Ohio's top riders—most of them professional trainers and several with Grand Prix horses—who all signed on for his first clinic. We held it at the stables where I kept Dancer, and it provided the perfect setting to introduce Miguel and demonstrate his expertise as a trainer and teacher. The clinic was a success. With Miguel's reputation established, we agreed to schedule quarterly clinics at a variety of facilities in the area.

Several months after the first clinic, the national magazine *Dressage Today* published a five-page article about the clinic and Miguel's training philosophy. The article was read by a Portuguese rider from Los Altos Hills, California named Sofia. She was particularly interested because her father had bred horses in Portugal called Lusitanos—an Iberian breed favored by the Portuguese, trained for both bullfighting and the classical art of dressage. Nuno Oliveira had been a friend of her father's and a devotee of the breed.

Sofia gave me a call. She owned an Arabian gelding she was training in dressage and wanted to host a clinic with Miguel in California. We agreed she would fly to Cleveland to meet Miguel at his upcoming clinic, and if he was on board, we would set up his first clinic outside of Ohio.

It was 1998 and still possible to meet an arriving passenger at the gate. Within the crowd disembarking the jetway, I saw a woman slightly under five feet tall, about my age, with an athletic build, pixie-like features, and a quick stride. Sofia was a dynamo with a ready sense of humor. She spoke a mile a minute—her staccato words filtered through a noticeable Portuguese accent—and her English was perfect. She had a special fondness for American slang and had mastered the use of four-letter words—the "f-bomb" being one of her favorites. She was sharp, well-educated, and passionate about her love for horses and dressage. We became instant friends and after a day with Miguel, they connected as fellow countrymen with a shared love for the art of classical equitation. Together we planned the first clinic in California.

Sofia had a large group of friends in and around Los Altos Hills. The dot-com bubble that had begun in 1995 was getting ready to burst, but Palo Alto and the rest of Silicon Valley were still thriving, and a lot of multi-millionaires were being made. Many of their wives were Sofia's friends and wanted to be part of the equestrian world and enjoy its prestige and elite lifestyle.

Sofia had meticulously organized the clinic logistics and held it at the historic Westwind Barn in Los Altos Hills. She put together a great collection of horses and riders that included a student of Miguel's from Australia who had married an American and moved to California. Miguel was thrilled to work with a rider he had previously trained who could demonstrate his methods. Several participants, as well as some who audited the sessions, wanted to ride in future clinics and said to Miguel: "We like your training methods and have learned a lot. But when you go back to Australia, how can we continue to learn your system of training?"

Miguel had an answer: "Gil is my protégé and teaches my system. He should come to teach when I am not here. Then I come back when Sofia brings me, and we go on." So, in addition to being Miguel's manager, I was endorsed as a teacher. That opened the door to my career as a professional trainer and I set up clinics in California, Pennsylvania, and Ohio with riders who wanted to learn Miguel's system of training.

My group of students grew quickly, and I dusted off Mastery in the Art of Equitation—the course I had designed in Australia—and offered it to them.

On a Saturday morning, while one of the winter's most aggressive blizzards was in full force, twelve dedicated students made the drive to attend the two-day program in Ohio. That inaugural course launched a program that remained successful until I stopped presenting it fifteen years later.

My dream had always been to own a horse farm and go to the Olympics as a rider. That dream still simmered in me, but I realized I was passionate about teaching and training and that I was good at it. But my commitment to this new endeavor was about to destroy one of the most meaningful relationships in my life.

48

Therapy

A horse in serious training needs to be ridden every day. With teaching, clinics, and consulting assignments, and no suitable rider to keep Dancer exercised when I was away, I decided to sell him.

I had made a video of a training session with him and sent it to a veterinarian in Florida who had seen my ad in *The Chronicle of the Horse*. She sent a local vet to examine him, and without coming to meet or ride Dancer, she bought him.

A large van pulled in on a Saturday morning to load him up with a group of racehorses heading for Florida. I felt the loss even before the van rolled off the property. Ten minutes later I headed home and while stopped at a traffic light, I saw the van at the gas station on the corner, filling its tanks for the trip. Dancer was standing on the side of the truck facing the road and the window by his head was open. He was nervous, I could tell. He neighed, and although I knew he was calling to the other horses, I couldn't help but feel it was a final goodbye call to me. I broke down in tears. I sobbed the whole way home and felt an incredible pang of guilt: *How could I have sold my best friend to a stranger? Did I just make a terrible mistake?*

A deeper level of depression set in than I had ever known. I stopped enjoying even the simplest of pleasures. Things that should have been important—working on my various projects, finishing to-do lists, or even returning phone calls—fell by the wayside. Nothing I did mattered.

Along with daily drinking, I added marijuana back into my nightly routine and woke up with the same sense of sorrow I had gone to bed with. It was like being trapped in a cycle with no breaks. My pain was no longer interrupted by occasional spurts of joy from working or riding—there was no escape.

After almost twenty years of struggling with my depression and addictions, it was time to find a therapist. As with most serious challenges in my life, I turned to Heather for help. She tapped into her professional network and found a therapist who referred me to an appropriate practitioner. Dr. Macbride's practice was a short drive from home, and I committed to two, one-hour weekly sessions. With very little preamble about how the process of therapy would work, we jumped right into the stories about my past and the challenges I was facing. At first, I downplayed my addiction to alcohol and drugs and focused on my depression. Before long we revealed my addictions were as serious a disease as my depression and began delving into the sources of them all. Then an unexpected event changed the focus of my therapy: Joe died.

49
R.I.P. Joe

In October of 1998, I got a phone call from a friend who had met Joe when they both worked at Schneider's Saddlery.

"I wasn't sure if you cared, but I thought I should tell you that Joe has died. You probably remember the young man who went with Joe from Ohio to South Carolina when he moved there in '86. He called to say that a lifetime of smoking, drinking, painkillers, and a horrible diet had finally taken their toll. The funeral will be in Durham, North Carolina. He'll be buried in a family plot next to his brother." Joe was fifty-four.

"Thanks for letting me know. Will you be going to the funeral?"

"I don't think so. I recently put down my retired horse. As you know, he had hung in there a long time and was old. He deserves his final rest in heaven, but I am still heartbroken. I may go a bit later and help sort through Joe's belongings, but I'm not up to a funeral right now."

"If you do go, could you do me a big favor? Joe kept an old cardboard shoe box—usually in his closet—filled with photos, most of them Polaroids. If he still had it, there may be pictures of me—naked, doing yoga. Would you please look for it, and if you find it, destroy everything? I am not the only boy he had photos of, and I think we all deserve to have that part of our past disappear." She assured me she would.

At that point in my life, many people close to me had died. With each passing, I believed I understood my emotions; they were different for each friend or family member but always included feelings of sorrow and loss. Not this time.

Joe had created a dream for me to live into and convinced me I could achieve it. He had devoted himself fully to me and had dedicated his life to my success. He had taught me to set goals and inspired the discipline in me that was required to achieve them. He provided the foundational dressage education that enabled me to train in Germany. That prepared me for my first ride with Miguel and the advanced education I was receiving from him.

These reflections brought a sense of closure, but I was unable to feel any sadness. The final chapter of Joe's perverted life had closed, and I could see the contribution it had made to mine, despite the abuse. Only therapy would reveal the true cost of that abuse.

I spent a lot of time in the following days thinking about him and our time together. I couldn't stop trying to justify everything that had happened with Joe as being an important part of my youth; so much of what we did together, especially in those years before Hiram, had been enjoyable. Being with Joe provided an escape from the nightmares of school and the sadness of living in a home that offered no refuge. I was beginning to accept the idea that I had been a victim of pedophilia, so I couldn't understand why I was trying so hard to justify everything as having been OK—except for that one "complication": abuse.

After escaping from Joe and moving in with Dennis, I continued to crave the kind of attention Joe had given me and searched for others who would confirm my physical attractiveness. I found it through anonymous sexual encounters that put me at significant risk—my need must have overridden my common sense. And even after a break, I worked my way back into Joe's world and participated with his vaulting team. *Why hadn't I been able to stay away?* I must have wanted something he had provided during our seven years together, so it was easy to believe I had enjoyed my relationship with Joe and was not, in fact, a victim.

As soon as my thoughts went down that path, scenes would come into my head and trigger horrible memories that reignited my feelings of having been abused: that first night sitting on his lap after my workout in his living room and the sexual encounter that followed; the nights in the parking lot in Fort Riley feeling the physical intimacy of his body on top of mine; Becky walking in on us while I was being fondled at the kitchen table; sleeping in the same bed at Erlenhof and the stench of the house; his vile nakedness draped on my body at the apartment in Hiram; stalking me on campus; inserting himself into my graduation ceremony; and harassing me after moving in with Dennis. Any of those thoughts brought me back to the reality of his crimes and should have brought relief that his death could bring closure to the most traumatic part of my life. But it didn't.

Surviving abuse and living with Complex PTSD created a myriad of emotions, often in conflict with one another. The resulting confusion and the frustration of not being able to resolve it became its own form of torment. That became the focus of my therapy. I was using alcohol and drugs to keep me from confronting the trauma and learning how to heal from it. It would be another twenty-two years before I would get help and begin that part of my mental and emotional health journey. The price I would pay during those years in the form of pain and suffering was beyond my comprehension in October 1998.

50

Lisbon

After several clinics in Ohio and California—in January of 1999—Miguel said he wanted to return to Cleveland in April for another clinic, and then take a trip to Lisbon. It had been seventeen years since he had left Portugal. At the time he left, he had been the Chief Instructor and Director of the Portuguese Military and Civilian Riding Academy in the town of Mafra, less than an hour northwest of Lisbon. The government had been going through a major reorganization in 1982—as was its military riding academy—and after twenty years of service, the Academy had not presented Miguel with the awards and formal recognition customary for someone of his stature. Miguel had been invited to return to Mafra for a ceremony to recognize his contributions to the Academy. Miguel invited Sofia and me to join him.

We gathered at the Newark International Airport for our flight to Lisbon and were as excited as a group of children heading on their first school trip to a new city. Miguel had stayed in touch with his friends in Portugal by letter and only rarely phoned, so he was overjoyed to be reconnecting with his friends and the memories from his early life.

Continental Airlines used an old and cramped, single-aisle Boeing 737 for the transatlantic flight, and since we had all opted for economy-class tickets, we were jammed in like sardines. When the flight attendant came through with the beverage cart, I honored my decades-long custom and ordered a screwdriver. As she was passing my glass, she asked Miguel what he wanted to drink. "I would like a jeen and tunic please." Because of his thick accent, she asked him to repeat. "A jeen tunic."

During the six years I had been with Miguel, I had never seen him have a drink—no beer, no wine, no hard liquor. People had told me Miguel was a recovering alcoholic, but prone to debilitating relapses. During my time with him, he arrived at the arena every morning at 6:30—after an hour of exercising in his study—freshly showered with his boots polished to a military shine. He was always energized for a full day of riding and teaching and appeared to be the picture of health. I knew all the signs of someone who drank, and he had shown none of them.

As he sipped his gin and tonic, I thought: *My God—what if he* does *have a problem? Could this be the beginning of a relapse, or is it only one small deviation because of the special occasion?* As I learned much later in life, the first drink for an alcoholic is never "only one small deviation." We both had a second drink and then did our best to sleep for a few hours.

The next morning, Miguel's friends picked us up and our first stop was at the home and stables of Dr. Guilherme Borba. They were nestled atop a hill in the same town where Dr. Borba's close friend, Nuno Oliveira, had lived and worked. Miguel had been a part of the tight-knit group of equestrians that shared Nuno's passion for the art of classical riding, and they had all trained together. Dr. Borba established the Escola Portuguese d'Art Equestre (Portuguese School of Equestrian Art) at the Sociedade Hípica Portuguesa, located in Campo Grande.

Miguel was given a heartfelt embrace when we entered the lounge, and both men had tears in their eyes. After introductions, Dr. Borba signaled for one of his servants to pass a silver tray of crystal glasses filled with one of the light-green port wines Portugal is famous for. Once everyone was served, Dr. Borba offered a welcome toast, followed by what must have been some very kind words from Miguel—there wasn't a dry eye in the lounge. The toasts were given in Portuguese, so Sofia translated for me.

After about an hour of drinks and socializing, Dr. Borba invited us outside to watch him ride one of his stallions. This one was his favorite, and we were mesmerized as they displayed the same harmony and brilliance I had watched in some rare videos of Nuno Oliveira. This was the first time I had seen dressage presented purely as an art form—classical riding as defined in the writings of the old masters.

After Dr. Borba's beautiful display of riding, we were driven to a nearby town for lunch at a bistro frequented by locals. Carafes of wine were automatically brought to the table throughout the two-hour meal, and we finished the gathering with another fine port. Miguel enjoyed the drinks as much as the others, and afterwards our driver took us to the next stop—the Lisbon Polo Club—to meet another friend from his close-knit circle, Filipe Graciosa. Another tearful reunion between dear friends became an occasion for drinks and celebration.

The next morning, we went on a special outing. Filipe was serving as Director of the Portuguese School of Equestrian Art and invited us to the gardens at the National Palace in Queluz to watch the morning training sessions. Like The Spanish Riding School in Vienna, there was a daily public performance with the Lusitano Stallions in an outdoor arena surrounded by flowers. Accompanied by Baroque music, it showcased up to eight horses riding figures and patterns—with Filipe leading the quadrille.

My love for the pure art of training dressage horses deepened over those two days, and I was proud to be introduced as Miguel's protégé. I was in awe of Miguel's rarefied history and the role it played in his life—all of which was to be recognized and celebrated the next day in Mafra.

When we arrived at the front gates of their stables, we were escorted into a carriage drawn by a pair of Lusitano mares and given a tour of the vast acreage making up the equestrian training grounds. The ride ended at the entrance to a banquet hall with a U-shaped table set for forty people. Major Tavora was given a hero's welcome and shown the respect any military cadre of peers would show an honored guest. After several speeches and generous rounds of applause, Miguel was presented with perhaps the most meaningful gift of his life: a traditional riding crop given only to past directors of the Academy. The institution had waited almost two decades to bestow this honor on him, and its reception was as poignant as if he had received it all those years ago.

After an afternoon of food, drinks, and camaraderie, we returned to the city and enjoyed dinner at a private home with some of Miguel's closest friends. It was the perfect end to a trip that had been filled with beautiful horses, fond memories of special times, reconnecting with old friends, the celebration of a rich military career ... and lots of alcohol. I had been drinking every day for the past twenty years but even I could feel the adverse effects of our heavy drinking. I had to wonder how it had affected Miguel and whether it was a temporary break from sobriety, or if it was the start of a downward spiral. My instincts told me the road ahead was going to be paved with challenges. Unfortunately, I was right.

51
Clay Feet

"I'm calling with bad news." Miguel's wife phoned after his return to Sydney. "Miguel was riding a horse at a clinic, and it spooked and reared up. The horse flipped over and landed on him. He fractured his pelvis and has had major surgery. He will probably need a year of rehabilitation before he can ride again."

I phoned Miguel every few weeks to check on his recovery, and by the spring of 2000 he said he was back to teaching full-time and expected to begin riding soon. His students in Ohio were excited to resume training after the long break; he was still in demand. I found a house to rent that was close to the stables, and lined up a full calendar of horses and riders who would train with Miguel over the three summer months. I set up the second floor of the house as a private suite for him, complete with an exercise room, bedroom, and private bath. I would stay downstairs in the guest bedroom.

The first months of Miguel's residency went well. I was at the stables every day to manage the logistics of having seven or eight horses arrive in the arena, tacked up and ready to go, at their appointed times. After a day's work, he was spending a lot of time with Paula—a student who was hosting his clinics at her farm—going out to dinner and then relaxing in the evening at our house, watching videos of international dressage competitions while he gave his critique and commentary. We all enjoyed a few drinks and always split up for an early night before another busy day of training.

Sofia was marrying her partner of many years, and they were taking their honeymoon in France. Since Sofia's horse was stabled at their home, she needed someone to stay there while they were away and look after him. I agreed to come out to Los Altos Hills, ride and care for her horse, and travel to some of the local stables to give lessons to riders from Miguel's clinics. In my absence, Paula agreed to manage the clinic.

The first week of this arrangement went well, and I was building a clientele at private stables in Woodside, Palo Alto, and Menlo Park—my new backyard in

Silicon Valley. But things with Miguel were turning out to be a disaster. Paula phoned with an urgent request: "Gil, you have to come back. Miguel is drinking heavily and some mornings he is not showing up to work. I have gone to the house to get him and found empty liquor bottles strewn about and some full bottles hidden behind the toilets or buried in closets. But there is a bigger problem. The seventeen-year-old girl who is working in the stables says Miguel has made inappropriate sexual advances and she refuses to come to work. I need you here to help me with this." I had also heard rumors of Miguel's inappropriate advances to women but never had reason to believe them. This news came as a shock.

It took two days to find someone to stay at Sofia's before I could go home to deal with the problems. Paula convinced Miguel to stop drinking for those two days and he was sober when I arrived. We sat at the kitchen table to talk things through, and Miguel declared it was the pain pills he was taking that were causing him trouble—not alcohol.

Miguel stopped drinking for a few more days, and I sat with him again to say, "Miguel, I understand you need the pain pills and I'm sure they help so you are able to work. But I know mixing alcohol with pills is never good. If you continue to drink, we have to end the program. I personally sponsor your HB-1 visa and am responsible if there should be an accident with you, a student, or a horse. You cannot drink while you are here." He assured me that would not be a problem and was irritated I had suggested it might have been.

The next Sunday he and Paula came back from dinner and Miguel was inebriated. He had stopped at the liquor store to buy a bottle of gin and was preparing to make a drink. There was one week left in the program, and I told him I was going to cancel all the lessons. When I asked him to change his air ticket and go home early, he became belligerent, made himself a drink, and went upstairs.

The next morning, I told Paula I was going to contact the same immigration attorney who had secured Miguel's working visa and have her initiate the process of having it revoked. As his sponsor, I could do that. I phoned the clients scheduled for the week and canceled their sessions. Several thanked me: they had noticed Miguel had not been "well" and had grown concerned. Miguel continued to go to the stables to train Paula's horses and then left for Sydney at the end of the week. We were no longer on speaking terms.

My hero had fallen, and I felt betrayed. All the work I had done to establish a business for Miguel in the U.S. had come to a disappointing and embarrassing end. I guessed Joe had been right—every hero does have his clay feet—and I realized my seven-year apprenticeship with Miguel was over. I was on my own again.

52
Go West, Young Man

Things went downhill in the months after Miguel left and I struggled to find a path forward without him. I was reaching an emotional breaking point, and the crash was going to be brutal.

Miguel's HB-1 visa had not yet been invalidated—the red tape was taking a while—but like any Australian citizen, he could enter the U.S. on a visitor's visa. Paula wanted to continue training with him, so she purchased a ticket for him to come at the end of September to teach and train at her farm. I was still liable for his actions in the U.S., so I went to the immigration office in Cleveland and explained my situation. They asked for his flight information, went to Cleveland Hopkins Airport to meet his flight, and escorted him off the plane. He was sent back to Sydney and told not to return to the U.S. until he had a renewed work visa.

I had the friend I admired and respected for over seven years deported from the country. I doubted he would ever forgive me. I felt I had ruined what should have been a lifetime friendship and I placed the blame on myself. I had never admired someone as much as I had Miguel, and my dream of competing at the Olympics, with Miguel as my coach, had been shattered.

Throughout the day on Sunday, October 1st, television was filled with scenes from the closing ceremonies of the 2000 Olympic Games in Sydney. Over 2.4 billion people watched what the president of the International Olympic Committee declared as the best summer Olympics ever.

I came home that evening and poured myself a drink. And then another, and another. I turned off the TV and stood in the middle of the living room, staring out from my eighth-floor apartment into the night. A combination of frustration, anger, sadness, and defeat dealt me the final blow and I threw myself onto the floor, slamming my forehand into the carpet. The pain shot through my head as I beat my fists and repeatedly howled the defeated cry: "I am *never* going to the Olympics!" My fit continued until my hands and arms went numb, my head felt ready to explode, and my throat grew hoarse. The sobbing went on for an hour, interrupted by short bursts of rage. A neighbor phoned to see if everything was alright. I lied and said it was.

I finished the bottle of vodka and passed out. The next morning, I looked at the bruise on my forehead, phoned in sick to my consulting client, and said I would be away for a few days. I felt guilty having to call in sick, but in truth, I *was* sick—I had had a mental breakdown.

After two days of isolation and grappling with my emotions, I committed to a plan of action. It was time to quit juggling a business career and a life with horses. Something had to give, and that something was the career. Repeated failures had marked twenty years in the corporate world, and I was no closer to achieving my financial goals than I had been when I abandoned my career with Mannesmann and struck out on my own.

If my Olympic dreams were ever to be realized, I would need to commit to a career with horses. Sofia had asked me several times why I didn't move out to California and start a full-time training business. I had established a client base and could grow it from there. A move to California seemed like the perfect solution.

I went to San Francisco to work out the details and we created a plan. Sofia and her husband had purchased the cabin they were renting in Los Altos Hills and there was room on the property for a camping trailer. I could live there in exchange for training Sofia and Malik, her horse.

With the thought of finally devoting my whole life to dressage, I snapped out of my debilitating depression. On the flight home I calculated the number of hours I had studied with Miguel: training horses at every level of dressage; watching him and his wife riding at home; and auditing his many clinics throughout Australia and the U.S. The number exceeded two thousand. I was confident I had learned Miguel's system of gymnastic training, and although I wasn't experienced enough to execute it at his level, I was qualified to go out on my own as a journeyman and teach it; I had already earned his endorsement as protégé.

There were a few loose ends I needed to tie up before heading out west. One was to end the two years of unsatisfactory "talk therapy" I had been enduring with Dr. Macbride. Although we uncovered that my addictions were as serious a disease as my depression, and delved into the sources of them all, I didn't feel we had made much progress.

Each session would begin the same way. I would sit on a couch—often dressed in my boots and breeches on my way to teach a lesson or ride a horse—and Dr. Macbride would look at me from behind her desk staying silent until I spoke. Sometimes I carried on with a topic from our last session, or I would bring up something that had happened since then. Dr. Macbride always asked questions about my remarks, but never tried to direct the conversation—that was up to me.

The questions she did ask were about how I let the sexual abuse with Joe go on for seven years; how I let Ted and Ben force me to perform oral sex on them; how I got into a situation where Dennis could rape me. The focus was on me taking ownership of my actions. I heard the word "trauma" for the first time and thought about my early teens in a new way, but I couldn't grasp how I had enabled the abuse with Joe, or how I had let this all play out as it did. Without providing a framework or tools to help me understand, I felt Dr. Macbride was leaving me on my own to figure it out.

I was drinking excessively and wondered why I could not stop, even when I felt I wanted to. I did not understand the disease of addiction and wanted information so I could. Dr. Macbride didn't provide that either. At one session when I commented on how I wished that there was wine without alcohol in it, she replied: "There is. It's called grape juice." That was the only explanation I received. I didn't find Dr. MacBride's "talk therapy" helpful. Moving west seemed the right time to end two years of confusion and frustration.

After announcing my decision to move to Los Altos Hills to my mother, Doug, Loren, and Heather, I resigned from my job, loaded up my three-year-old Chevy Blazer, and made the four-day drive to California. During the two days I crossed through the plains of Indiana, Iowa, and Nebraska, my thoughts went to the road trip with Joe to Fort Riley—twenty-eight years before—when the dream of going to the Olympics was new and had become the impetus for my decisions.

The day I looked into Mr. Button's eye and connected with his soul had started me on this journey and it was time to bring it to its conclusion. I had been betrayed many times along the way and wondered how I had stayed so resolute in my quest to master the art of equitation. But after hours of thought, the answer came to me. The spark that ignited in me every time I looked in a horse's eye, and the exhilaration I felt as I swung my leg over a horse's back and settled into the saddle, had never abandoned me. I would turn that reliable spark into a roaring fire. I was ready.

Part Three

SALUTE

Preparation, the Olympic dream, and saying goodbye

53
Dressage Royalty

My trailer was a far cry from the multi-million-dollar homes where most of my clients lived. Many were venture capitalists and private equity investors enjoying the windfall of their incredible gains from the dot-com bubble. When I arrived in Silicon Valley in November of 2000, the NASDAQ had risen by almost 400 percent over the past five years and was beginning its downward spiral. It would fall by almost 80 percent over the next two years and the dot-com bubble would have burst—but we weren't there yet.

Sofia and her husband owned a 580-square-foot cabin at the foot of a hill adjacent to their small barn. There was enough room next to the cabin for my fifteen-foot trailer but there was no water hookup. So, I joined a fitness center and every morning at 6:30, showered after my workout, pulling on my breeches and boots for a full day of training and teaching. I returned to the cabin at the end of each day and joined Sofia and her husband for a fabulous home-cooked dinner, along with several martinis.

After Miguel's first clinic in Los Altos Hills, our trip to Lisbon, and my teaching engagements in the valley, Sofia and I became close friends. Sofia was an accredited massage therapist—for horses. Like any athlete, a horse gets stiff muscles and neurological blockages and benefits from a massage. Because horses can't tell us where they hurt, a massage therapist needs to be able to "read" a horse's energy field by touch and then locate the exact source of tension or pain. Sofia had a sixth sense for that, and her services were in demand. She traveled to many of the local horse facilities and promoted me as a new trainer in the area. Her clients trusted her and started to take lessons from me. Before long I had a full schedule teaching at private farms in Woodside and public barns throughout the valley. Every day included a training session with Sofia and her Arabian gelding, Malik.

In the spring of 2001, Sofia got her dream car: a silver and black BMW Z2. The car suited her personality to a tee—small, powerful, and zippy. When May rolled around, she suggested we enjoy the car and take a weekend trip to Hanford—in the middle of the Central Valley—to attend the annual dressage show at the DG Bar Ranch. One of the largest shows in the country, it attracted most of California's top riders and was a "not to be missed" event.

Sofia and I arrived in time for the afternoon classes, one of which was for the international Prix St. Georges—two levels away from Grand Prix. The covered arena, packed with spectators, went silent as the announcer introduced the next competitor: "Ladies and gentlemen, next to ride is our two-time Olympian, Guenter Seidel—returning from his bronze medal win at the Sydney Olympic Games—with his new Bavarian warmblood, Aragon. Aragon is owned by his long-time sponsors, Dick and Jane Brown."

We were sitting on the ground, only ten feet from the side of the arena, when Guenter and Aragon came powering by. The ground shook as they passed, and their presence took my breath away. Guenter was the most elegant rider I had ever seen. He was over six feet tall and as handsome as a runway model. He was impeccably turned out in a top hat and tails, with white breeches, matching gloves, and spit-polished black boots—the required attire for international-level competition. He embodied my vision of an Olympic dressage rider, and I was in awe throughout their ride.

Every Friday evening at the annual show they held a barbecue inside a tent that could accommodate well over a hundred guests. Sofia and I found a table near one of the open sides and were enjoying dinner when we heard the roar of laughter from a table in the middle of the tent. Standing beside the table was Guenter, and in front of him was an elegant couple who appeared to be in their late sixties, dressed in a fashion that said, "old money." They were the owners of Guenter's horse and had sponsored him for the past thirteen years, beginning when Guenter emigrated from Bavaria to Rancho Santa Fe in southern California. Dick and Jane Brown were "dressage royalty" and were holding court at the VIP table.

I had been reading about the Browns in *The Chronicle of the Horse* since the beginning of their partnership with Guenter. Their horses had won team bronze medals at the 1996 Atlanta Olympics, and most recently, in Sydney. They had competed at World Cup events and World Championships throughout Europe and always had several top-quality horses in training that were working their way to Grand Prix. Guenter had never been without an international horse and was one of the country's most decorated dressage riders.

The Browns provided Guenter with everything he needed for a successful career as an Olympian and people in the horse community joked that he was "the son they never had." All their wealth was in service to the success of Guenter and their horses, and he rode exclusively for them. As I watched their interactions, it would never have dawned on me that, one day, I would become part of this equestrian royal family.

My enthusiasm from the weekend at DG Bar followed me home and I jumped into the next week's training with new vigor. The timing was perfect because one evening at dinner, Sofia shared a great opportunity with me.

The largest horse facility in the area was the Portola Valley Training Center in Menlo Park. Its sixty acres were home to six separate barns—each with over a dozen stalls—and run by trainers with their own businesses and private clients. Sofia had learned that one of them was moving out of his barn and it was going to be available to lease. Sofia had a good relationship with the owners of the facility and set up a meeting for us. They were convinced I was a credible trainer with a growing clientele and gave me the lease on the vacated barn. Three weeks later I opened the "Gil Merrick Dressage Academy" and my clients moved in.

Although I was only leasing the stables, I felt I had accomplished an important part of my dream: I was an accomplished equestrian with his own training facility; I didn't own it, but it was *my* business, free to run the way I wanted. With that in place, it was time to move on to the next part of the dream and find my way to the Olympics.

54

Burnout

One of my clients, Elaine Johnson, was the granddaughter of a billionaire oil baron and owned a large estate in Los Altos Hills. With the launch of my academy, I let my clients know they were welcome to move into my facility and train every day, but I would no longer travel to their farms. I made an exception for Elaine.

When I began teaching her, Elaine had an older warmblood gelding that she rode as often as her time allowed. I agreed to continue coming to her farm every day to ride her horses, and to give her lessons when she was available. Elaine maintained a professional distance, making it clear our relationship would not become a friendship; I was there to do a job. Given her family's wealth and stature, their privacy was of paramount importance, and I understood that.

My barn at the Portola Valley Training Center had twelve large stalls and an area at the end of the center aisle where two horses could be tied for grooming, tacking up, and post-exercise showers. One morning while standing at the grooming area, a familiar man and woman walked into the barn. I had met Kevin and Marsha Bachman on a visit to the equestrian center where they trained. Kevin had recently sold his company and Marsha was from a wealthy family; they had the time and resources to enjoy the sport of dressage. Kevin was a Grand Prix–level rider and trained his own horses, and Marsha learned from him, so they did not need a trainer. What they needed was a full-service facility that could take care of their two horses and the young warmbloods they would be importing from Germany. Full service meant that when they arrived at the barn their horses would be groomed, tacked up, and ready to ride. When finished riding, they could hand the horses back to the grooms and leave. That was the service I provided. I had room for their horses and assured them I could expand my facility if it became necessary—and it would.

* * *

As the summer of 2002 was nearing an end, I was excited to have Heather visit. My training operation was in full swing, and I was proud to show it to her. The Bachmans had brought back a group of horses from Germany that I was riding every day to prepare for sale. My favorite was a bay gelding named Wilson. He had the sweet personality of my beloved Dancer, but he was an even better athlete, more comfortable to ride, and had the potential to become an international-level dressage horse. He had passed his veterinary inspection in Germany, transported well to the U.S., and was fit and healthy. On my recommendation, Heather bought Wilson for herself and left him with me for training until she moved him to her new farm, not far from Hiram.

As October approached, I was training up to nine horses a day, six days a week. I fueled my days with Red Bull and anesthetized myself at night with vodka. Riding and teaching in the sun for ten hours a day was exhausting, and it was taking its toll—mentally and physically. I still went to the gym every morning, and one day as I was showering, I heard the little voice in my head pose a disgruntled question: *Oh God—how many horses do I have to ride today?*

I froze as if ice water were coming out of the faucet.

Did I just say what I think I said? It shocked me.

For thirty-five years, riding horses had been my passion—the one thing that lit me up and kept me going, no matter what life threw at me. *How could I be dreading the thought of riding horses? Have I made the mistake everyone warned me of: "Be careful; it's not always wise to turn your avocation into your vocation—it changes things, and you could lose your passion."* That was what had happened: I was burned out.

Those thoughts led to other questions: *Should I go back to a lifestyle I truly enjoyed—working in corporate America and riding a horse like Dancer for nobody's pleasure but my own, with no clients to please, and no stress on my body?*

For two years, I had been training world-class horses belonging to my elite clientele, and I was as close to having my own horse farm as I was going to get. *Why would I want to give this up? Surely, this is a major part of my dream come true.*

My client, Elaine Johnson, inadvertently helped me answer the question.

Planning was underway for Elaine and her husband to renovate their stables and upgrade the entire training facility. They showed me the architectural plans and it was going to be magnificent—a horse trainer's utopia. Elaine told me that when the renovations were complete, she wanted to purchase some more horses and offered me the chance to train and teach full-time at her new facility. It was an incredible offer. I had already taken one trip to Germany to buy a warmblood mare for Elaine, and she had paid for Sofia and me to travel to Portugal to search for a suitable Lusitano. Elaine intended on buying additional horses she could ride and enjoy, and one of those, she indicated, could be a horse I could train to Grand Prix and compete with.

The offer seemed too good to be true, and after some careful thought, I decided it was. Although I had fantasized about having a sponsorship like Guenter Seidel had with the Browns and imagined achieving my Olympic dream as a competitor, this was different. The Browns did not ride—they were patriots who wanted to bring honor to the U.S. by sponsoring horses that won medals for our country. Elaine wanted to enjoy the solitude of her farm while riding for pleasure when her schedule allowed.

As her full-time trainer, I would be beholden to her and the demands of one of America's wealthiest, most private, and potentially most demanding families. I knew many trainers who had worked in similar situations and there seemed to be two outcomes: one where everything went brilliantly and provided everyone with a rewarding experience; and another where challenges that could not have been foreseen led to tumultuous breakups. As tempting as Elaine's offer was, I was not willing to take the risk of an upsetting ending. I had experienced enough uncertainty in my life. And after more than three thousand hours of teaching and training in California, I was burnt out. It was time to move on.

I let the Portola Valley Training Center and my clients know I would be closing the business in sixty days. I upset a lot of people—some of whom became angry, including Sofia. Wealthy people are used to getting what they want, and each client had been getting what they wanted. Seventeen horses needed new homes, including Heather's Wilson, and over a dozen riders needed a new trainer. For two years I had been the new kid on the block—the flavor of the month—and I was leaving everyone with a sour taste in their mouth.

55

Diane

Heather, on the other hand, was living my dream. She had purchased a hundred-acre farm with an eight-stall barn, turn-out paddocks, an indoor riding arena, and miles of trails that wound through the woods. It was a beautiful set-up with space for Wilson.

Wilson was arriving from his cross-country trip to Ohio in December. I was at Heather's the night he arrived and I helped him settle in and adjust to his new life of luxury. I talked to Heather about an offer I had received to establish myself in Gaithersburg, Maryland. A student of mine had moved there and suggested I pursue my new corporate career in Washington, D.C., where she had a lot of high-level business contacts. The circumstances were ideal for fulfilling my new goals and I decided to move there. I told Heather I would come to Cleveland regularly and help her with Wilson and her other horses. Because I was already known as a trainer in northeast Ohio, I could also teach lessons at local barns and use that income to carry me along.

I rented an apartment in Gaithersburg and assembled a small group of riding students in the Virginia suburbs to generate some income while I looked for a job. And that is where I met Diane. Diane leased a stable in Clifton, where she ran a boarding and teaching business. She owned a warmblood she was training in dressage and wanted some help. So, I made the one-hour drive to meet her to see if I could provide it.

It was a sunny January morning when I drove into the stable area. Diane was already in the outdoor arena and walking around on her black gelding, Pepper. As I was heading down the hill to join her, I was struck by how elegantly she sat on her horse. I was impressed by how fit she was, and with only the slightest amount of mascara and a hint of eye shadow, she radiated natural beauty. I was charmed by what I thought was a Southern accent. She was bright and eloquent and laced all her remarks with an endearing hint of humor. In fact, I thought everything about her was endearing—and beautiful. We hit it off and she had a fantastic ride.

After returning Pepper to the stables, we sat at a picnic table in front of my car and talked for over an hour. One of her students arrived and we needed to wrap up, but we scheduled her next lesson and agreed we would continue to work together for as long as I was available. I couldn't wait to come back.

We ended up seeing each other twice a week and finished each training session with a long talk—sometimes at the picnic table, and sometimes at a local coffee shop. We were getting to know each other well and our attraction to each other was obvious. A week before Valentine's Day, Diane asked if I would join her for dinner at her favorite restaurant, L'Auberge Chez Francois, in Great Falls. It would be our first date.

Diane was getting a divorce and had three teenage children. Looking at Diane's petite figure, I would never have guessed she had given birth to one child—let alone three. We were the same height and had the same lean build; we were physical twins. My attraction to her allowed me to put any concerns about her family situation aside, and I accepted her invitation to a romantic dinner on Valentine's Day.

Our evening was perfect in every way. After cocktails and five courses of French cuisine with beautifully paired wines, we stepped into a foggy night. I walked Diane to her car and knew the evening would end in a kiss. With the mist falling lightly under the overhead floodlight, I took her in my arms, and we savored a long kiss. She surprised me as I felt her weight drop and her knees buckle—she had swooned.

In March, Diane left her husband and children to live in an apartment thirty minutes away from their home. We took our relationship to the next level and began spending nights together—mostly at her place, and sometimes at mine. The lovemaking was passionate and frequent. We spent evenings on her balcony sharing the stories of our past—many of Diane's bringing her to tears. The last few years had been rough.

According to Diane, her husband had been verbally and physically abusive and had threatened to harm her if she ever tried to leave. She had orchestrated an escape with the help of a girlfriend and had gotten herself and her belongings out when he was at work. After she had moved out, he continued to phone her daily and was using her children to spy on her, as I discovered one night when her son knocked on the door at 1 a.m. with the excuse he had lost his wallet and needed her help. Her husband wanted to know if we were sleeping together. I also had received a strange letter from "someone" laying out a host of reasons why I should stay clear of Diane—accusing her of being "unstable." Her eldest daughter had signed it, but Diane said it had come from her husband. Either way, it set the tone for what lay ahead.

In April an event was being held at the Kentucky Horse Park in Lexington. The park covered over 1200 acres in the heart of the Bluegrass and had state-of-the-art training facilities for every discipline of riding. A dressage symposium was being held featuring a Finnish Olympian named Kyra Kyklund. She would present her teaching clinic over two days with close to five hundred spectators, including Diane and me.

We made the eight-hour drive to Lexington in Diane's cobalt-blue Ford F-250 pickup—the one she used to transport horses to and from her stables. Diane shared details about her childhood as we drove. In her telling of things, she was the great-granddaughter of Henry Ford—the namesake of her truck. Her father had married one of Henry's granddaughters and established a successful paper mill in Lexington. He had a passion for thoroughbreds and used his wealth from the business to breed some of the world's finest racehorses; buyers came from around the world to see them. Diane shared extensive details about visits to the stud by Saudi Arabian Sheiks; the lavish dinners with rare wines from her father's private collection; the opulent stables with cathedral ceilings and sterling-silver water buckets; a home filled with scores of cooks, servants, and governesses; and long summer afternoons playing in the pastures and helping in the stables. The house was an antebellum mansion where she and her siblings often got lost but were forbidden to go into the secret room in the basement where clandestine meetings of her father's friends were held. Her childhood had been privileged and filled with adventure. Her father died years earlier and her mother had moved to Clarksville, Tennessee. Her mother was leasing out the farm, but upon her death, Diane was to inherit the estate—all 1500 acres of it.

The dressage symposium ended mid-afternoon on Sunday, and we planned to spend the night at the Marriott Courtyard and head back to Virginia in the morning. As we were pulling out of the Kentucky Horse Park, I said, "Honey, it's a beautiful afternoon and we have the rest of the day free. I would love to take a drive and see all the nearby horse farms. Wouldn't it be fun to go see your farm—where you grew up and had all those wonderful experiences? Since it will be yours one day, you must be interested in seeing it."

There was a pause, and she said, "Baby, it's been so darned long since I've been here, I don't think I could find it. If you want to drive around a bit and see all the farms, I'll sing out if I see it. I'm sure I'd recognize it—I just don't know how to get there."

2003 was too early for cell phones with GPS or Google Maps, so I acquiesced and took us on a driving tour of the Bluegrass. We never found the estate.

56

Friendships Die

Every job lead in D.C. had come to a dead end and I was frustrated. Then Diane presented me with some exciting news after her morning ride.

"Sweetie, I have something wonderful to tell you. I think I told you about my friend Myrl. She's a horse buddy and president of a big organization in D.C. that does something with the healthcare industry. She is looking for a new Vice President for Finance and Administration and I told her I would ask you to send her your résumé. Here's her email."

It *was* exciting news. Myrl Weinberg was Chief Executive Officer of The National Health Council. The NHC was a membership organization on M Street—five blocks from the White House—that served the healthcare community. Myrl invited me to come for an interview that week.

It was May and I had already made a few trips to Cleveland to work with Heather and her horses. On my last trip, Heather made me an offer. She was planning to expand her farm by renovating her barn and purchasing some new horses. She asked me to consider staying in Ohio to be her dedicated trainer. It was not a full-time position but might become one after she acquired more horses. If I came on board, she would pay me for my time and ensure I enjoyed the full benefits of having access to top-quality horses at a world-class facility. It felt like an opportunity to partner with my best friend in fulfilling a dream we both shared: success at the international levels of dressage.

Heather was traveling a lot for her business and needed me to be available whenever she was. That meant my schedule would vary from week to week. When I wasn't working with her, I was free to train other students—with one caveat: her schedule needed to be my priority and take precedence over my other clients. I told her I would give it some thought.

I had promised to be in Ohio the same week Myrl invited me for the interview. On Tuesday morning I sent Heather an email and apologized for having to cancel my trip to work with her. I let her know how excited I was about the prospect of getting the job at the NHC, making it obvious I was giving that offer priority over hers.

I went to the interview later that week without having heard back from Heather. It struck me as odd since she was rigorous about managing her email. I was also surprised I didn't get any words of encouragement about my upcoming interview. Myrl offered me the job; the salary was attractive, and the 401K plan was generous. I accepted the offer.

Every day while sitting in the train on my commute to work I asked myself why Heather had never gotten back to me. It turned out that a lifetime friendship had ended with that one email, and I had no idea why. Communicating about the silence should have been easy. Somehow it wasn't, and neither of us did.

* * *

A few months later Diane told me that through a girlfriend who worked as a mortgage broker, she had secured a loan and bought a small house in the Virginia suburb of West Falls Church. It was 2004 and the great housing bubble was inflating with the kind of sub-prime loans Diane received. With no steady income, no recent job history, no down payment, and a pending divorce, she was an ideal candidate for that kind of loan. A 1200-square-foot home became hers, and in March, I moved in.

We spent weekends doing yard work and I mowed a lawn again for the first time since I was eleven and earning money for riding lessons. We were regulars at the Home Depot, and I acquired handyman skills I would put to good use for several years. At night we engaged in our favorite evening activities: drinking cocktails and smoking. Diane smoked Virginia Slims and drank rum and Coke. I drank martinis and we both smoked pot. Smoking and drinking were two things we had in common, and we happily enabled each other's addictions. It was part of our attraction to each other. We were the perfect Boomer couple, living the perfect life in suburbia. Then things got complicated.

Diane's divorce turned ugly, especially around custody of her two young girls. Her ex-husband, Jack, was fighting tooth and nail to retain it and he was winning. Diane's long calls with him and the screaming that went with them interrupted every evening at home. When Diane picked the girls up for visitation, Jack always came to the car to menace us. The girls were unhappy, Diane was anxious and distraught, and I was miserable. I had no idea what I had signed up for. I was beginning to wonder if some things Diane had been accused of in that anonymous letter may have been true. She was acting irrationally about many things and crying at the drop of a hat. I was being closed out as she struggled to win her battle with Jack, and I needed some relief: the alcohol and marijuana were not getting the job done and I could not cope with the confrontations and anger—two major triggers to my PTSD. I told Diane we could continue to see each other, but that I was moving into a studio apartment close to my office.

By June I had been working for the NHC for over a year and took a much-needed vacation. Mary Gober, who had first trained my staff in Sydney and then at Heather's company, had become a close friend. She had based herself in London and her business was thriving. I booked a first-class ticket from Dulles to Heathrow.

I needed that trip. I visited Mary in her new offices, we enjoyed a beautiful dinner and a night at the theater, walked through Mayfair and did some shopping, and took a ride on the London Eye to take in the view of all the new skyscrapers going up in the Financial District. It was the perfect escape, but the days went by too quickly. Spending a few days in her presence reignited my enthusiasm for my work and I was eager to return to the NHC, refreshed and able to jump back in without the daily stresses of being at home with Diane.

The high I was riding on came to an abrupt halt when I got home. My brother called. Loren had died. She had been going through an especially rough period and had not worked for several years—her addictions had become debilitating. She had been living alone and did not answer the phone one evening when her mother called. A lifetime of physical and emotional stress had taken its toll and Loren had died of heart failure. Her mother found her on the living room floor.

The funeral was held the day before I returned from London. I went to Cleveland and spent an evening with her parents. The next day I drove to the cemetery to say goodbye. The stone had not been laid and the earth was still bare, but I lay prostrate on my stomach and sent all my love to her. I lay there and cried until I ran out of memories about all our wonderful times together: sludging through the mud at Red Raider and circling the wagons on Indian Day; hundreds of evenings eating, drinking, and dancing to excess; and countless hours talking about our lives and the pain we carried with us from our childhood. We both had masked our challenges with mind-numbing addictions, but I had somehow managed to stay functional. My struggles were far from over—but at the age of forty-seven, hers were. I don't think I had ever been sadder.

57

Breakdown

I had been living with depression my entire life. Sometimes it felt like a steady drain of emotional energy—a yearning to shut down and turn my brain off. That was what the alcohol was for. Other times it went deeper and made me question whether anything I had done in my life had mattered. And sometimes it made me painfully sad. In February of 2005, all three versions came together.

My job at the NHC was going well. It was mostly administrative, and although I interacted daily with my colleagues—along with the staff and leadership of all our members—I managed projects, not teams. In my state of depression, I was unable to appreciate the job and was feeling unfulfilled.

Diane and I went out on the weekends and enjoyed events at the Kennedy Center or dinners in Georgetown, but we were no longer spending nights together. My evenings became the same as in New York: leaving the office, going to the gym, drinking, calling in dinner, smoking pot, stretching, and going to bed. I knew my increased drinking exacerbated my depression, but I continued to search for that elusive *click*. Of course, it never came. I went down a dark tunnel thinking about the people close to me who had died over the years—and I had made and lost just as many friends, including Mark, Dennis, Alexandra, and Sofia. The losses that hurt most were the friendships with Miguel and Heather.

As spring approached, I was in the depths of my depression, and I isolated myself. I wrote Diane a long letter and told her we could no longer see each other. I stopped answering her calls and she left voicemails pleading with me—she only wanted to hear my voice and know I was alright. I wasn't and didn't know how to face her.

One Friday evening, after several strong drinks and listening to an especially emotional voicemail from Diane, I broke down. I buried my head in a pillow and sobbed; they were the sobs one makes when grieving the loss of a loved one. After so many days dwelling on the loss of family members and friendships, I was saturated with unshed tears. The intensity of my crying increased over the hour and culminated with me violently tensing all my muscles—like isometric stretching on steroids—accompanied by a pounding of my hands and feet on the mattress. A wave of hopelessness and despair took over, causing me to clench my buttocks while arching my back and emitting a primal scream into the pillow. As the hysteria abated, I felt a searing pain in my lower back—I had herniated a disc in my sacrum.

The effects of the strong drinks kicked in and I unplugged the phone before passing out in bed. I stayed there until the next afternoon before plugging the phone back in. The instant I did, it rang, and I picked up, knowing it was Diane. Even with our separation, it was clear we still loved each other. Within an hour of hearing about my back injury, Diane was at my door. She stayed with me and took me to the doctor on Monday morning. The herniation was slight, and I was already getting some mobility back. But the pain was intense, and I went home with a supply of oxycodone. The only drugs I had ever taken were recreational, and I discovered I was a lightweight when it came to narcotic painkillers. It did not help that I was washing down my evening dose with vodka.

Diane's rescue mission, along with the numbness from oxycodone, erased my debilitating thoughts about things being hopeless and that only my mother and brother were left to love me. I stayed at Diane's house the following weekend and we rekindled all our passion, albeit delicately. By the time I got home, I had decided: I wanted to spend the rest of my life with her. The thought of being alone was terrifying, and my love for Diane had not died. Many questions remained unsolved—about her divorce, custody of her children, and her own emotional stability—but I believed all relationships had their challenges and that the right one was worth fighting for. I thought I understood our challenges and was willing to take them on. My life needed to change, and being married to Diane felt like the right choice.

Diane and I had taken many weekend drives to the heart of Virginia's fox-hunting country: Middleburg. For decades it had been the fox-hunting grounds for families like the Duponts and Kennedys, and in the center of town was The Red Fox Inn and Tavern. Established in 1728, it had retained its old-world Virginia charm and was home to a fabulous restaurant. We had spent many afternoons driving by the horse estates, walking through the town streets, and shopping at the antique stores and tack shops that catered to the English hunting clientele. Every trip included a meal at the Red Fox Inn; Middleburg was our happy place.

In early April I asked Diane to dinner there, but this time it was for a special occasion she did not know I had planned. Diane was chatty that night, and when she finished her entrée, I excused myself to go to the restroom. Having phoned ahead, I sought out the Tavern manager and asked her to bring me the vase of Kennedy roses I had ordered. Everyone who worked in the restaurant was privy to my plan—Diane was not. With all eyes upon us, I tapped into my hidden romantic, presented the flowers to Diane, and got on my knee. I proposed, she said yes, I put the ring on her finger, and the restaurant erupted in applause. Apparently, the woman seated next to Diane knew of the plan, and when Diane's crying had stopped, she turned to Diane and in a light Southern drawl said, "Honey—I didn't think you were *ever* gunna finish eatin' that damned steak! Congratulations to you both—finally."

We spent the night at Diane's and then rode the Metro into Georgetown on Sunday for brunch by the Potomac. It was the first week in April and the cherry blossoms were in full bloom. We strolled through the Tidal Basin to take in their beauty and finished the afternoon with cocktails at the Hay-Adams Hotel by the White House. It was the perfect end to a magical weekend.

I walked Diane to the Metro station for her ride back to West Falls Church, and while passing by Dupont Circle on my way home I caught the end of an impromptu jazz concert in the center of the roundabout. Despite the levity of the music and the enthusiastic crowd, I started feeling depressed and ended up going home and getting drunk. I did not want to accept my reality. I had committed before to many ideals, jobs, projects, and goals—but I had never made a lifetime commitment to another person, about anything. Deep down, I was terrified, and I couldn't help but wonder if I had made a huge mistake. It took me two years to confirm I had.

58

Finding Marital Bliss

Diane's mother, Evelyn, was the sweetest little woman I had ever met. She lived in a tiny brick home on the outskirts of Clarksville, a lower-income city about an hour northwest of Nashville. Diane and I were there to give Evelyn the news of our engagement.

Evelyn was in her eighties but as spright and lively as a woman twenty years younger. She was a devout Catholic and had raised all twelve of her children in the Catholic faith. She lived modestly in her two-bedroom home. The furniture was inexpensive, and the wall hangings and knickknacks were sparse. Given the stories Diane had shared about Evelyn being an heiress to part of the Ford fortune—and her fond memories of growing up on a farm in Lexington with lavish stables and a house full of servants—the trappings of this modest home didn't make sense. Evelyn lived like someone reliant solely on Social Security benefits and not like a wealthy widow.

Her mother was thrilled at our news, and we left with her blessing. We said we would let her know the date of the wedding as soon as it was set.

Diane had planned a surprise for our drive home. She had already found a wedding gift for me and wanted us to stop and see if I wanted it. Diane had seen an ad in *The Chronicle of the Horse* for a five-year-old American warmblood gelding that was for sale. He lived on a farm in Shelbyville, Kentucky—about halfway between Louisville and Lexington—and was to be my wedding present, provided I fell in love with him on our first meeting. I would have to get to know him from the ground because he had never been ridden. His owner was a retired college professor from Sweden named Stig. He and his wife had purchased a twelve-acre farm in the middle of nowhere so Stig could recover from a recent heart attack and live a stress-free life in the country. With a lifetime love for horses, he bought the large grey gelding, named him Anders, and cared for him like a child. He did not, however, get around to putting a saddle on his back.

There was no question Anders had a sweet personality. He had known nothing but pampering and affection from Stig, but Stig was also a good disciplinarian and Anders's manners were impeccable. We watched him run about the pasture and show us his flashy gaits, and with that, we agreed he would be ours—I knew how to break a young horse to ride. We asked if Anders could stay on the farm while Diane and I figured out where we wanted to live after we married.

After a few minutes, Stig prodded us by asking where we were planning to live. When we said we weren't sure, he proposed: "I moved here after a forty-year teaching career to recover from a blasted heart attack. Well, I have recovered and am bored out of my mind. I have an offer to go to New England and teach again—that's why I must sell Anders." Then he added, "This farm is for sale and might be the perfect home for you two newlyweds. Didn't you say that you were here visiting Diane's mother in Tennessee?"

Diane said she would love to be closer to her mother and asked to see the house. It was a ranch with three bedrooms on the west end and a guest suite on the east. There was a large living room, a family room, a dining room, and a breakfast nook off the kitchen. The three-stall barn was in good repair and attached to a structure that housed his tractor and mowing equipment. Nine of the twelve acres were fenced-in pasture and there was plenty of level ground for riding.

The price was more than fair, and Stig said Anders would be a gift-with-purchase if we went ahead with the sale. On the way home, Diane and I discussed the prospect of moving to Kentucky and decided we were on board. Diane wanted to escape from the drama in Virginia—her divorce had been granted, but her ex had been awarded custody of the children—and I was ready for a change. We could both live our shared dream of having a farm and training our own horses, for our own purposes, with no clients to manage. I could once again have a relationship with a horse like I had with Dancer and begin training it while searching for a coach to help me find my way onto an Olympic team. It would be the perfect plan. Anders would never be a top-level dressage horse, but he could be trained and sold for a profit which could be put toward buying a more athletic horse.

It was 2005 and the housing bubble was on its way to bursting, but Diane's girlfriend was able to swing another sub-prime loan for her. We were on our way to owning a horse farm in the Kentucky Bluegrass—ready to begin our new journey toward matrimonial bliss. However, we would never reach that destination.

59
Head Honcho

The move to Kentucky did not start well. When I arrived at Diane's from D.C. with all my belongings to help with the move, I was shocked by what I saw when I stepped inside. It looked like a bomb had gone off in her house. Diane had pulled things off the shelves and put them on the floor. She had dragged clothes and shoes out of closets and thrown them on the beds. She had emptied all the kitchen cupboards and drawers onto the table and counters. Nothing had been packed. Nothing.

Movers were coming the next day to load their vans and follow us to Shelbyville. We stayed up all night packing, but with countless cigarette breaks and several meltdowns, Diane was of minimal help. The vans arrived mid-morning and we began the frenzied game of "can we pack boxes as quickly as the movers are loading the truck?" Somehow, we succeeded and sent the vans on their way while we spent another two hours loading the pickup. Pepper had been left at the stables until we could drive back to get him—Anders would have to wait a while for his new pasture mate to join him. Diane had turned over her horse business to a new trainer and I had given my notice at the National Health Council.

We were both jobless as we ventured off to our new home in Kentucky, but we were excited by the thrill of the unknown. Everyone who knew us said we were crazy—and perhaps we were—but this move put me straight on the path toward fulfilling my Olympic dream.

After settling in, I spent the mornings putting my landscaping skills to work and the afternoons job-hunting. Since we were located between Louisville and Lexington, I was searching online for positions in both areas and was networking through some people in Washington who had contacts in both cities.

After sending out over a dozen résumés, I came across an online job posting at the United States Equestrian Federation in Lexington. The USEF was the national governing body for equestrian sport and managed the programs offered to the dozens of breed groups and sport disciplines that were members. That included all the Olympic disciplines: Jumping, Eventing, Para-Equestrian, and Dressage. They were hiring a Managing Director of Dressage—and because its Olympic team coach was a native German, the ad said fluency in the language was a plus. With prior experience as a Managing Director, a career as a professional horseman with Grand Prix experience, and fluency in German, I submitted my résumé. I told Diane I had every reason to believe I would at least get an interview—I must have met their search criteria—but after several weeks, I heard nothing. Disappointed, I carried on with my search.

My networking efforts put me in touch with the Vice President for Finance at Churchill Downs in Louisville. Although the racetrack did not have an opening, she offered to spend time getting to know me and to see if she could help me with leads. Toward the end of our meeting, she asked if I knew their previous Executive Vice President, John Long. He had left Churchill Downs to join the USEF as its CEO. I told her about the job I had applied for and said how surprised I was I hadn't heard from them. She promised to give John a call and make sure he knew I had applied.

While I was driving home, my phone rang. It was John's administrative assistant, asking if I could interview the next day. The Executive Director for Sports Programs was in Lexington and John wanted me to meet him.

The USEF was headquartered at the Kentucky Horse Park—an hour's drive from Shelbyville. I arrived at 2 p.m. and was taken directly to John's office, where the Executive Director, Jim Wolf, was seated. The first twenty minutes were a review of my résumé, after which we spent another twenty minutes talking about my dressage experience and how I had become fluent in German. A read of their body language and the eye contact between John and Jim signaled to me the interview was headed in the right direction. Then John dove into the details.

"If we offer you the position, it is important you understand what it entails. You would be responsible for the administration of every national and international dressage program at the USEF. There is a National Dressage Director who manages the Young Horse Program, the North American Junior and Young Rider Program, and the National Dressage Championships. The High-Performance Dressage Director manages all the international programs. They include the annual World Cup Finals and the quadrennial programs: the Pan American Games, the World Equestrian Games, and the Olympic Games. Both directors would report to you, and you would report to Jim. This would be a big job."

I laughed and said, "No kidding."

Then Jim weighed in. "This won't be like any job you've had before. You will eat, drink, breathe, and sleep 'dressage.' This job is 24/7. We will give you a Blackberry and from the time we hand it to you, you will never turn it off. You will travel extensively throughout the States and overseas. One championship or high-performance training event leads smack into the next and you will rarely have time to catch your breath."

"It definitely sounds like a lot," I said, "and thanks for being upfront about what's involved—but I believe I have both the management experience and the passion for dressage the job requires, and I would love to have it."

"If we offered you the position, when could you start?" Jim said.

"How soon could you get me the Blackberry?"

"Well, that is the easy part," John said.

I left feeling confident and while driving back to Shelbyville I got a call from Jim.

"I am calling to offer you the position," Jim said. "But be warned, the salary will not even be close to what you're used to earning. You'd be taking the job because of your love for the sport and the doors that would open up to you as the country's head honcho for dressage."

The salary was half of what I had been earning in Washington. I accepted the job and spent the rest of the drive home wondering how I was going to break the news to Diane—she was going to have to step up her game and get a job too. Otherwise, we'd be eating a lot of Ramen noodles.

Solving that problem seemed insignificant as I pinched myself in disbelief—after all those years, it was going to happen. I was headed to the Olympics—not as a rider, as I had imagined so many years ago—but as the Olympic team leader and the executive in charge of all our country's national and international dressage programs. Every choice I had made in my adult life—after each high, and each low—had culminated in this opportunity. *So that's how fate works*, I thought. And then I realized: It had not been fate, or chance, or luck. It had been by design. I had set a goal decades ago and had committed to fulfilling it—no matter what. My passion had determined my choices, and although the path after each decision had never been clear, the destination had been. *And that's the essence of how living life masterfully works*, I determined. And I have held on to that belief ever since.

60
Meet Dick Brown

The village of Wellington is one of the largest playgrounds in the world for the rich, and the super-rich. It is where the "1 percent"—and the ".01 percent"—go during the winter to enjoy equestrian sport. It is affectionately known within the horse-set as "Welly World" and there is nothing else like it anywhere.

The village is about thirty square miles and is a twenty-minute drive from Palm Beach. In 2006 it was home to the Palm Beach International Polo Club (where King Charles III and other royals have played), a gated community with its own airfield called the Aero Club, and at its heart, the Palm Beach International Equestrian Center: 160 acres that was host every year to the Winter Equestrian Festival. It was one of the largest and longest-running equestrian competitions in the world and from January through April, it attracted Olympians, professional trainers, and amateur riders from more than forty countries. There was a horse show every week for jumping and dressage, where dozens of barns, hundreds of stalls, and eighteen international-caliber arenas were used to ensure that the top riders in the world attended. Many of the horse shows were qualifying events for athletes earning their way onto teams that would compete at international championships. Diane and I were there in March of 2006 for one of those qualifying events.

I was five months into my job with the USEF and my boss, Jim, wanted me to attend the show so he could educate me on how the qualifying process worked and see firsthand how the needs of our country's elite riders were provided for. Jim suggested I bring Diane along so she could enjoy the experience and take part in the many social events that surround the horse show. The equestrian community is very social, with *lots* of social events.

People are in Wellington to enjoy the luxuries their riches provide, and a big part of my job was to ensure they did. The price tag for a champion horse began at one million dollars and the sky was the limit from there. The horse owners have multi-million-dollar homes in the Wellington and Palm Beach areas and are accustomed to having the finest of everything. From the time their private jets land at Palm Beach International Airport, the riders and horse owners are there to win prizes, and they take winning as seriously as they do earning and spending their wealth. There was a lot for me to learn, and Jim was the best possible teacher.

On Friday evening there was a fundraising gala held in the hospitality pavilion in front of the International Stadium. Although the jumping competition was the main event in the stadium, the real action was going on in the pavilion. A table for eight cost around $20,000 for the entire season. It came with lavish buffets from breakfast through dinner and an open bar. The placement of one's table was as important as who sat there—and some very important people did. The adult children of Bill Gates, Bruce Springsteen, Steve Jobs, Michael Bloomberg, Lou Dobbs, and other well-known celebrities were there. Lesser-known financial barons, tech entrepreneurs, and media giants had tables. So did the families of many horse owners, riders, and those who donated to the sport— founders of companies with familiar names like Johnson & Johnson, Campbell, Mars, Singer, Proctor and Gamble, General Motors, Wrigley, and Cargill. Their tables were all at the front, and right beside them was a table for equestrian sport's governing body: the USEF. That's where Diane and I sat.

At one point I looked across the room and saw a table with some familiar faces. Heather and a group of friends from Ohio—some of whom I knew from Red Raider—were attending the event. Diane and I were being introduced to a lot of people and we stayed engaged in conversation throughout the evening, so I never had the occasion to speak with Heather. But the next morning Diane and I were walking through the vendor village and about a hundred feet down the path I saw Heather walking toward us. We were the only ones there and as our distance closed, I asked myself: *Well, is this when we finally break the silence and at least exchange some pleasantries?* Heather avoided eye contact until she was ten feet in front of us. At that point, she lifted her head, broke a weak smile, lowered her eyes, and walked past.

Although our paths crossed a few more times at horse shows, we would only engage in brief casual conversations and move on. Neither of us extended a hand to rekindle the friendship.

* * *

The next event I attended was at the Los Angeles Equestrian Center in Burbank.

It was a qualifying event for the World Cup Finals and Jim wanted me to try a solo run. As I was walking across the upper deck of the competition arena, I spotted a tall and lanky man in his mid-seventies coming toward me with a stiff, military-like stride. He stopped in front of me and said, "Hey. You must be the new USEF guy."

"Yes. My name is Gil Merrick, and I am the Managing Director for Dressage at the USEF."

I noticed a few quirks in this man: a slight twitch in his left eye, a high-pitched voice—almost like a cartoon character—and his habit of wearing the waist of his pants slightly below his armpits. He was impeccably dressed in a plaid dress shirt and conservative tan pants that all appeared to be custom made. His suede Gucci loafers looked like they were on their first outing. He looked at my feet and said, "Wow! Would you look at those shoes? Yours, not mine. Very nice. Nice polish job. I think I'm going to like you." I had just met Dick Brown.

I told Dick how nice it was to meet him and congratulated him on their bronze medal win with Aragon at the 2004 Olympics in Athens. I was only at the show for two days and did not have the chance to meet Dick's wife, Jane, but everyone assured me that once I did, I would never forget her. Everyone was right.

61
Ramen Noodles

When I wasn't traveling for the USEF, I was settling into my life as a Kentucky farmer. I didn't grow any crops, but caring for a twelve-acre property with two horses was a far cry from an urban lifestyle. I got up early every day to feed the horses, clean their stalls, and turn them out in the pasture before leaving for the Kentucky Horse Park. Anders and Pepper had bonded and were fast friends; they were living the life of leisure. My job had precluded breaking Anders to ride, and we had not built our riding ring yet, so without any nearby trails, Diane was not riding Pepper. In fact, I was not sure what Diane *was* doing all day. One thing was for sure, she was not actively looking for a job.

I knew she snapped on the television mid-morning and spent many hours on the couch—smoking, talking on the phone with girlfriends, and watching her favorite shows. Diane did not do the grocery shopping, run errands, or cook on her own. All those activities were done with me. Every evening began with cocktail hour—rum and Cokes for Diane, vodka martinis for me—and the drinking continued until we went to bed. On weekends we smoked what she called "Happy-Time," and any night of the week was good for lovemaking.

Overall, we were doing "OK" as a couple, but something was off: a piece of Diane I couldn't figure out. In Virginia, she had been energetic, focused on her teaching business, and enthusiastic about sharing a new life. The excitement was slipping away and each day she became more complacent. I was paying the mortgage and most of the bills; she was paying for enhancements to the house, stables, and landscaping. But she showed no interest in getting a job and we needed a second income. I had drained my 401K from the National Health Council when we moved, and that had carried us along until I started my job, but my small salary was not going to be enough to keep us going without incurring some debt along the way. Her lack of concern about our financial situation worried me, but I had learned to never bring it up.

On the infrequent occasion I asked why something had not been done or asked how things were going with the job search, she exploded. Her crying was accompanied by disconnected, random comments that had nothing to do with my question. Each meltdown ended with the same declaration: "Oh dear Mary—mother of Jesus—I know I am not worthy of your love. I know I am failing you and your blessed son. Help, Mother Mary—help me find my way. I am lost and unworthy!" The cries of anguish sounded as if I had attacked her. After the hysteria, she would withdraw into silence and then change the topic. She seemed to have two personalities and could be thrown from one to the other with so much as a hint that she was insufficient in any way. But true to my survival mechanism, I would step over the incident, tell her I loved her, and then figure out how long until cocktail hour.

* * *

In the late spring of 2006, Doug phoned to say that our mother needed to be moved from her independent living facility into one that offered assisted care. She had been instructed to use her walker at home but had found it to be a nuisance and opted not to. That resulted in numerous falls with fractured or broken bones, and the facility said their repeated calls for an ambulance indicated my mother could no longer live independently.

Doug and I spent a long weekend looking at several assisted living facilities, but fortunately, my mother knew of one nearby where a friend of hers was living. She said if she had to move, that is where she wanted to go. She surrendered the few financial assets she had and signed over her Social Security benefits. Since Doug was working as a landscaper and living paycheck to paycheck, and my sister was accumulating unplanned medical expenses due to an as-yet undiagnosed condition, I took on financial responsibility for any uncovered expenses.

Diane was going to have to step it up and bring in a second income. Things had changed and many more changes lay ahead.

62
Meet Jane Brown

I met Jane Brown at the Dressage Festival of Champions—the event where the short-list of athletes would be named for the 2006 World Equestrian Games team. Guenter was riding the Browns' horse, Aragon, and given his bronze medal win two years earlier at the Athens Olympics, unless Aragon became ill or was lame, they were a shoo-in for the team.

As Diane and I walked into the foyer of the stables at Hamilton Farms in Gladstone, New Jersey, there was a flurry of activity in the center of the room and Jim motioned me over to the small group that had gathered to welcome the royal couple of dressage. Jim said, "Dick, Jane—I want to introduce you to our new Managing Director for Dressage, Gil Merrick." Dick stared at me as if we had never met. Jane was saying hello to her many friends and gave me a passing glance.

Before I could welcome them, Jane turned to no one in particular, lifted her chin, and said, "Well, I *must* head over to the mansion to take care of unpacking my wardrobe." The mansion had previously been the residence of the estate's owners, and the Browns were staying there. Jane intentionally spoke with the exalted air of aristocracy—it was her way of being funny. I would soon learn that the "air" was only slightly exaggerated. She spoke in a manner Hollywood would call "Mid-Atlantic": not quite British, not quite New Yorker. It is a dialect where the "R's" at the end of words are dropped and "mother" becomes "muth-ah," "theater" becomes "the-a-tah," and "dinner" is always "sup-pah." She laced that affect with her native New Yorker accent and a lot of animated hand gestures.

Her hairdo was part of her curated look—one she had sported for fifty years. It was a thick wave of chestnut brown with a distinct blonde streak, dramatically swept up from her forehead and feathered back along the sides. Her makeup was as important to her look as her coiffure. Her foundation was a beige cream about three shades darker than her skin: a fact confirmed by the sharp line under her chin where it stopped. Fake eyelashes, smokey-grey eye shadow, and purply-red lipstick finished the look. Her signature feature was her jewelry, and she made sure everyone noticed it. On her left hand was a thirteen-carat, internally perfect, yellow diamond in a simple platinum setting. On the right was a ten-millimeter sapphire encircled in small diamonds. Her earrings were large pearls surrounded by diamonds, and around her neck was a one-inch gold link collar no one had ever seen removed.

Jane had a loud voice and made sure it was heard. She demanded to be the center of attention and would monopolize any conversation. She was animated, funny, and bold. Jane was also demanding—*very* demanding. She was a woman who had spent her entire life getting what she wanted, when she wanted it. If she set her sights on something, she was like a dog with a bone until she got it and— as I would find out—she *always* got it.

Dick and Jane had been born with silver spoons in their mouths and grew up living privileged lives just four blocks away from each other on Park Avenue. When Jane was ten years old, she saw Dick walking around their New York neighborhood, having dinner with his parents at the Harmonie Club in Manhattan, and playing golf at the Fairview Country Club in Greenwich. That is when she said to her mother: "One day, I am going to marry Dick Brown." Ten years later, in 1954, when Dick was released from the Army, Jane got what she wanted.

After twenty-five years in the costume jewelry business, the Browns sold their company and invested in the stock market. In 1985 the Dow was at 800 and they invested in blue chip stocks. They had also made friends with a man named Roy Kroc when they visited California and bought some shares in a new company of his called McDonald's. Since Dick was invested in hamburgers, he thought it would make sense to also invest in chips, so he bought some shares in a chip manufacturer called Intel. Over the next thirty years, the Dow would grow to over 10,000 and the Browns became very wealthy.

The Browns had often spent weekends at the La Costa Resort in Carlsbad, just north of San Diego, playing golf and socializing. La Costa was owned and run by the mob and everything there was the best of the best. Dick and Jane fell in love with the lifestyle but hated the commute from Los Angeles, so they purchased a one-acre dirt lot on a street overlooking the golf course and built the home they would live in for the rest of their lives.

Dick had ridden jumpers as a young man with an Olympic icon from New Jersey, William Steinkraus, and in his retirement, Dick wanted to ride horses again. Although there was a small stable near La Costa where he rode occasionally, friends had told him he should investigate keeping a horse nearby at the Rancho Riding Club in the upscale enclave of Rancho Santa Fe. He did, and that is where Dick and Jane Brown met Guenter Seidel. It was the beginning of a twenty-year journey toward equestrian celebrity for Guenter and the Browns.

63
World Championships

The 2006 World Equestrian Games were being held in Aachen, Germany at the show venue I had visited as a college student. Our High-Performance Director was to serve as team leader at the event, but after years of battling lupus, she left her position at the USEF to take care of her well-being. That left me to serve as team leader.

In August, our riders would travel to Rosendahl, Germany—near the east border of the Netherlands—for two weeks of intensive training at the private stables of our national dressage coach, Klaus Balkenhol.

Klaus was one of Germany's dressage heroes. His career had started as a mounted policeman in Düsseldorf. Since the police department had a limited budget, his horse, Goldstern, was considered to be an "average" horse. But Klaus made lie to the notion of "average." He had trained Goldstern to the Grand Prix level and enjoyed an illustrious career. Among his most notable successes with Goldstern were individual bronze and team gold medals at the 1992 Olympics in Barcelona, and another team gold medal at the 1996 Olympics in Atlanta. So much for Goldstern being "average."

I landed in Amsterdam on a Monday morning and went by train to Enschede, where one of our riders picked me up for the short drive to Klaus's farm. I knew all the riders stabled there, but I had never met Klaus. A barrel-chested man with chiseled features, a full head of greying hair, and a broad smile, Klaus was soft-spoken and kind. At sixty-seven he had mastered the art of dressage and was sought after throughout Europe as a trainer for elite riders. He had been the U.S. dressage coach since 2000 when he coached our team to a bronze medal at the Sydney Olympics. It was an honor to meet him, and hard to believe we would be glued to each other's hips for at least two years—until his contract ended—traveling throughout Europe, South America, and Asia in a quest for medals for the U.S. dressage team.

Klaus and I hit it off well and he especially liked that my fluency in German allowed me to serve as a translator for the riders who did not speak much German. It was clear from the start I was going to make his life as the U.S. coach a lot easier.

Guenter and Aragon had been named to the team, along with Debbie McDonald and her chestnut mare, Brentina. Debbie and Brentina were fan favorites throughout the world, but especially in the U.S. Brentina was big, bold, and beautiful, and Debbie always rode her spectacularly. They had won the individual and team gold medals at the 1999 Pan American Games, a team silver medal at the 2002 World Championships, and a team bronze at the 2004 Olympics. In 2003 they were the first American combination to ever win the World Cup Finals.

The third rider was Steffen Peters on the chestnut gelding Floriano. They had finished in third place at the World Cup Finals in Las Vegas earlier that year and then won the National Dressage Championships in Gladstone.

Our fourth team member was Leslie Morse with her Swedish Warmblood stallion, Tip Top. Leslie purchased Tip Top in Europe from Kyra Kyrklund—the trainer Diane and I had traveled to the Kentucky Horse Park to see. Leslie had trained her stallion to Grand Prix and they were at the top of their game, having recently returned from the World Cup Finals in Amsterdam.

On August 16th we finished our training at Klaus's farm and traveled to Aachen to join the U.S. delegation. As a colleague and I were walking across the showgrounds, I stopped for a moment to share a thought: "You know, it's funny how things work out in life. Thirty years ago, I was walking on these grounds, hoping for the chance to see some of the world's top dressage riders. Today, I have access to every venue at these world championships, and I'm a big part of making the event happen. Back then, I was flat broke. I couldn't afford a ticket to sit in the bleachers. I even planned to spend the night under a tree. It's amazing how things change."

"Did you ever think you'd be back in Aachen?"

"To tell you the truth, my dream had been to ride in a World Championship one day, and from there, to make it to the Olympics. I never knew if competing in Aachen would have been part of that journey."

"Well, here you are—team leader for the United States Dressage Team. And in two years you will be in China, for the Olympics. Looks like you made it after all. Now, let's see what we can do to help our athletes win a medal!"

The Grand Prix competition for the team medals ran over two days. We had two riders scheduled on each day with the starting time for their tests set to the minute. Each rider knew how much time they wanted to warm up before moving from the training arena to the ten-minute holding ring while the previous athlete was in the stadium performing their test. Last-minute adjustments were made to the tack, the horse and rider received a final polish from the groom, and the coaches gave their last words of advice. From that point on, the rider was on their own.

The main stadium could hold 50,000 spectators, and on most days, it was full. The horse and rider have the competition arena in the center of the stadium to themselves as the crowd watches in silence. But once the test is complete, spectators explode with applause, stomp their feet, wave flags and banners, and throw bouquets of flowers into the arena. And that is the cue for the next rider to enter the arena and claim the stage for the next ten minutes.

While Steffen and Floriano were in the holding area, there was silence everywhere. The rider in the stadium was favored to win, and the crowd was hushed as they performed. Klaus had given Steffen his last words of encouragement, his groom had finished the polishing, and Steffen, now alone, directed a laser focus to the job at hand.

The ring steward started the countdown: "Five minutes, Steffen." "Two minutes, Steffen"—at which point Steffen walked Floriano to the end of the arena. And then ... up went the roar of the crowd. The previous rider had turned in a spectacular ride and the spectators went wild. Klaus and I jogged behind Steffen as he and Floriano made their way down the chute that led to the stadium. They trotted off as they entered the arena, with Steffen having to shut out the cheers of the crowd as he made his first lap around the perimeter of the ring. The judge gave the signal for them to enter the competition arena, and the crowd went silent. Steffen halted in front of the judges, removed his top hat in salute, and gathered his reins.

Every dressage test—from the most elementary level to the international Grand Prix—begins the same way: enter, halt, salute. As the rider collects the reins and prepares to execute the dozens of exercises that make up one test, the outcome of the next seven minutes is unknown. Everything could go wrong: the horse could become distracted and miss a cue; the rider could make a navigation error and perform the wrong exercise; or the horse or rider could be fatigued and simply not be "on their game." In the face of the day's unknown circumstances, the test could go off the rails and the rider would have what is commonly referred to as "a train wreck"—years of training and preparation falling apart in what feels like an instant. Or, the sun, the moon, and the stars could all align, and the rider can receive the highest score of their career on that horse and achieve "their personal best"—the goal of every competition rider, at every level.

On that day, Steffen rode one of the best tests of his life and the crowd roared with approval. His score would be the fifth highest for the event and, combined with the other team members' scores, the U.S.A. won the bronze medal.

Other events in my life had raised goosebumps, but they were nothing like the ones I experienced watching our team step onto the podium to receive their medals. The president of the International Equestrian Federation—HRH Princess Haya Bint Al Hussein of Jordan—presented the medals and bouquets to the winning teams as part of a ceremony an athlete works their entire life to experience. I was honored to be there to share it with them.

Managing our team at The World Equestrian Games had not been without its challenges and there had been a good deal of drama, but that was all part of the job. The tour had been a success, but compared to what lay ahead at the 2007 Pan American Games and the 2008 Olympics—Aachen had been a walk in the park.

64

Duped and Betrayed

I was only fourteen when I embraced the dream of one day going to the Olympics. Thirty-five years later, in 2007, while pulling into the driveway of The Olympic Plaza in Colorado Springs, the next phase of fulfilling that dream unfolded.

The Olympic Plaza was home to the U.S. Olympic Committee and served as its official training center. Jim and our group of team leaders were there for a series of meetings with the USOC, along with the leaders of all the other sports that would be contested at the Pan American Games in Rio de Janeiro, Brazil. It was February, and there were five months left to prepare for the Games. The USOC spent the next three days giving us an overview of Brazil's history, customs, and politics; reviewing the logistics for each team; and briefing everyone on measures the U.S. Department of State would take to provide security.

Until 1985, Brazil had been ruled by a military dictatorship, and although the country's first nationally elected president, Lula da Silva, had been sworn in on January 1, 2003, the country was facing major economic challenges. More than one out of four Brazilians lived on less than one dollar a day, and although incomes had been slowly rising since 2003, and Lula had been reelected in October 2006, his government was accused of corruption on a massive scale and was increasingly unpopular. With social unrest barely held at bay, and with drug cartels and militias running the crime-ridden *favelas* (slums), Rio de Janeiro was not safe. The Department of State would assign each team a driver and van that would serve as their security detail.

The USOC ran like a well-oiled machine. The logistics of bringing the U.S. delegation to compete every four years at the Winter or Summer Olympics, or every four years at the Pan American Games, are complicated and must be executed with military precision. The USOC was in the business of managing those logistics for dozens of teams and hundreds of athletes, every year. It was a machine that never turned off, and I was thrilled to be part of it.

* * *

After I returned from Colorado, I had a month at home and used that time to see if I could make any progress with Diane. She still had not looked for work, and with bills for my mother's assisted living coming in, a second income was essential. I also wanted to know if Diane was serious about setting a date for our wedding.

At the risk of provoking one of her meltdowns, I said, "We've been here for two years, and we still don't have a wedding date set. I don't understand why?"

"Baby, there's one obstacle we need to overcome in order for us to marry and I've been afraid to bring it up."

After reminding me she was a devout Catholic, she said, "Because I am divorced, I can't marry in a Catholic church if you are not a Catholic. We would need to meet with my pastor and see if he would marry us in his church, most likely on the condition you converted to Catholicism."

"Well, let me get this upcoming trip to Rio under my belt, and then we can think about it and put a plan in place."

Diane agreed and added that she would like us to take a trip to Clarksville to visit her mother, Evelyn. One of Diane's sisters was there, and she had not seen her in ages. We were having beautiful spring weather, so while Diane was inside catching up with her sister, I sat on the back porch with her mother and brother-in-law, Eric, sipping iced tea and getting to know them.

Eric was interested in learning more about his wife's childhood and began asking Evelyn some questions about it. Thinking Evelyn was going to share details about raising a large family in a mansion on a thoroughbred horse farm in Lexington, I was surprised when she began talking about their cramped and modest home in Clarksville. Evelyn told some amusing stories about her days looking after the family-owned business in Clarksville—a bowling alley. She shared memories of hand-me-downs being passed from boys to girls, and how cute they all looked when dressed for church. She even added, "Money was always tight, but their daddy was a good man and always made sure we had enough. We certainly weren't wealthy, but we were usually pretty happy."

On our drive back home, I addressed the discrepancies in Diane's stories. "Honey, you said you were raised on a horse farm in Lexington, but your mother said you were all raised in Clarksville, and that your father owned a bowling alley, not a paper mill."

After a pause, Diane reacted as if I had thrown acid in her face. "I can't believe Eric made my mother go through that! She has never gotten over the loss of my daddy and she can't bear to talk about him or their past. My poor, dear mother—it is so painful for her. She tries to be brave and hide her pain, but when someone like Eric comes along and opens the wounds, it tears her apart. She always loved to bowl, and because my daddy was such a kind man, he bought her a bowling alley."

None of that made sense given the pure joy Evelyn had shown while sharing her stories about what seemed like a modest, but happy, past ... in Clarksville. And then came the hysterics: "Oh dear Mary, mother of our sweet Lord Jesus, why must our lives be so tortured? What have I done to deserve this? I know I am not worthy of your love, but why must I be punished so? I know I am a sinner and need redemption. Please help me, Mother Mary." The outburst was followed by a few minutes of sobbing, then silence.

Then she asked if I wanted to stop for lunch.

Everything Diane had told me about her past had been lies: all of it. I was in shock. *How could she have made up so many details, and repeated them dozens and dozens of times over the past four years as if it were all true? And if those were all lies, what else was she lying about?* There was something wrong with Diane and I had ignored it for four years. Her instantaneous jumps from one set of emotions to another were unexplainable. And what was the reason for her paranoia? I was the last person who would harm her, but she reacted as if I were her enemy.

She was a pathological liar and I had fallen for everything. I had trusted her, and she betrayed me. I showed up in her life when she was trying to escape her marriage and she latched on to me. All the pieces were falling into place: I had been duped and I felt like an idiot. I was also furious—at her for lying, and at myself for being so naïve.

I spent the next two weeks drinking a copious amount in the evenings and smoking pot on the weekends. Any thoughts that my depression was somehow lessening in the face of all my international dressage adventures, were fading away. I had a new reality to deal with and knew I needed to change things. I would have to end the relationship and move out: as soon as I got back from Rio.

65
Brazil

It was time to head for Rio. The athletes and the horses were flying out of Miami International Airport. The cargo plane that would carry the horses was scheduled to depart at 11 p.m. for the nine-hour flight to Brazil. To minimize the time the horses would have to stand in the hot, crowded van, they arrived at 9:30 p.m. so they could be loaded onto the plane straightaway.

A concerned shipping manager met the van. He told Tim Dutta—the man who managed all the logistics of flying the USEF's horses to international events—that the plane had an engine problem and repairs would take at least an hour. After that, the plane would need to take off and land to ensure everything was operational. The delay would be at least two hours.

We waited on the steaming tarmac, listening to the drone of idling jet engines across from the loading area, and crossed our fingers. After an hour the agent told us the repairs were complete and we watched as the plane took off for its test flight. It returned twenty minutes later. The repairs were not complete, and a new part would need to be ordered. They could get the part overnight, but the horses could not leave until the next day.

The horses and their grooms were driven back to the stables and the team checked into a local Hampton Inn. We would only get a few hours' sleep before our 7 a.m. flight to Sao Paulo. When we arrived in Rio, Jim and our security detail took us to the administration offices to get our credentials. There we learned the horses would arrive the next morning at six.

The flight arrived on time, and we were all at the cargo terminal to meet them. Dr. Rick Mitchell—our team veterinarian—came over to the chain link fence separating us from the tarmac and told us all the horses had traveled well and were in good shape. That was the last piece of good news we would have that day.

When horses fly, they typically stand in a container with three stalls; that is economy class. Horses in first-class stand two stalls to a container, so it's roomier—our horses flew first class. The containers are moved planeside with a small truck equipped with a scissor lift. They are lifted from the tarmac up to the plane's loading door and slid onto a system of in-floor rollers that guide the container to its spot in the cargo hold. Once the container is in place, the horses receive a net full of hay and a big bucket of water—their version of cabin service.

After parking on the tarmac in Rio, the scissor lifts removed the containers from the plane and moved them into the quarantine stables. The horses were given a physical exam, checked for any signs of distress, and hooked up to an IV to administer a saline solution that prevents dehydration. After an hour, the horses would be loaded on a van and taken to the competition stables.

An hour came and went—and then, another. Because it was a quarantine facility, we had no access to the barn. Understandably, all the riders were anxious and wanted information about the delay. Tim and Rick alternately came to the fence to give us updates, and Tim finally said, "We have no idea what is taking these clowns so long. They have assigned one of their people to unload all the veterinary trunks and lay everything out for inspection. We have a complete inventory list, but they want to inspect everything themselves."

Tim returned thirty minutes later. "The horses will be on the van shortly. It was all a ruse. What they wanted was a bribe. I've been to this rodeo before, so I greased his palm and Rick is reloading the trunks. Welcome to Brazil."

* * *

Our State Department van and driver followed the horse van to our competition venue, the Deodora Military Club. The drive immersed us in Rio's poverty.

Within two minutes of turning out of the driveway, we were crawling through the slums of the city. The houses and shops were dilapidated, and most had only corrugated tin for roofs. There was a stench of rotting garbage hanging in the air, laced with the occasional waft of raw sewage that collected in the bays and harbor. The roads were overrun with carts pulled by skeletal donkeys and horses—some being driven gladiator-style, zigging and zagging across the roads while jumping curbs and meridians to avoid traffic. A look to the hillside revealed the masses of shanties that formed the *favelas*: slums established by people who had moved from rural areas to the city in search of work, and who were allowed to squat on any piece of land they could find.

When our van approached the front gate, armed soldiers surrounded it to confirm we were who we said, and that we were not carrying weapons or contraband. After a fifteen-minute delay, we were told to drive to a different gate, where we went through the same interrogation. We were finally let in and shown where to park, anxiously waiting for the grooms to unload the horses. Tim, Rick, and Jim had another conversation with someone in charge who wanted a bribe to open the van, and this time, they refused to pay. We were at a USOC competition venue and under the jurisdiction of the International Equestrian Federation—it was time for the bribes to stop. An argument ensued and the tension escalated when a rider called out, "Fire! The van is on fire!"

Black smoke bellowed out of an electrical box behind the cab while the horses were still inside. Because the horses had come from a quarantine facility, the back door was sealed and could only be broken by a Brazilian official, who was not there. Our group ran to the back of the van and was stopped by two guards—their rifles pointed directly at us—who demanded we stop our attempts to break the seal. Jim yelled, "Seriously? You are going to shoot us? Well, have at it—those horses are coming out, *now*!" Before he could finish his sentence, the others had broken the seal and were removing the horses from the burning van.

Two tons of equipment were in a separate van still at the Rio cargo terminal. We desperately needed the water filtration system, buckets, hay, grain, and all the other essential equipment to ensure the horses' well-being. There was no sign of that van. Tim phoned the cargo terminal and was told since it was the weekend, the person responsible for releasing the equipment was off duty and would not be back until Monday. That was the final straw.

Jim whipped his Blackberry out of its holster and phoned the one person he knew could help us: HRH Princess Haya Bint Hussein. Not only was she the president of the International Equestrian Federation, but she was also the daughter of the late King Hussein of Jordan, and the second wife of Sheikh Mohammed, Crown Prince of Dubai. Due to its tremendous oil wealth, Dubai did a lot of international trade with Brazil. So, Princess Haya spoke to Sheikh Mohammed, the sheikh phoned Brazil's president, Lula de Silva, and forty-five minutes later the van with our equipment arrived.

* * *

The Pan American Games ended on July 29th. As anticipated, our athletes won the team gold medal as well as the individual gold and silver. Everyone returned to the States safe and sound, and I breathed a sigh of relief knowing I had come through what had been my training event for the upcoming Olympics. I was sure I was ready for Hong Kong.

66

The Great Escape

I came home to disaster. Diane was in the kitchen when I walked in and the sight of her, and the room, stopped me in my tracks. The additional grey in her hair told me she had stopped touching up her roots—something she had done since the day we met. She had parted it in the middle, swept the front pieces to the sides, and affixed each with a bobby pin—the kind you can get a hundred for with nineteen cents at the Dollar Store. She had no makeup, which was unusual— she almost always wore some mascara and a hint of eye shadow. Her grey, waffle-weave Henley T-shirt had holes under the armpits and around the neck, and her jeans had tears in the knees—not the intentional ones that became fashionable a decade later, but the ones that come from wearing clothes beyond their "use-by" date. Diane had stopped caring for herself.

However, her unkempt look was outdone by that of the kitchen.

The trash can was overflowing with empty food containers, unwashed dishes languished in the sink, old newspapers and junk mail splashed across the counters, the linoleum tiles were sticky under my shoes, and the overhead light fixture was home to numerous spider webs.

Diane greeted me with a warm hug and said, "Hey, baby. Welcome home. I've already had something to eat, but I'll bet you'd enjoy a cocktail after your long trip. Bar's open!"

Unsure of what else I would discover, I said, "Sure. Let me take my suitcases to our room and then I'll fix us a drink."

The rest of the house was worse. There was clutter everywhere: on, in front of, and under the furniture. There were used ashtrays scattered throughout the rooms, and they stank. The plants were dying. All the toilet bowls had green rings along the water lines, there was hair stuck in the shower drains, and the wastebaskets were overflowing. The site of our impeccable home in a state of squalor shocked me and I didn't know what to say other than, "I'm gunna run out to the barn and see the horses—I missed them—then I'll fix us that drink."

"OK, baby. Hurry back and we can relax on the front porch while you tell me all about your trip. I'll bet you'd also enjoy some Happy Time—I'm sure they didn't have *that* in Brazil."

The final horrors were waiting for me when I walked out to the barn. On the morning I left for the Pan Am tour, Diane had turned the horses out in the pasture and never brought them back in. She had thrown them some flakes of hay when she remembered, but their watering trough was half empty and lined with algae. Cobwebs and dust were on every surface of a barn I normally cleaned to the standard of an operating room.

And then there were the snakes. In front of the barn and inside the stalls. When one fell from the rafters and landed on my shoulder, I knew the grounds were infested. With the barn vacant and filled with old manure, it was the perfect feeding ground for snakes with its ample supply of small rodents and spiders. It was like living through a nightmare.

Diane had spent the six weeks sitting on the couch, smoking pot and Virginia Slims, talking to her girlfriends, and watching TV. The empty rum bottles and Coke cans confirmed she had continued our habit of evening cocktails. She was unwilling to acknowledge anything was amiss and acted like none of it bothered her. I was in no mood for a confrontation and had no idea how to address the situation.

I handled it all in my usual manner: I went to the office each day and stewed about the intolerable situation at home, drove back each night to get lost in a fog of vodka and pot, and shoved the problem under the rug until I figured out a plan of escape.

Diane's daughters had come to Kentucky the first two summers, but this was the third summer and they refused to come. I could understand why teenagers would hate being in rural Kentucky, but Diane was certain her ex had conspired to keep them away, so she decided she would drive to Virginia and spend time with them there, whether he approved or not. That would leave me at home to clean up her messes. As soon as Diane was out of the driveway, I sprang into action.

A few days before Diane was due home, I rented a small truck and began loading it up to move my things into storage. As I was finishing, Diane called. The nosey next-door neighbor had seen me loading the truck and called her.

"Teresa said you are packing up a *huge* truck and stealing everything out of the house!" Diane said. "I bought *all* that furniture and those are *my* things. I'm calling the police and telling them I am being robbed. How dare you do this to me when I'm away and then run out on me?!"

"Calm down," I said. "I have a seven-foot U-Haul and am moving my office furniture and some boxes into storage because, yes, I am going to be leaving you—but not until you get back. I have found a place to live but will continue to pay your mortgage until you decide if you are going to sell the farm or stay. If you sell it, you won't lose the equity you have in it. If you stay, I'll stop paying the mortgage after six months. At that point, you are going to have to get a job. I will be here when you get back—I would never abandon the horses."

Diane returned and tore through the house in a fury, determined to identify all the items I had stolen in her absence. There were none. As with all good knock-down, drag-out fights, ours devolved into a screaming match—rife with accusations about all the misdeeds we had wrought upon each other during our four years together. But then it got ugly.

"I was in the attic when you were away," Diane said, "and I was looking for something in a box and came across a journal you kept." That journal was wedged between years of tax returns, bank statements, health records, and every other personal item I had saved. Diane had gone through all my things—piece by piece—aggressively invading my privacy.

"And when I read your journal, I found out you are gay! My girlfriends had been telling me all along you were. They said a good-looking man who was so kind, caring, and impeccably put together, could not be straight. Now I know they were right!" And then she threw a punch to my gut. "I always wondered why you didn't want me to give you blow jobs. I guess you only wanted those from men."

The journal had no entries about the Pataki brothers' rape—a violent attack, whose memories continued to haunt me. Diane had read the entries in my journal from 1979 after I had broken away from Joe. She read about my nights at the gay discos and partying with Dennis and then coming out as gay to Heather, my friends, and my family.

She went on: "Well, I read all about the man you had been in love with for so many years—Joe. And after you broke up with him, you moved right on to the next boyfriend—Dennis. So don't tell me you aren't gay!"

"Of course, you are right," I retorted. "And that explains why we made passionate love hundreds of times over the past four years." Not to be outdone, I landed my own low blow, "I guess we both mastered the art of faking orgasms.

Can we get Academy Awards for that?"

With only my clothes to pack, I left the house before I let out more of my rage. Diane had set off more triggers in fifteen minutes than a year of intense psychotherapy could have evoked. She phoned me two times on my drive into Lexington, where I had already sublet a furnished apartment. After a few minutes of the second call, I hung up. I had never verbally abused anyone—ever—and I was hating myself for who I had become that night. I had lost control and let my emotions take over. I was devastated.

I stopped at the liquor store and before the door to the apartment closed behind me, I opened the bottle of Smirnoff and downed a large gulp. My adrenaline had been raging for over two hours and my nerves were jangled. I was far too agitated to sleep, so I sat on the faux leather sofa, sipping my vodka, staring into a dark room, trying to convince myself that leaving Diane had been the right decision. It was Saturday night and I had nothing pressing to do on Sunday, so I drank the entire bottle of Smirnoff. I don't remember the next day.

67

So Long, Debbie

The next year was going to be one of the busiest of my life. My calendar was filled with over a dozen trips as part of the Olympic tour, and I had just added an unexpected one to California.

On September 1st I got a call from my brother. Doug had always been good about keeping in touch with our sister and her family—much better than I had been, so it was Doug who my brother-in-law Legarde phoned to give us an update on Debbie's health.

Debbie had been a smoker since her early teens—not at all uncommon in the seventies—but she had never been able to quit. She spent her adult years trying various ways to break the addiction, but none of them had worked long-term. She had developed a cough several years back that continued to worsen, and late in 2006, she was diagnosed with lung cancer. Legarde was phoning to tell Doug the cancer had advanced to stage four and that Debbie was in home hospice, receiving palliative care while waiting for the inevitable. She was fifty-three— only four years older than my father had been when he died.

Doug and I agreed to do whatever was needed to take our mother to visit Debbie, aware it would be the last time she would see her daughter. Given Mother's mobility issues, there would be some logistical challenges on the trip, but I assured Doug if I could get a small herd of horses, thousands of pounds of equipment, and a couple of dozen people halfway around the world and back, I could fly the three of us out to California.

Debbie's situation was worse than we had expected. She perked up when she saw us walk in, but that provoked a coughing spell lasting several minutes. Debbie could only speak in a whisper—because she was so weak, but also because anything louder would have provoked more coughing. She was confined to her La-Z-Boy, surrounded by everything she needed for her comfort: the most valuable of which was Legarde. Since the early days of her cancer diagnosis, Legarde had been by her side 24/7. He had become her hospice nurse and administered all her palliative care. He had eased into that role over many months, having gone on extended leave from his job. Legarde's caring for Debbie was the most generous display of love I had ever seen. He was watching his wife of thirty years slipping away and I could only imagine how devastating that must have been for him.

We spent the morning in the living room, talking to Debbie and Legarde and watching her nod and smile to let us know she was taking everything in. Her children, Carrie and Aubrey, joined us in the afternoon and we took a drive to a local park so Debbie could get some fresh air and sunshine. Doug and I knew the drill for moving our mother about, as Debbie's family did for her, so like a small military maneuver, we made our way to the park and enjoyed a sunny afternoon together.

Two days later, when it was time to head back to Cleveland, none of us knew how to say our final goodbyes; it was something we had never done with a family member. There were hugs all around and a lot of held-back tears—nobody wanted Debbie to be upset—so we made lots of vague comments like: "Now you hang in there. Legarde is doing a great job. Try to make the best of things. Know we love you. So glad we could be here." None of us said what we felt or expressed our true emotions—not because we were stoic WASPS and unable to, but because we were terrified of breaking down in front of Debbie and having to openly deal with our own pain. It is hard to know how to die, but Debbie seemed okay with it all. The rest of us were at a complete loss.

Unfortunately, this had only been the dress rehearsal for our return trip—three weeks later—for Debbie's funeral. Mother could not make that trip.

* * *

All Debbie's friends attended the celebration of life service, and many went to the podium to share their remembrances. So many people spoke that afternoon, and the words from her daughters tore our hearts out. No one tried to hold back any tears as we listened to each confirmation of my sister's sweet nature, abundant kindness, and the pure joy she spread with her eternally optimistic outlook on life and her ability to find something nice to say to anyone about anything.

As I listened to those moving words, my thoughts went to childhood memories and the aggression she used to show toward me. I knew Debbie had struggled as a teenager—maybe because our father was absent, or because we had an emotionally unavailable mother, or even because she was the first-born child. Whatever the reason, she was often a frustrated and angry child. I remembered being at the receiving end of her aggression and how I had learned to deal with her constant bullying—both verbal and physical. But *that* sister had disappeared on the day she married Legarde.

Even though Debbie and Legarde had eloped and left for Tokyo as soon as he joined the Navy, we had enough contact over the ensuing years to know that Debbie had changed. We recognized her for the beautiful person she had become; marriage to Legarde had transformed her into a caring and giving mother and wife. That was the woman being eulogized by her friends and family.

I had never realized how much I loved her.

68
So Long, Mother

Things only got worse in the months following Debbie's funeral.

After returning from California, Doug made time to visit Mother more often than usual, but each time he said goodbye, she was left alone to deal with her grief, which sent her into a deep depression from which she never escaped.

On a Saturday morning in January, I got a call from Doug. Mom's depression had caused her to stop eating properly and her immune system was suppressed. She had caught a cold, but in her weakened state, it had turned into pneumonia. She was hospitalized for treatment and Doug felt I should be there. I arrived on Sunday evening and understood why he said I should come.

Mother was in the intensive care unit, hooked up for around-the-clock monitoring. Her respiratory problems were being treated aggressively and she was wearing an oxygen mask day and night. Doug was working for a landscape company, and it being winter, he was on call for snow-plowing assignments, but he had stayed with her in between callouts. Once I arrived, one of us was always with her over the next two days.

But on Wednesday, January 23rd, things took a turn for the worse. By late afternoon she was writhing in pain—despite the morphine drip—and she struggled with the discomfort of her oxygen mask. Doug and I watched on, wondering what else we could do to make her more comfortable. We called for a nurse and were standing bedside when she came into the room. Mother saw the nurse and made a gesture to have the mask removed so she could speak. As the mask was being taken off, my mother uttered the clearest words I had heard her speak in the thirty-five years since she underwent her electroshock treatments.

"Let me go."

Doug and I looked at each other, and then at the nurse. "What can we do?" I said. "She clearly doesn't want to live like this. I know she has a living will on file here and it states she does not want to be kept on life support. If the pneumonia can't be cured, then we need to grant her request and let her go."

The nurse left to consult with her team and returned to confirm that the appropriate documents were on file. The doctors declared our mother's condition to be incurable and began the process of letting her die. They increased the morphine dosage to stop the pain and removed the oxygen. For hours—maybe ten, maybe twenty, maybe more—our mother's heart would weaken, her lungs would start shutting down, and she would die.

Doug and I held vigil throughout the night. Shortly before sunrise, I glanced into the courtyard outside Mother's room. It was a perfectly still night and a heavy snow was falling—the kind with large, thick flakes that stick to everything they touch. They sparkled as they reflected the few strands of light streaming into the courtyard, and it was the picture of tranquility—the most beautiful snow I had ever seen.

Around eleven o'clock that morning, Mother's vital signs dropped. Within an hour, the pace of repetitive beeps from the monitors slowed and the peaks and valleys on the digital displays were flattening. With a final sigh, she let out her last breath and everything flat-lined. Doug leaned down to kiss our mother on the forehead and whispered his final words to her, "I love you, Mom." As he lifted his head to step away, we heard the familiar beeping from the monitors resume and saw digital displays dancing. Mother had sprung back to life—if ever so briefly—as if to say *thank you* to Doug. About ten minutes later the machines went quiet, and after seventy-nine challenging years, Mother was at peace.

* * *

I knew that my mother had had a difficult life: growing up with an alcoholic and abusive father; marrying a kind but alcoholic husband; living with debilitating depression; enduring three miscarriages; going through the loss of her sister to suicide; and living with an array of health problems that had lessened her quality of life, every day, for thirty-five years. Maybe it was the combination of all those factors that rendered her unable to show emotion to her children. Doug and I had no memory of ever hearing her say the words "I love you" or of being hugged or kissed.

After she died, I reflected on her strong spirit and willingness to accept her life for what it was—never letting herself fall into the role of victim or complain about her struggles. But something much stronger took over my feelings of admiration and respect: a profound sense of guilt.

Why didn't I visit her more often? How could I have left Doug alone to carry the burden of looking after her from the time he was twelve? Why couldn't I have been more sympathetic to her own limitations? And why was it always so hard for me to experience true feelings of love and gratitude for all she was able to do for us, despite everything?

I had always given serious questions like those only cursory thought. When answers became too hard to find or too painful to accept, I defaulted to my familiar coping mechanisms: I drank and kept myself very busy. I knew no better way to escape the pain of reality; grieving was not part of my skill set.

My job at the USEF would provide the perfect vehicle over the next two years for staying busy. I would ensconce myself in the social fabric of the equestrian world, fueled by endless parties and the ever-abundant supply of alcohol that accompanies them. I knew where to seek refuge and was anxious to get there.

69

Dreams Really Do Come True

My first port of refuge was an international dressage competition in Hagen, Germany. Two Grand Prix riders who were not in contention for a place on the U.S. Olympic team were competing there to gain more experience at European shows. Klaus was ostensibly there to support those riders, but he otherwise had a very full agenda.

When Klaus was not working with U.S. riders—either at competitions or in private training sessions—he was busy training elite European riders. All of Klaus's clients were potential buyers of horses whose purchase could yield him handsome commissions. But those riders were also competing against the U.S. riders Klaus was meant to be coaching, so there was a conflict of interest, and our riders consistently complained about it.

Laura Bechtolsheimer was a British rider whose mother was Ursula Bechtolsheimer-Kipp, a German-born heiress with a fortune estimated to be worth over a billion pounds sterling. Klaus was a close friend of the Bechtolsheimers and Laura was in Hagen preparing for the Olympics.

Princess Nathalie zu Sayn-Wittgenstein-Berleburg was another of Klaus's European clients. She is the daughter of Princess Benedikte of Denmark and Prince Richard of Sayn-Wittgenstein-Berleburg. Nathalie was preparing to represent Denmark in Hong Kong. (Because the competition venue for equestrian sports requires dozens of stables, multiple training rings, and large competition arenas, they are usually held apart from the host city's Olympic stadium. In the case of the Beijing Olympics, we would be competing at a racetrack in Hong Kong.)

Klaus was keeping an eye on them to make sure they would be in top form for the Olympics; never mind they would all be competing against his U.S. riders. I was seeing firsthand why Klaus's politics, and priorities, were such a point of contention for our riders—a problem that would reach a boiling point in Hong Kong.

On the last day of the competition, I was heading to the VIP tent to grab some lunch and passed through the outdoor terrace. Someone had told me Rosemarie Springer was at the show, and to my delight, I found myself walking right up to her. We had not seen each other in almost twenty years, but she had not changed a bit. She was sitting alone and invited me to join her. We spent an hour catching up and I told her what I had been feeling for so many years: "Rosemarie, thank you from the bottom of my heart for all the opportunities you provided me from the first day we met. You believed in me when I was young and only had raw talent, but your generosity helped turn that into a meaningful career with dressage. I am so glad to be here today to thank you in person."

"And I am thrilled everything has worked out so well for you," she said. "You have obviously met with success and now you have a very important job. I'm certain you will do well with it." I held back the tears long enough to say *auf Wiedersehen*—a wonderful German expression that means, "until we see each other again"—and then found my way behind the VIP tent for a quick cry. Rosemarie passed away eleven years later at the age of ninety-eight; we did not see each other after talking in Hagen. It turned out an informal *tschüß* would have been a more appropriate salutation that day: it means goodbye.

* * *

After the horse show, I flew from Amsterdam to Vienna to conduct some business at The Spanish Riding School on behalf of a friend in Lexington. It resulted in a VIP invitation by the School's Managing Director to watch the famous Lipizzaner stallions' training sessions in their historic Baroque riding hall.

With other guests, I was directed to the front row of the royal box and was seated beneath the portrait of Emperor Charles VI, which the riders always salute before they ride. Classical Viennese music played throughout the training sessions and its melodies carried my thoughts back to 1976—when I was nineteen and had brought my friends from college to watch the stallions perform. I was a poor student and could only afford a standing room place on the top tier of the arena, but at the time, being there had been a dream come true. I had fantasized about what it would be like to be seated in the royal box, watching what I believed was a living monument to classical equitation.

Sitting there with the other guests and hearing the stallions' rhythmical breathing—smelling the sweat and leather as they floated past us—was almost surreal. We were guests of honor at The Spanish Riding School, watching the training of horses that were the progeny of Pluto Alga—the stallion at Erlenhof on whom I had given my own Grand Prix exhibitions—and I was on my way to China to serve as Team Leader for the U.S. Olympic Team. The hour I sat there, reflecting on the amazing path my life had taken, was the first time in many years I knew what happiness felt like. All my childhood dreams were coming true.

70
The Team Is Ready

Winning a place on the United States Olympic Team is a dream come true that crowns an athlete's career. We were ready to select the team to represent the U.S. in Hong Kong.

During 2007, and until the end of May of 2008, riders throughout the U.S. rode in internationally sanctioned competitions to gain scores on a ranking list. At the end of that qualifying period, the top twelve horse and rider combinations received an invitation to compete at the USEF National Dressage Championships in San Juan Capistrano, California. When the competition finished on Sunday, June 29th, the USEF High Performance Dressage Committee named the team and alternates for the 2008 Beijing Olympics.

Top of the list was Steffan Peters and his horse Ravel. After the 2006 World Equestrian Games, Steffen ended his sponsorship with the Browning family, and Floriano was given to their son to ride. Steffen's new sponsor was Akiko Yamazaki, an amateur Grand Prix rider who had the financial wherewithal to sponsor an Olympian like Steffen: her husband was Jerry Yang, the founder of Yahoo. Steffen's new horse, Ravel, was a powerful Dutch warmblood gelding and they had won the National Championships—earning them their place at the top of the list for the team.

Debbie McDonald had given her big chestnut mare, Brentina, time off after the World Championships in Aachen, and the resting period had paid off. They came back stronger than ever and finished in second place; they were also named to the team.

Courtney King-Dye was a seasoned international competitor who rode a large Dutch warmblood gelding that could more than hold his own against Ravel. Her horse was Harmony's Mythilus and was owned by Leslie Malone. Leslie's husband, John Malone, was the billionaire chairman of Liberty Media and perhaps the largest private landowner in the United States. Leslie owned a large breeding operation in Colorado called Harmony Sporthorses and dreamed of one day seeing the U.S. win a gold medal at an Olympic Games. It was an effort she actively supported, and her sponsorship of Courtney was part of it. Courtney and Mythilus finished the Championships in third place and were named to the team.

Leslie Morse had two talented Grand Prix stallions. Tip Top was the Swedish warmblood she had ridden to a bronze medal at the World Championships in Aachen. Just as magnificent was her Dutch warmblood stallion, Kingston. He was a seasoned competitor and had been the alternate horse for the 2004 Olympic team. Leslie had elected to qualify Kingston for the upcoming Olympics, and he was once again named as the "traveling reserve." That meant he would travel with the team to Hong Kong, but since only three riders compete for medals, Kingston would be brought into service if Steffen, Debbie, or Courtney could not ride.

The team would be traveling to the competition facility in Aachen and quarantined from July 18th to the 30th. Using an abundance of caution, we brought an additional rider and horse with us on the outside chance one of the horse and rider combinations could not make the trip to Hong Kong. Michael Barisone was a Grand Prix rider with extensive international competition experience; he and his sponsor's horse, Neruda, would also come to Aachen.

* * *

Two weeks after the team had been selected, all five horses were brought to a stabling facility on the grounds of the Los Angeles International Airport to prepare for their flight to Amsterdam's Schiphol Airport.

We flew in a specially equipped KLM 747-400 called a Combi: the front two-thirds of the cabin was for passengers, and the other third had room for our horses in the aft cargo hold. Our team sat in the main cabin, but the riders could walk back to the galley, and with an escort from a flight attendant, enter the cargo hold to check on their horses. The only way other passengers knew there were horses on board was if they detected a stray piece of hay in a rider's hair and asked about its origin.

Dr. Rick Mitchell—our team veterinarian—flew in the hold with the horses, along with two of our grooms and an equine attendant provided by KLM. After the containers were secured and Rick was confident the horses were relaxed and ready to fly, the team members took their seats in the main cabin, and we settled in for our long flight to Amsterdam. I had an aisle seat in the economy cabin and enjoyed several screwdrivers before dinner—and a couple of glasses of wine with dinner—missing the comforts of first-class air travel. My job at the USEF came with a lot of perks, but flying first class was not one of them.

As I was slipping into my familiar alcoholic fog, the reality of the day set in. Going to the Olympics had lived for me as a dream in multiple versions, but it had never occurred to me that going as a Team Leader was an option. There had been no way to foresee the series of seemingly disconnected events that led me to the USEF. I rarely let myself play the "what if" game and I found no value in doing it on the flight, so I accepted that things always seem to work out the way they should and did not question too deeply how I had gotten there; I was just grateful I had.

I was on my way to the Olympics, and it was up to me to make sure everyone on the team had a safe and successful journey. As I drifted off to sleep, I welcomed the challenges that I knew lay ahead and I embraced my new vision of what going to the Olympic Games looked like. However, I had greatly underestimated the challenges.

71

Bumpy Start

All the horses were fit and healthy when we landed at Schiphol. They remained in their flight containers and were taken to a livestock import facility adjacent to the airport. Plastic tarps at the front of the container stalls had been rolled down to help keep the horses calm after landing. The containers were set onto large loading docks inside the doors of the import facility where the horses would be untied and led down ramps to their stalls.

The grooms, Tim and Rick, arrived at the stables first to receive the horses. The rest of the team arrived a few minutes later. My car was the last to pull into the stable yard, and as I started over to the barn, Leslie came charging out to meet me. "The front of Kingston's container was opened before I could get there—he got excited when he saw the other horses and reared straight up! He smacked his front leg on the front of the stall, and it is already starting to swell." That kind of injury could take a long time to heal, and Leslie's panic was understandable.

After arriving at the stables, Rick confirmed Kingston had injured a flexor tendon in his front leg. For the next week, Leslie and her groom intermittently soaked the leg in ice water and then bandaged it for light compression.

Seven days and a hundred bags of ice later, Rick made the final call: Kingston would not be fit to compete and had to be sent back to California. Leslie was devastated. She acquiesced to Rick's decision, asked her groom to take care of Kingston until he was safe in his stall at home, and left. Years of preparation for a chance that her prize stallion could perform on the world stage ended abruptly because of an accident that took less than ten seconds to unfold. Leslie had experienced a train wreck before she and Kingston even got into the arena. As a result, Leslie would join the ranks of countless athletes who had lost their chance of going to the Olympics because fate had dealt them a bad hand. We needed a new reserve horse to send to Hong Kong, and that brought Michael Barisone and Neruda into service. Our abundance of caution had paid off.

I instantly liked Michael when I met him. Standing next to his six-foot-four frame made me look like a dwarf, but we were compatible in every other way. Michael was a big man with a heart of gold; some said behind his booming baritone voice and bold self-confidence, there was a marshmallow inside. Although not weak, Michael had a charming softness that came through when empathy or compassion was needed. Everything he did, he did with gusto, and if he said he was going to do something, his word was his bond. He combined integrity with humor and was always looking to help others. He would become the glue that held our team together in the face of devastating circumstances, and although I felt sorry for Leslie and Kingston, I was thrilled Michael was on the team.

* * *

After two weeks of training at the quarantine facility on Aachen's showgrounds, Tim kicked into high gear and began one of the largest airlifts of horses the world had ever seen. Finally, the horses and their riders were on their way to the 2008 Beijing Olympics.

From Aachen, the horses traveled by van to Schiphol for their nonstop flight to Hong Kong. The flight path for the eleven-hour trip routed them over Dubai in case an unexpected stop was needed for fuel or maintenance. Dubai's airport was equipped with a state-of-the-art veterinary clinic and personnel who knew how to handle horses.

When the planes arrived at the Hong Kong International Airport, a group of vans was waiting on the tarmac, and the horses were driven convoy-style to the Sha Tin Racecourse, complete with a police escort to ensure a seamless ride through the crowded city. The stabling had been designated as a quarantine facility, so the horses could go straight to their air-conditioned stalls and recuperate after their long journey.

Rick's first job was to examine each horse and make sure there were no signs of stress. Our faces froze as he removed his stethoscope from Mythilus's chest and said, "Something's not right. This horse's heartbeat is irregular. Courtney, has Mythilus ever had any trouble with his heart?"

"No—not that I'm aware of."

"Well, let's keep a close eye on him. I don't like what I'm hearing."

That was just one omen predicting the many challenges that lay ahead. The heat, with temperatures above ninety, and the relentless humidity were among them. But weather would be the least of our problems—even with typhoons. Our problems were going to be of our own making, not Mother Nature's.

72

Abandoned

Home base for the U.S. Equestrian Team was the Sheraton Hotel in Kowloon: located in the heart of the city's business, shopping, and entertainment district in Tsim Sha Tsui. With panoramic views of Victoria Harbor from its rooftop terrace, no one in the U.S. delegation had reason to complain about their accommodations. And for the horses, everything at the Sha Tin Racecourse was state-of-the-art, including the training arenas. It was one of the largest racetracks in the world and it had been built to impress.

We gave the horses a day to relax after moving into the stables and then began a program of light training to regain their fitness. After the second day of training, Courtney complained that Mythilus was lethargic and somewhat unsteady in his gait. Rick conducted another examination and this time the stethoscope flashed red: there appeared to be a murmur in Mythilus' heart, and it required immediate treatment. He was checked into the veterinary clinic, where it was determined he needed to remain for around-the-clock monitoring. Treatment options would be limited due to drug restrictions for horses in competition, but the veterinarians partnered with Rick and treated Mythilus as aggressively as possible.

Uncertain whether Mythilus would have a full recovery, Michael was told the chances of Neruda being used as the reserve horse had increased substantially. The reserve rider at any international team championship is placed in a horrible situation: they must train every day as if they are going to compete for a medal, knowing it would only happen if another horse or rider dropped out. *Schadenfreude,* the anticipated joy at someone else's misfortune, is an emotion no one would admit to, but it is experienced by every reserve rider.

As Mythilus languished in the clinic for the next four days, our team trained so their horses would peak at the exact minute they entered the competition arena. Every day Mythilus was in the clinic was a lost training day for Courtney, putting her at a disadvantage to the other riders. But the treatments proved successful, and Rick declared him fit to compete.

The riders were anxious about Courtney and Mythilus's ability to peak for the first event—the Nations Cup. It was a team event, so all three horses would need to be at the top of their game if they were to win a medal. With forty-seven horses in the team competition, one-hour training slots were allocated among the three outdoor rings to each team. It would be the only time riders were guaranteed a training space to themselves.

On the day Mythilus returned to work we were scheduled to train at 11 a.m.—when temperatures were reaching their peak. I approached our arena at 11:10, my shirt already plastered to my back, and saw our four riders circling their horses outside the ring. Courtney's husband came running over and shouted, "What is Klaus doing? He is in *our* arena with Laura Bechtolsheimer, and we are losing valuable training time. Courtney needs to train! Get Laura out of there!" He was right, Klaus had appropriated the U.S. team's arena for a competitor's training—training he was delivering. Laura left and Klaus grudgingly turned his attention to Courtney while the others trained on their own. Courtney had lost even more valuable time.

The van ride back to the Sheraton was painfully silent. The riders were upset with Klaus, and he sat in the front seat, unwilling to talk. In the hotel lobby, a rider stopped me. "Gil, I don't know what's up with that childish German, but if he doesn't get his act together and start supporting this team, he will go home in a box. He is destroying team morale, and we would be better off without him."

It was time for me to confront Klaus, so I asked him to join me in the lobby.

"Klaus, what is going on? You are clearly upset about something and demoralizing our riders." I looked at him intently and added, "This must end, and it must end now. What is wrong?"

"What is wrong? You know what is wrong," Klaus snapped. "The USEF is going to fire me after this, and they have already hired my replacement. That is what's wrong."

"Klaus, we already told you the USEF is creating a new position, and it will require someone to be based in the U.S., so it can't be you. But you knew that. We haven't even begun looking for a new person."

"Well, that is not what my sources tell me." Klaus scowled and added, "I happen to know that the USEF has already made an offer to the Dutch team coach. He has accepted it, and you will be paying him a lot more than you pay me!"

"I have no idea what you are talking about. I manage all committees that determine this, so I would certainly know if that had happened. I can assure you it has not." Then I added, "Klaus, you have been given bad information that you want to believe. If someone is out to sabotage our team, they are playing you for a fool and doing a great job of it."

I arranged a meeting with Jim and the USEF CEO where they confirmed to Klaus what I had already told him. The matter was closed, but Klaus walked away only partially mollified.

The next day at lunch, the entire team sat together. Klaus was with us, but only in body—his mind was elsewhere. Klaus and I were facing the door and could see the Bechtolsheimer family being seated at a table near the window. Without saying a word to anyone, Klaus left our table, greeted the Bechtolsheimers, and joined them for lunch. Klaus let the team know where his priorities lay; it was a clear gesture of abandonment on the day before the competition began.

73
Thrill of Victory, Agony of Defeat

On the evening of Wednesday, August 13th, Mythilus was the first U.S. horse to enter the floodlit stadium and perform his Grand Prix test for the Nations Cup. Despite the challenges leading up to the event, Courtney and Mythilus finished in seventh place with a score high enough to have us think a team medal was within reach.

The following evening—with temperatures still above eighty degrees and humidity to match—the next train wreck was about to happen. Klaus and I stood ringside at the ten-minute holding box and left Debbie McDonald in silence as she put the final touches on Brentina. When her name was announced, they walked down the chute and boldly trotted into the stadium, with Klaus and I taking our places in the Kiss-and-Cry stand. The judge rang a bell to indicate Debbie could enter the dressage arena, and as she halted in the center to salute the judge, the only sounds we could hear were the beating of our hearts ... and the roar of what sounded like a jet engine.

In the far corner of the stadium was a fifty-foot tower holding a cauldron with the Olympic flame—a flame that burned throughout the Games, powered by gas. When the stadium was quiet, it sounded like a massive blow torch, and on that night, the wind was carrying the sound across the competition arena and into Brentina's sensitive ears. As Brentina made her first turn in front of the judges, the roar from the cauldron filled the arena, and Brentina's flight response kicked in. Debbie felt her horse tense up and knew Brentina was on the verge of panic. Even after a decade of competing in noisy venues throughout the world, Brentina was only afraid of two things: the sound of a diesel truck or a jet engine—and that is what she thought she was hearing as she began her test. Already in a state of panic, Brentina made her next turn to go diagonally across the arena in a bold trot and headed straight for a live-feed Jumbotron projecting an image of a horse and rider eight times her size. She never recovered her nerve.

It was a testament to Debbie's talent and Brentina's trust in her that they made it through the entire test. Due to the tension in her body, Brentina's movements were stiff and uneven, and the performance lacked any of the suppleness and harmony the judges award points for. They finished in thirty-sixth place—unheard of at any point in their long and illustrious career. In the world of dressage competition, the circumstances of the day came together to deliver every rider's worst nightmare: a train wreck.

Debbie walked out of the arena with her head bowed and tears streaming down her cheeks. As she passed our group she said, "I am sorry, guys. I am so sorry I let the team down. I am really sorry." Debbie was wrecked.

Debbie was the quintessential team player and was there to contribute to a medal—both for the other team members and for the U.S.—and there was nothing any of us could do to help ease the pain of what had happened. "The thrill of victory—the agony of defeat," as NBC Sports liked to say. Olympians pay a high price for their place on a team and very few people understand what the personal cost can be to an athlete. It broke my heart to watch Debbie pay.

Our last rider to go in the Nations Cup was Steffen, but even if he had scored higher than ever before, it would not have been enough to make up for Brentina's low score. He and Ravel finished in tenth place in the Grand Prix, putting the U.S. team in fourth place in the Nations Cup: Germany had won the gold medal, the Dutch silver, and the Danish bronze. If Debbie and Brentina had turned in a score even close to what was customary, we most likely would have won the bronze medal.

In the spirit of good sportsmanship, we all attended the medals ceremony. Debbie's sunglasses could not hide the profound disappointment she felt as the Danish team stepped up to the podium to accept their bronze medal. I wondered if Klaus felt proud to see his student, Princess Nathalie of Denmark, on that podium.

But in the end, even if Debbie and Brentina had not received a low score, it would not have mattered. We would find out on August 19th that the U.S. Dressage Team had been provisionally eliminated from the Nations Cup competition: any medal the team had won would have been forfeited. The team elimination would live forever as a black mark on the historical record, yet I doubt it would have helped Debbie to know that as we looked on—and I would have given anything that day to help relieve her pain.

74

Zero Tolerance

On Tuesday, August 19th, just as tropical storm Nuri was leaving Japan and heading across the East China Sea toward Hong Kong, I received a call from Jim.

"I need you to call Courtney and come to the conference room right away—we have a situation on our hands. I have called the other team leaders and asked them to join us."

With a seriousness I had never seen, Jim said, "We were just informed that in the random drug testing after the Grand Prix Freestyle, Mythilus tested positive for Felbinac. We are not that familiar with it, but it is a non-steroidal anti-inflammatory drug and is a prohibited substance. The veterinary panel will conduct a B-test, and if it is also positive, Mythilus will be put on suspension until a hearing can be held in Lausanne on September 5th. His scores have not been formally accepted, and if the charges stand, the team will be eliminated from the Nations Cup and Courtney's scores from the individual events will also be eliminated."

Rick jumped right in, "We have nothing—*nothing*—in our veterinary supplies that could contain Felbinac. We suspect Mythilus came into contact with it during his four days of treatment in the veterinary clinic. The veterinarians are following up on our request for an investigation. Exposure in the clinic is the only possible way Mythilus could have come into contact with it."

You could have heard a pin drop while we waited for Jim's next words. Everyone avoided making eye contact with Courtney, who looked as if someone had hit the pause button and put her image on hold. Seeing her look of disbelief, I asked Jim, "What happens next? What do you need us to do?"

USEF's general counsel would manage the appeal process, but we had to share the information with the team and do all public relations. A firestorm in the press would be harmful to the team's morale and to the media-shy billionaire whose wife owned Mythilus: John Malone.

We would have to manage the fallout as we awaited Nuri's arrival. Hong

Kong is accustomed to summer typhoons and initiated its standard protocols for tropical storms: cars were removed from the streets; everyone was relegated to traveling by subway; shops were closed; the metal storm shutters were lowered on the windows; and we all hunkered in to ride out the storm.

The grooms were staying at the racecourse and would be with the horses. Rick and Michael took the subway from the hotel to make sure everyone was prepared and came back to report that things at the stables were secured. The only thing to do was to settle in at the rooftop lounge, enjoy a lot of cocktails, and marvel at how the tall buildings could sway in the hurricane-force winds without so much as creaking.

* * *

As the "Person Responsible," Courtney appeared in front of the International Equestrian Federation's Tribunal in Lausanne, Switzerland on September 5th. On September 22nd they handed down their ruling: Courtney and the entire U.S. Dressage Team had been disqualified from the Olympic Games.

Per their ruling, the Tribunal "... found the evidence of the Person Responsible (PR) and the U.S. Dressage Team Vet to be credible and believed that neither the PR nor anyone on her behalf or related to the USEF had knowingly administered the medication to the horse." The Tribunal went on to state that despite "...the possibility of contamination, [and] the excellent stable management practiced by the U.S. team..." the ruling of a positive drug test would stand, and the U.S. team would be eliminated. It was the ultimate definition of "zero tolerance" in the world of equine drug testing and our team had now established what would be a new benchmark for it.

* * *

My lifetime dream of going to the Olympics had been fulfilled, albeit in a role I had never anticipated. I learned a lot about the realities of being on an Olympic team. I saw firsthand the great personal cost athletes pay to realize their dreams.

A lifetime of hard work, dedication, and innumerable personal sacrifices provides no guarantee that a trip to the Olympics will bring long-term rewards. Performance on any given day is unpredictable, and equestrians have the added challenge of competing together with a four-legged partner who has a mind of its own. No amount of hard work can insulate an athlete from the disappointments Debbie and Courtney experienced. Michael had trained as rigorously as any athlete at the Games—ready to jump in at a moment's notice and do his part to help win a medal—all for naught. Steffen had to suffer the consequences of being disqualified through no fault of his own.

Olympians face the same unpredictability in life as everyone else. Less than two years later, the horse Courtney was riding tripped and fell. She hit her head and suffered a traumatic brain injury. She has remained physically and cognitively disabled ever since.

Debbie became the U.S. Dressage Team's most successful coach, but in 2019 allegations were made that in the mid-1970s she was guilty of negligently supervising two minors who were accusing her husband of sexual abuse. All allegations were proven to be false but before they were, Debbie had been removed from her position as national coach.

After competing in two more Olympic Games, Steffen suffered from debilitating depression and considered retiring from competition. He was overwhelmed by feelings of self-doubt after a disappointing performance at the 2018 WEG. The stress of maintaining his success had become overwhelming and he only returned to competition after months-long therapy.

Michael returned to his training facility in New Jersey, where a client launched a campaign of online attacks toward him that included allegations of child abuse that were proven to be false. The torment became so extreme that Michael confronted the client in his stables and shot her in the chest. The client survived, and Michael was charged with attempted murder. He was incarcerated while awaiting his trial and was subsequently released to a psychiatric treatment center after being found not guilty by reason of insanity.

Ironically, the lives of Olympians can play out in the same way a dressage test does. After the rider enters, halts, and salutes—anything can happen. Their fate will be determined by the circumstances life throws at them—circumstances that can lead to either a trainwreck or to a victory in achieving their personal best.

Fulfilling the Olympic dream and pursuing fame and glory can involve dealing with harsh realities: just ask the 500 sexual abuse victims of U.S. Gymnastics doctor Larry Nassar—or me, after seven years of sexual abuse and the lifetime of addiction that followed.

I turned off the light and put my Olympic dream to rest after Hong Kong, but I still did not know how high the costs of fulfilling that dream had been. I would need to struggle for another twelve years before I could finally pay the piper and stop the emotional bleeding.

75
I Quit

After the Olympics, Jim asked me to join him for dinner; the USEF CEO and the board president would be there. We discussed how things were going with the search for Klaus's replacement, debriefed the events from Hong Kong, and shared information about the World Equestrian Games that were being held the following year in Lexington. After eating, Jim opened a new conversation.

"Dressage is the second largest discipline at the USEF, and we know it isn't an easy one to manage—you have some tricky characters to work with and the politics at the International Equestrian Federation are a mess right now. You are doing a great job, and we appreciate it."

"Thanks, Jim. I couldn't do it on my own. You always have my back and are a great teacher. I really appreciate it."

"Well, that brings me to my next topic. We would like to offer you a promotion—to Assistant Executive Director. You would keep all your responsibilities as Managing Director for Dressage, but you would also be responsible for Driving, Endurance, Reining, and Vaulting."

He paused for a moment before adding, "It's a big job—you would have a Sport Director reporting to you for each discipline—and put you in a position to one day take over my job."

"Wow. That's an amazing offer, and unexpected."

Jim explained further, "You would have my full support and I would help you get your arms around the nuances and politics of each new discipline. I'd teach you everything I know, and after the London Olympics, you would be ready to move into my job and I could move on to other things in the sport."

Then the CEO weighed in. "The three of us at this table run the whole show, and if you accepted the offer, you'd become part of the inner circle and join us in running things. It is a ton of work, but there are a lot of benefits—for you and for the USEF. I hope you'll accept."

The president added: "There are a lot of exciting things on the horizon for horse sport in the U.S., and we think you'd be a great addition to our team."

Something I have always responded well to is recognition for a job well done and an acknowledgment of my talent. Their comments played into my fundamental need to be liked and to feel special. My decision was automatic.

"Guys, that sounds fantastic. I accept your offer. I can't thank you enough and I promise I won't let you down."

"We know you won't," the CEO said. "That's why we made the offer."

We finished the evening with another cocktail and shared a round of high-fives as we left the restaurant. Later, I would wish I had given it more thought.

* * *

The following months went as Jim had promised. The Sport Directors reported to me, and we got to work preparing for the WEG. The countdown was underway—September 2010 would arrive before we knew it—and the city of Lexington was experiencing an abundance of pre-Games excitement. The transition into my new role was going well and I was confident I could succeed—if only I wanted the job.

The USEF had very clear expectations of me: I would serve as Assistant Executive Director through the 2012 London Olympics, and if all went to plan, I would move into Jim's role as Executive Director after that. When I interviewed with Jim in 2005, he had promised me I would eat, drink, sleep, and breathe dressage. He had well and truly delivered on his promise. All I did was work, and travel, and then work and travel some more. The job never turned off. The prospect of four more years with five sport disciplines, followed by four years with accountability for eight disciplines—at an even more hectic pace—no longer appealed to me. I had always marveled at how well Jim did his job, but I knew what that entailed, and it was not what I wanted to do.

I met with Jim, gave him my reasons, and resigned, effective August 26th, 2009.

* * *

The equestrian press published a lot of articles after my resignation, and reading them caused me to reflect on my decision to leave. I had made a lot of friends over the years, and I had a Rolodex filled with phone numbers for some of the wealthiest and most influential people in the world. Other than my memories of many incredible experiences—some good, and many not so good—the friendships I had made were my most valuable takeaways from the job and I hoped I could retain the ones that were meaningful to me.

There was a sadness to leaving that had nothing to do with saying goodbye to the job and the lifestyle that came with it, and I could feel my depression deepening. Handing in my resignation after four successful years—on the heels of being offered a once-in-a-lifetime opportunity to go to the Olympics as many times as I wanted—felt too familiar, and it disturbed me.

What's wrong with me? I had accomplished the goals I had set when I was fourteen years old: becoming an accomplished equestrian and being a member of an Olympic dressage team. In the face of all my difficult circumstances, I had always made choices that led to the fulfillment of my dreams. I was leaving the USEF without a new dream—without any clear aspirations for what I wanted to build in my life from that point forward. *Am I sabotaging myself in the face of my success?* I wasn't sure what questions I needed to answer, but something felt wrong. I was a decade away from understanding the impact my childhood trauma had on my decision-making process, so I was reacting to feelings that were buried deep within me. Some insidious force was driving my decision-making process, and it was my enemy.

I suspected treating my depression with alcohol was making things worse, but I couldn't imagine getting through a day without it; alcohol had not stopped playing its role as the Great Deceiver. It is lonely when alcohol is your only friend, and I had a long way to go before that would change. I had no idea what lay ahead, but one thing was certain: I was bringing my only friend along for the ride. The worst was yet to come.

Part Four

TRAIN WRECK

Lost, addicted, and without a dream

76
Catalyst for Growth

It was time to plan the next phase of my life. I needed to figure out what I was passionate about and then design a career around that; one that would be challenging, enjoyable, and provide a sense of fulfillment.

I delivered the first Mastery Course to my students from northeast Ohio and western Pennsylvania in 1999. I knew it was a marketable product, and I was passionate about it: I had created it from nothing, and it was my baby. I expanded the course to focus on organizational development concepts and deliver it to corporations. Designing and delivering those courses would be challenging and enjoyable, and if I were training people both inside and outside of the horse world, I would be fulfilled on many levels.

In a leadership program I had taken years ago, students were asked to define their purpose in life with only three words—which I discovered was no small challenge. But when I honed in on the sense of fulfillment I experienced when I was training and developing others, I landed on it: *Catalyst for Growth*. I was committed to providing the tools and training to people interested in self-improvement; I had a passion for teaching. I spent two months redesigning my courses and developing the marketing materials to promote them. In October 2009, I registered "Mastery Concepts LLC" as my new business and declared myself to be a professional Catalyst for Growth.

During my time at the USEF, I got to know Debbie McDonald well. She retired from competition after Hong Kong and was named the USEF Developing Coach: the person responsible for identifying future High-Performance riders and developing them into successful international competitors.

I told Debbie about The Mastery Course and she offered to host it for a group of her students at a hotel conference center in Sun Valley. That weekend launched my career in the equestrian world as a Catalyst for Growth and established my brand as a teacher with a passion for mastery.

Scott Hassler was the USEF National Young Horse Coach. His job was to identify horses—four, five, and six years old—who had the talent to compete on the global stage, and then partner with their riders to get them there. Debbie and Scott worked closely and were good friends. After Debbie told Scott about The Mastery Course, he contacted me to schedule one at his training center in Chesapeake City, Maryland. He brought together a group of passionate riders and trainers at John and Leslie Malone's six-hundred-acre estate. He declared the weekend a success.

The endorsement of The Mastery Course by the USEF's top national coaches, along with several successes presenting my organizational development programs within corporations, told me I was on the right track.

During that time, I also began teaching dressage clinics across the country. I incorporated the education gained by watching the world's top dressage athletes train and compete, into the classical gymnastic training program I had learned from Miguel. The clinics were popular, and the demand was strong. I was booked almost every weekend.

Six months after leaving the USEF, Mastery Concepts LLC was a fully developed business and I had established a new identity in the horse world—one that combined my skills as a manager and trainer with my passions for horses and business. I was off and running.

77

Fun With Dick and Jane

Jane Brown had gotten to know me well after our first meeting in Gladstone. Knowing I was teaching and training in southern California, Jane invited me to spend the weekend at their home and to join Dick and her at the "Dressage Affair"—an international dressage competition at the Del Mar Show Park where Guenter was competing several of their horses.

Jane had arranged for La Costa Limousine—her car service of many years—to pick me up at the San Diego airport and bring me to Carlsbad and their house on Almaden Lane.

Dick and Jane emerged to greet my limo as if I were arriving at Claridge's in London—the model for hospitality Jane strove to provide every guest at their home. "Welcome to our abode," Jane said, sweeping her arm as if inviting me into a grand reception hall. "We built it in 1982 as a weekend home—never imagining we would live here full time—and I designed every inch myself. Let me give you a tour."

"I'll be in the den, watching the news," Dick said. It was Friday afternoon and he needed to see how the stock market had closed.

The double front doors of the Mission Revival home were solid mahogany and opened into a foyer built with the same red bricks as the exterior of the house. Two steps down from the foyer was the dining room, and the living room was to the left. Both rooms had cathedral ceilings and sliding glass doors running the length of the rooms. Above the doors were arched windows stretched to the ceiling that looked out to a large patio surrounding an in-ground pool and colorful gardens. The house, perched two hundred feet above the thirty-six-hole golf course belonging to the prestigious La Costa Resort, offered sweeping views of its lush greenery.

"The house was built by Mueller Custom Homes," Jane said. "They are building Mitt Romney's new home in La Jolla right now. We are good friends with the Romneys. In fact," she said, pointing to the wall leading to the dining room, "that is a torch from the 2002 Salt Lake City Olympic Games; Mitt was in charge of those Olympics. He gave us the torch."

During the extensive tour, I learned about the provenance of every item on display; each had a detailed and dramatic story. Jane had designed the house—and its contents—to be a statement of wealth and good taste.

But Jane's pride and joy was her "Wall of Fame," just off the main hallway where a torch from the 2004 Athens Olympics hung. The area resembled a narrow art gallery—filled with shadow boxes containing a ribbon and photo from every major competition their horses had won, along with the hind shoes the horse had been wearing when they competed. That wall held two decades of joyful memories she and Dick shared from three Olympics, two World Equestrian Games, two World Cup Finals, and numerous National Championships. After telling stories about the victories represented in each of those frames, she said: "And it was a privilege to bring honor to our country and hear the national anthem played as the medals were awarded to our horses." Her tears were immediate and genuine; Dick and Jane Brown, above all else, were patriots.

We found Dick on the sofa in his den, in front of the TV, asleep. He sat up and said the market had done well and that he had made some money that day. The nap seemed well deserved; Dick looked tired.

Jane went off to prepare dinner and I stayed to talk with Dick—mostly about the stock market. "You know," Dick said, "I had a very simple investing strategy: only buy blue chips that pay a dividend and hold on to them—and always dividend reinvest. Of course, we needed to sell some stocks from time to time. Those damned horses are expensive. Do you know how much I've spent on them over the past twenty years? Huh? Do ya?"

"No, but I can imagine."

"*No*, you can't. How could you imagine? Do you know how many horses we've had? Do you know what we pay for Guenter and the training, flying the horses all over the world for horse shows and training with Klaus, and my God, the vet bills? Geez, the vet bills—we've had nothing but vet bills. Big ones. Some horse always seems to be lame."

Rather than trying to show that after a lifetime with horses and a four-year career managing international dressage teams, I did know what things cost, I said, "Well, I guess I could *only* imagine."

"Ten million dollars! We've spent ten million dollars over the past twenty years—and that doesn't include the cost of buying the horses. Oh no—buying the horses is not included. I'm not sure off-hand how much that would be. I know we've bought over a dozen horses—oh yeah, at least a dozen—at least. But I'll figure it out on the weekend and let you know. Geez. That's gunna be a doozie of a number."

After an hour of Dick peppering me with questions about the "who, what, where, when and hows" of the USEF and its operations, Jane called us to dinner. The smells from the kitchen had stoked my appetite and I enjoyed every bite of the meal. Jane was a fabulous cook.

The next morning, Jane had set the breakfast table with her finest Limoges China and Baccarat glasses and treated me to a spread worthy of the Plaza Hotel. By 9 a.m. Dick and Jane had loaded up the car and we were ready to head to Del Mar for the horse show.

As we were getting in the car, Jane said, "Now, dear—I'm sorry this is *only* a Lexus. I have owned two Rolls Royces, Dick and I have each had a Bentley, and Dick had an Aston Martin for a while—but he was too tall and couldn't get out of it easily. This is a limited-edition sedan with an additional thirteen inches of legroom in the back and only fifty-two were ever made. I trust you'll be comfortable." I was.

Early in the afternoon, Jane sought me out and said, "Gil, dear. I am so sorry to inconvenience you, but could you please do me a huge favor? Dick is exhausted and not feeling well. Might you drive him home and then come back to get me? I have some people I still need to talk to and can't leave yet."

The drive home started quietly, but after a few minutes, Dick wanted to share something with me. "Don't ever take your health for granted; being sick is no fun. I used to go all day with no problems. But not anymore. I have non-Hodgkin's lymphoma and it is no fun. They tried some chemo—it wasn't too bad; I kept my hair. Now I'm on some drug. Can't tell if it helps or not, but they say I'm not going to die from lymphoma. But geez I feel lousy. Woozy. That's how I feel: woozy. No, no fun. Never take your health for granted." At least I understood why Dick looked so tired.

I spent Saturday night at the Browns' and La Costa Limousine took me back to the airport on Sunday morning. As I was walking toward the airport entrance, I looked back at the car and thought, *This was fun. I would enjoy spending more time with them, and I think they enjoyed my company. I hope we can do it again.*

78

Smartest Man in the Room

My calendar was going to be full for the rest of the year. I scheduled training clinics and Mastery Courses in Atlanta, Los Angeles, Lexington, and Boston. And I had a unique opportunity that had come my way via a friend from the USEF.

It was a long-term project that would be based in Birmingham, Michigan, a suburb of Detroit. The founder of a start-up was developing a website catering to the horse community, and he was looking for people to join his leadership team. His name was Jett and my friend suggested I call him.

Jett was enthusiastic and full of promises during his pitch. He believed that with my business experience, credibility in the horse world, and extensive network of contacts, adding me to his team would ensure the backing of his private investors. I went to Michigan for a presentation to them.

The conference table seated twelve, and it was full. I had no idea who anyone was, or what role they played, but my job was to introduce myself to the group, talk about my experience in the business world and my time managing international equestrian sports, and sell them on the idea I would be an invaluable asset to the company—should it be funded.

Among all the unknown faces, one attendee sitting on the side of the room caught my attention and I was interested in hearing his introduction. He was a handsome man of about thirty in a crisp white dress shirt, with a full head of short-cropped brown hair, and a trendy three-day beard. Even slumped in his chair, he appeared to be at least six feet tall and had the build of a Navy SEAL. He was seated when I got there. Whatever was happening on his laptop was more interesting than what was going on in the room. At first glance, he appeared to be bored, but as the morning went on and everyone was making their introductions, I had the feeling he might be the smartest guy in the room.

Jett gave each person a quick set-up and then asked them to introduce themselves. "I'd like to introduce you to an associate of mine who is working on several projects with me," Jett said, pointing to the smartest guy in the room. "He is a tech genius and would be a valuable asset to the team for both developing the website and managing it once it is launched. Tony, would you like to introduce yourself?"

"Yeah. I'm a software developer and inventor. My partner and I are working on an algorithm for day trading that we'll market as a web-based app, and we've got some other projects in the works. I'm not really sure why I'm here today, except that Jett asked me to be."

When the presentations were over, the large group dispersed, and the investors stepped outside the conference room for a private meeting with Jett. Tony stayed behind and was there when Jett came back, grinning like the Cheshire Cat. "Well, guys—we did it. They gave me a guarantee for the first million dollars, and we are on our way! They said if you are on board, then they are on board. Looks like we have a company."

I assumed that meant if I accepted his offer to join the company, I would work closely with Tony—the man I knew so little about. When Jett finished with his proclamation, Tony looked away from him and glanced at me with a mischievous grin. I decided on the spot he was someone I could work with. Little did I know, he would become my closest friend.

79

The Club

My fun with Dick and Jane was just getting underway. When Jane learned I was heading out to California in March, she said, "Guenter is going to be showing our Grand Prix horse, UII, in Del Mar. Darling, would you be able to come that weekend and stay with us? We would love to have you back and it would help me tremendously to have you with me at the show. I'm not sure Dick will be able to come; things are still not great with his health." I accepted the invitation and arrived for another weekend of Jane's hospitality on Almaden Lane.

On the Monday morning after the horse show, Dick and Jane headed to Los Angeles and invited me to join them. Jane drove us on the two-hour trip with Dick in the front seat, reclined for a nap after reading his *Wall Street Journal*, and demanded there be silence in the car. He was having respiratory problems, and his "wooziness" was getting worse. His hearing was failing, and he was losing his sense of taste, but his biggest problem was fatigue. He did not seem to want to make the trip to Los Angeles, but he did not want to deprive Jane of the pleasure of spending a few days at her beloved California Club.

Located on Flower Street in the heart of the Los Angeles business district, The California Club was an exclusive social club that had been an icon in the city for more than a century. Membership was only possible through the invitation of current members, and the application process was rigorous. The Club's members were the "Who's Who" of southern California's business and professional communities and included people from the financial world like Charlie Munger and founding families like the Irvines. Jane thrived at the Club; it suited her to a tee. It was old-world elegance in an opulent setting.

Jane pulled into the ground floor garage and three uniformed attendants swarmed to the Lexus to open each of our doors.

"Hello, Mrs. Brown, how was your drive up?" asked an attendant.

"The traffic on the 5 was horrible but thank goodness we've made it in time for lunch. I'm starving!"

"Good to see you, Mrs. Brown—as always." As the attendant walked to the trunk Jane said to me, "That's Guatemala—it's not his real name, but that's what I call him. Every time he goes home to visit, he brings me back a pound of coffee. It's quite good."

While Guatemala loaded the bellman's cart, one of his associates was helping Dick out of the front seat and said, "Good morning, Mr. Brown. Good to see you. Did you have a pleasant ride?" Dick walked past him as if he didn't exist and made his way into the hallway.

The ground floor of the garage could hold about fifty cars and it was already filling up with the lunch crowd. Among the Bentleys, Porsches, Rolls Royces, and Jaguars, Jane's Lexus looked like the poor stepchild. The granite epoxy floor sparkled and seemed suitably luxurious for the livery it hosted—there was not a tire mark to be found.

The bellmen took the luggage to the overnight rooms on the fourth floor. We headed to the reception desk on the first floor, and as we stepped out of the elevator, the General Manager greeted us. Peter Schaub was tall and handsome. He appeared to be in his late thirties, with a full head of neatly combed, short brown hair, and a dark-grey suit perfectly tailored to his lean frame. Upon seeing us, he brought his feet together, clasped his hands behind his back, and tipped his head as if greeting royalty. "Welcome back to The California Club. It's always nice to see you. And this must be Mr. Merrick. It's nice to have you here. I hope you enjoy your stay."

"Mr. Merrick was the head of dressage for the United States and stays with us when he is in California. This is his first time at the Club, so I'm sure you will do all you can to make his visit special," Jane said.

"Of course we will, Mrs. Brown. That's what we do here."

Dick was fading and needed to sit. He lifted his right hand and slowly pulsed his extended fingers up and down to signal Jane it was time to stop talking and move along. I had seen the gesture before and understood it to be Dick's way of telling Jane to shut up—in fact, I had seen it often.

Dick had grown impatient while Jane and I went to get our room keys and had already gone upstairs when we got back to the elevators. He was in the suite and yelling at the bellman who had dared ask where to hang the suit bags. Jane promised a complete tour of the Club's seven floors after lunch when Dick would retire for a nap.

Lunch was in the third-floor dining room, where we sat at the Browns' regular table. A cluster of people approached to push in Jane's chair, fill water glasses, place a breadbasket in the center, deliver menus, and spread napkins on our laps. To no one in particular, Dick waved his hand and said, "Get those out of here. We don't need them." We would not be enjoying olive oil or balsamic vinegar with our bread.

In an instant, a tall Hispanic man in a tuxedo arrived at the table. "Mario," Jane said, "it is *freezing* in here. Can you call an engineer and have him warm up the room? Why must it always be so cold in here?"

"Yes, Mrs. Brown. Good to see you. Rios will be right over to take your order."

Jane started gazing about the room, in search of something. An older busser in a pressed grey jacket and black slacks was shuffling by the table and Jane waved to flag him down.

"Where is my iced tea? It is usually waiting on the table. I need a water glass with very little tea—only this much ..."—holding her thumb and forefinger a half-inch apart—"... and *lots* of ice. And you'll bring two lemons—the wrapped ones—and some sugar. Lots of sugar. Why is the sugar never on the table? Is Peter afraid someone will steal it?" The gentleman did not speak English, so he trotted off to find Rios.

I would learn Rios was always assigned to wait on the Browns. He was from Mexico, and although hard of hearing, he spoke better English than most of the servers and knew all the Browns' special requirements. He was already apologizing as he approached the table: "I'm sorry about the iced tea, Mrs. Brown. I will get it right away. Hello, Mr. Brown, would you like something to drink?"

"A Diet Coke. And I want that sandwich with the corned beef and turkey, but none of that white goop they put on it. And only one piece of bread—leave the top off—and don't toast it. And give me some potato salad, but not too cold. They always take it right out of the refrigerator and it's too cold." Looking at the breadbasket, he added under his breath, "But who cares anyway? I can't taste a damned thing."

Jane ordered a lobster salad—asking for about half of the customary ingredients to be left off—and made sure there would be extra thousand island dressing on the side. I ordered a fruit salad and some club soda.

As promised, Dick went to lie down after lunch and Jane gave me a tour of the Club. She knew the history of every room, on every floor, and had stories to tell about events they had attended in each of them.

The next evening, Mario greeted us and took us to our table in the main dining room as a piano and violin played in the corner. Dick and I wore the mandatory suit and tie and looked like everyone else. Jane had chosen her favorite Escada dress, Louboutin heels, four-strand pearls, and a broach with twenty-one diamonds that her father's good friend, Harry Winston, had given her on her twenty-first birthday. She did not look like everyone else. It was intentional.

While enjoying drinks and contemplating our first pass at the buffet, I realized how much I had always enjoyed the sophistication and charm of old-world social clubs. I felt at home there and sensed the California Club was a place I would spend a lot of time. Lots, and lots of time.

80

Red Tracton's

Come July, Jane decided we would celebrate our birthdays together.

"Gil, dear, we thought we would go to Red Tracton's tonight. It's Sunday, which means they have fried chicken. It's a *whole* fried chicken! It's the most wonderful fried chicken we've ever had. I don't know how they make it, but there isn't a bit of grease in it."

I could not imagine Jane—who would be dressed in a St. John knit outfit and bedecked with jewels—picking apart a fried chicken carcass, and I was looking forward to seeing it. Tony had gotten to know Jane and suggested I snap a photo to document the event. After Jane told me the bartender had a heavy hand, it seemed like an entertaining way to celebrate.

Tracy Tracton had inherited the restaurant from her father, Red. It was located across from the Del Mar Racetrack and had a decades-long reputation for its rowdy sports bar with lots of single ladies, generous drinks, and large portions of quality food. It was a regular haunt for the racing crowd and was always busy.

Still daylight when we stepped inside, it took a minute before my eyes adjusted to the darkness. The sound from the bar and the dining rooms was deafening. The acoustics in the dining rooms seemed to amplify the noise from the bar, so guests needed to raise their voices to be heard above the crowd. I couldn't believe Dick and Jane enjoyed eating there.

Tracy was at the desk when we walked in. "Hello, Dick. Hi, Jane. Your table's ready and Zandra will be taking care of you tonight. Enjoy."

Dick went straight to the banquette to claim his regular seat, and Jane stopped on the way to talk to an acquaintance. I was waiting for Jane to finish and saw a tall woman with jet-black hair, pulled tightly back from her face and braided at the side, heading toward Jane. Her black shirt and slacks suggested she was a server, and the large hair clip with rhinestones and a feather suggested she had some flair. She stood behind Jane until the conversation ended and then tapped her on the shoulder.

"Oh—Zandra!" Jane said. "I didn't see you. How are you, darling? This is Mr. Merrick, from Michigan. He also drinks *lévriers*, so get cracking—we both could use a drink—and, of course, I have the juice in my bag. Dick will have a Diet Coke. And I hope you got here early tonight so you had time to pluck a chicken for us." That seemed to be a standing joke.

Dick was studying his menu when we sat down and he barely acknowledged our arrival. He had napped for most of the afternoon but appeared exhausted. His health had taken a turn for the worse during the short time I had been away.

"That was Zandra," Jane said. "We have known her for almost twenty years. She used to be our server at the Inn at Rancho Santa Fe until ... what ... about ten years ago, Dick?" He gave a disinterested nod. "We adore her. She is always pleasant and has a wonderful sense of humor. Did you see her hair clip? It's tame compared to some that she wears."

Zandra returned with two tall water glasses, filled with ice, a white wine glass, also filled with ice, a rocks glass filled with Kettle One vodka (no ice), and a rocks glass filled with green olives. "Thank you, dear. Oh good—you remembered to take the pimentos out of the olives. And I have the juice right here. They squeezed it for me at the Club on Friday, so it's fresh."

And with that, Jane filled her wine glass with Kettle One and topped it with Ruby Red grapefruit juice. Through the course of the evening, she would alternately add ice, Kettle One, and juice to her wine glass; the olives were for snacking. Jane told me that although vodka and grapefruit juice was called a "greyhound" in the U.S., she had tried her first one after an exhausting afternoon in Monte Carlo when the bartender suggested she might find a *lévrier* refreshing. From that day forward she refused to let anyone in her presence refer to her drink by its common name: a "greyhound" would always be a *lévrier*.

Zandra had brought me a large rocks glass, filled with both ice and vodka, and I had to take a large sip to make room for the juice. The bartender was indeed heavy-handed, and that suited me just fine. The second drink went down as smoothly as the first and I enjoyed both my buzz and the sight of Jane delicately picking up each drumstick and thigh and nibbling away at the fried batter. The oil dripping off her chin made lie to her claim the fried chicken was greaseless.

Over the next ten years, I would eat hundreds of pieces of that chicken and can attest that it never came in a grease-free version. But I could always look forward to Zandra's doting service and bottomless *lévriers*—Tracton's would become our Happy Place.

81
End of an Era

Three months after my July visit, I got a call from Jane. Dick had woken in the night with debilitating abdominal pain, and she had taken him to the University of California San Diego (UCSD) hospital's emergency room in La Jolla. During emergency surgery, they removed five tumors from his kidneys. They had gone undetected in previous ultrasounds.

"Thank heavens they were able to remove them all," Jane said. "They think they got everything, and Dick should be OK, but he is going to be here for a while. He has all sorts of tubes attached to him and one of them is a morphine drip. He is pretty much knocked out, but the pain is mostly gone. I guess that morphine really does the trick."

"And how are *you* doing?"

"Well, I'm not leaving his side. I don't trust any of these doctors, and the nurses are as cold as fish. I called Chris [the housekeeper], and she is bringing me some undergarments, my toothbrush, and more makeup. I'll bathe standing in a plastic tub in the bathroom. I don't care how long he's here—I'm not leaving."

"I'm sorry I'm not there. I'm on my way to Rancho Murietta and then I go to Merced for another clinic. I really can't cancel any of those trips."

"There's nothing you can do while Dick's in the hospital. They think it might be a week before he can go home. I *hate* hospitals."

"Please call and let me know how things are going."

Four days later, she called. It was not the call I expected.

"Well, it happened," Jane blurted. "Dick just fired Guenter."

"Was Guenter at the hospital?"

"No, he phoned. I told him Dick was resting and couldn't talk, but he insisted—you know how Guenter can be. I could only hear what Dick was saying, but they argued about how many grooms we should have. Can you believe it? He called Dick after four days in the hospital to argue about *that*?"

"What did Dick say?"

"He told him he was lying in a hospital bed and did not want to talk about it. Darling, he's been on morphine for four days. What the *hell* was Guenter thinking?"

"Did Dick give him an answer?"

"Yes. He said he had had enough—of everything—and told him he was fired. They've been arguing a lot recently and this was the final straw. Actually, that day in Del Mar when he told Dick I was a 'fucking bitch' and threatened to quit, that was really the turning point. So, Dick just hung up and now he is upset."

"When did this all happen?"

"I said—he *just* hung up. But I know Dick; once he makes up his mind, that's it. He is done with Guenter. *We* are done."

* * *

Dick stayed in the hospital for twelve days—his respiratory problems and fatigue had complicated his recovery. After a couple of weeks at home, he and Jane found a private farm in Rancho Santa Fe to board their three retired horses, and UII.

Kelly was a trainer at the farm and agreed to ride UII. She was not a dressage rider, but since UII was now retired from competition, he only needed to be exercised every day to keep fit. I drove to the farm with Dick and Jane and could see that their horses were going to be well cared for. It was a beautiful farm, and only twenty minutes from Almaden Lane, so they could come out on the weekends to give them treats and thank them for winning so many championships for our country.

After more than two decades together, news of Guenter's separation from the Browns spread quickly. Jane gave an interview to the publisher of *Dressage-News.com*—a leading website for international dressage coverage—and gave a quote with a passage from Ecclesiastes: "'For everything there is a season, and a time for every matter under heaven, a time to be born, and a time to die' ... and a time to part."

82

Falling Out

For twenty years, Dick and Jane had spent the last week of December and the first week of January at the J.W. Marriott Camelback Resort in Scottsdale. There were over 450 privately owned casitas on the 125-acre property, nestled between Camelback and Mummy mountains. Dick and Jane had discovered the resort when Dick was traveling from Denver to sell costume jewelry in Arizona, and they fell in love with it.

The owners of their favorite casita, 558, made it available to them every year for the holidays. Dick and Jane would also visit around Easter, and work in a trip in the fall, depending on what horse events were going on. Casita 558 was on the far side of the property, away from pedestrian traffic, and overlooked a vegetable garden that supplied many of the resort's restaurants. It was the most peaceful place on the property.

There had been an incident with a TSA agent at the Los Angeles airport: the underwire in Jane's bra had set off the metal detector, and after several unsuccessful attempts to locate the offending metal object with a wand, Jane ripped open her top and exposed her bra so the agent could see what the problem was. Dick and Jane vowed to never fly commercially again. They had been spoiled after flying in their friend Gwendolyn's Citation CJ5, Hawker 400, and Gulfstream jets and reimbursed Gwendolyn for the planes' operating expenses in exchange for their use. They always took the CJ5 on their one-hour flight to Scottsdale, which allowed Jane to bring enough luggage and Christmas decorations to fill a small house. She also brought a large duffle with an entire portable kitchen—electric fry pan, coffee makers, dinnerware, Tupperware, cutlery—and several thermal bags loaded with frozen food she could heat up on nights they didn't feel like going out to eat.

Dick and Jane invited me to join them there for a few days after Christmas. I flew into Phoenix and moved into the casita next door to theirs, casita 559. I stayed for three nights and joined them for their return trip to Carlsbad. The bellmen loaded their many things into the rental car, and we headed off to the private air terminal at the Scottsdale airport. The CJ5's pilots were at the bottom of the steps, waiting to greet us.

Everyone knew the departure drill—Dick and Jane had flown often with the crew—and fifteen minutes later the tail was loaded, the door was shut, and we were on our way. After demanding silence from Jane and me, Dick lay back and slept through the entire flight.

When we got home, I offered to help unpack the car and Jane said, "Oh, honey—don't bother. The houseman will be here tomorrow, and he can do all that. Go relax and we can meet for drinks at 5:30—I'm *sure* we will need one."

La Costa Limousine took me to the airport the next morning and I went back to Detroit. During the next seven years, I would take more than fifty flights to and from Scottsdale for what would be over three hundred nights in Casita 559. A new era had just begun.

* * *

I was back in California in June to conduct more clinics and stayed with Dick and Jane over the weekend. On Sunday morning, I went into the kitchen to greet Jane; Dick was in his den.

"Good morning, darling. I have a favor to ask. Dick has told me many times recently that he is ...well ... upset with you. He has asked you several times if you would come to the stables and ride UII for him. He loves that horse and would really like to see him strut his stuff. Kelly is a lovely rider, but she only jumps. Dick doesn't have any interest in watching her ride—he wants to see UII with a good dressage rider. He keeps saying, 'Every time I ask Gil to ride UII, he has some excuse not to.' He says you always have your riding clothes when you are here, and you can always make time to go to your clinics, so he doesn't understand why you can't make time to ride UII."

I had been dreading this conversation.

Guenter had been telling his friends in the dressage community I had had him fired because I wanted to ride the Browns' horses. In his telling, if it had not been for me, he would have ridden at the 2012 London Olympics. UII had been at the top of the ranking list and would have most likely been named to the team with Guenter as his rider—if Guenter had not been fired.

To make sure no one ever had a reason to say, "I heard Gil Merrick rode UII the other day," I had always made up an excuse when Dick asked me to ride.

However, like Jane, Dick was used to getting what he wanted, and I wasn't giving it to him. I knew he was upset about this, and I wondered when things would come to a head.

"May I suggest something?" Jane said. "Why don't you go into the den and ask Dick for Kelly's phone number? You can say you had been thinking about arranging a time you could join us at the farm and ride UII. I think that would make him happy, and he wouldn't suspect I had said anything to you."

I didn't like the idea because Dick would think I was finally going to do what he wanted. I had no intention of ever riding UII, but I thought I could at least ask for Kelly's number and then continue to make up excuses for not calling her or coming to the farm. I was leaving on Monday, so there was no risk of anything happening that day, and from then on, I could plan to only visit Dick and Jane when they were at the Club in Los Angeles.

Dick was behind his desk reading the *New York Times* when I walked in. "Good morning. Dick, could you give me Kelly's phone number? I don't seem to have it, and I thought I might give her a call on one of these visits and see if she could schedule a ride for me—you know, when you and Jane go to see the horses."

"Now? *Now* you get around to asking for her number? First of all, *you* don't need her number—I can *tell* her what to do. After all the times I've asked you to ride UII—after all the excuses you've made—*now* you want to call her? All I asked was one small favor—ride my horse. Everything we do for you—staying here, the dinners at Tracton's, going to the Club, an expensive room at Camelback—and you pretend to be our friend? You're not a friend—if you were, you would do something nice for me. You ride everybody else's horses, but you won't ride mine? No, you're not a friend." Dick was yelling and had stood up from his desk to meet me eye to eye.

"Dick, I'm sorry, but ..."

"No! You're *not* sorry. If you were sorry, you would have ridden my damned horse. But no, you couldn't be bothered. You were too busy riding everyone else's horses—everyone's but mine. Some friend!"

Jane had come in and said, "Dick, please calm down. Gil is only trying to ..."

"I *won't* calm down! You are always trying to help him out—always looking out for Gil. How about looking out for me for once? Or don't I count anymore? Maybe Gil's more important than me."

Jane was crying. "Dick, don't be like that. Why does everything have to be so hard with you? Why are you always so angry about everything? I can't stand it anymore. You are just so negative these days!"

Dick came within inches of my face, and we locked eyes. "See? See the problems you cause? That's all you bring into this house—problems."

"Well, then that is certainly easy to fix. I'll simply leave—and then the problems will go out the door *with* me: problems solved."

"NO! You can't leave!" Jane bellowed. "I count on you too much to help *me*. I have problems too, you know. Dick—just stop it! Stop doing this."

"Well then—maybe Gil *is* more important to you than me."

At that point, I had had enough. "The last thing I want is to be a problem, and obviously, I am one. I'll change my flight and you can sort things out yourselves. It is clearly best if I leave."

"For good!? You can't!" Jane was in a state of panic and Dick's anger had turned his face a shade of red I had never seen on a man before; I was afraid he might have a heart attack.

"I'm going to stay in my room for the day and let you work this out. I'm sure I can get a flight out this evening. If not, I'll stay at the airport and get a flight in the morning. Either way, it's best if I leave."

Dick and Jane went to their bedroom and shut the door. I called Tony to ask for his advice, and a few minutes later Jane came to my room. "I'm sorry, dear. I don't know why Dick is being like this. Please, don't leave today. Ride with us to the Club tomorrow like we planned. We can have lunch together and then you can leave for LAX."

Jane made dinner that night, but Dick did not join us. The drive to the Club on Monday morning was awkward, but because Dick had always demanded silence and slept the whole way, it wasn't hard to avoid conversation. He never made eye contact during lunch and barely spoke to Jane or the servers. At 12:45, I said my car was waiting, and excused myself to get my bag from my room and head downstairs. As I walked past, I put my hand on his shoulder and said, "Goodbye, Dick. Take care." That was the last time I ever spoke to Dick Brown.

83

To New York With Dick

"We've lost Dick!" It was September 5th, and I was pouring my second drink when Jane called. Before I could respond, she said: "We were at the doctor's office—another damned doctor—and the nurse came to get us. Dick was breathing hard—he'd been having more trouble—but he couldn't get up. The nurse got the doctor and they put him in an ambulance—I thought he was having a heart attack. So, I left the car there and went in the ambulance. I asked the person how long it was going to take to get him to the hospital—I *insisted* on UCSD—and she said I didn't need to worry about it. She said, 'He's not going to make it.' My God—can you believe she said that to me? They got him there, but she was right. He died shortly after he went in. Dick is gone."

Her friend Bonnie was there when Jane got the news. I took the morning flight to San Diego and arrived at the house before noon.

I expected Jane to be an emotional wreck; she was not. She was in full "take charge and get things done" mode. Like an officer commanding her troops, she was working the phones to plan Dick's funeral. Dick's grandfather had built a family mausoleum at Woodlawn Cemetery in the Bronx. Dick's grandparents and parents, plus Dick's aunt and her two husbands, were interned there. The mausoleum had been built for eight, so Jane had been told either she or Dick would have to be placed in the floor. It looked like the floor would be hers; she had always resented the aunt's second husband for taking one of their places.

Jane's first order of business was to get Dick's body flown to New York for the burial. "I talked to Gwendolyn, but she doesn't want to let me use her Hawker; she can't stand the thought of having a dead body in the cabin. I told her Dick was *not* going to be treated like a piece of freight and he was *not* going in the belly of the plane. So, I called John."

John was a close friend and owned a horse transport company. For two decades he had driven Dick and Jane's horses around the West Coast for horse shows and flights from LAX. He was married to the daughter of a billionaire (whose father had used John's company to transport his many racehorses), and they always flew in private jets.

"John was a sweetheart. He said he would talk to his father-in-law and see what he could do. If John can manage to get Bill Gates's daughter's horses wherever they need to go, he can get Dick to New York—and *not* in the cargo hold!"

John found a charter company willing to carry Dick's corpse in the passenger cabin. The Cessna 680 Sovereign had a banquette at the rear and seating for six, so it would do the trick. All the other details were in place, and we planned to depart from the Palomar Airport in Carlsbad on the following Thursday.

John had partnered with Owen, Jane's household manager of twenty years, to make sure everything went like clockwork at the airport. They needed to get Dick's body through the small cabin door, strapped into the banquette, and covered with blankets before Jane boarded. I was at home with Jane, waiting for their call to say the deed had been done, so I didn't see the operation, but according to John, it had not been easy. John and Owen were coming with us to New York, so they stayed on the plane with Dick.

Two of Jane's closest friends—Bonnie and Patty—had met us at the house and would join us on the trip.

After getting the "all-clear" from John, we piled into the Lexus and pulled up to the plane about fifteen minutes later. Jane got to the top of the steps and froze. She had spent a week feverishly managing all the details for the burial in New York and had focused only on that. But seeing the form of Dick's body lying on the banquette, covered in blankets, brought home the reality of the situation and she fell apart. John and Owen were in the cabin when we arrived, so they helped her to her seat. She insisted on sitting at the rear of the cabin, across from the banquette, so she could be with Dick.

The Frank E. Campbell Funeral Chapel was on Madison Avenue at 81st Street and known as the "Undertaker to the Stars." Rudolph Valentino, Jacqueline Kennedy Onassis, Judy Garland, and Joan Crawford had all been "clients." All of Dick's family, and all of Jane's family, had been served by the home and they knew Jane's family well.

After assuring the director she wanted the best of everything and that money was no object, Jane selected a handsome casket with a simple silk lining, absent of any frills or lace. When we returned to the office she said, "Now I want you to start a file for me—for my funeral—and I want *exactly* what Dick is having.

If you must order my coffin now and put it in storage, that's fine—I'll pay for it now—but I want the same thing. You won't have to store it for long, I don't plan to live much longer. I want to be with Dick."

Jane had booked us all rooms five blocks away at the Carlyle Hotel. She had reserved a table in their main dining room, and after drinks in the bar (I had never seen Jane drink a *lévrier* so fast), we went to dinner. It was an elegant dining room with fabulous food and world-class service, and as we ate and drank our way through the evening, I could see Jane transforming. She was in her element: playing the gracious hostess, entertaining in a lavish setting, and being the center of attention. Without Dick tapping his hand up and down to silence her or create tension for everyone by treating the servers poorly, Jane was able to relax and take back control of her life. And everyone else's.

The casket was already laid upon a stand in front of the mausoleum when our limousine pulled up and the six of us got out and encircled it. There was no religious service, no music, and no eulogy. Jane stared at the casket and was alone with her thoughts. After a few minutes, she went inside to make sure the shelf under the stained-glass window had been prepared to receive a small bronze statue of a horse Dick had always admired. She inspected the area where Dick's casket would be placed, as well as her future resting place in the floor, and after declaring everything to be in order, we left for the airport.

Jane's relief was palpable. The flight attendant served us lunch after takeoff and afterwards we all got up to sit with Jane; the banquette had been freed up for living passengers. We slipped a bit of vodka into our drinks and let Jane hold court and entertain us with her stories. Five hours later we arrived at Palomar.

It was time for Jane to begin her new life as a widow, and I was soon to find out I would be with her, every step of the way.

84

First Invitations

Thanksgiving came right on the heels of Dick's funeral, and it was Jane's first holiday in sixty years without him. She had always hosted lavish dinners at her home. Jane declared she would never eat another meal at the formal dining room table—without Dick it would be too hard—so she hosted her friends at Red Tracton's. It was a grand affair with exquisite centerpieces, multiple side dishes she had made and brought from home, and lots of toasts with her favorite champagne, Dom Perignon.

Jane was the happiest I had seen her in years. She was like a bird that had been freed from its cage and she was able to shine again. As Dick's health declined, Jane had become his full-time nurse. After a lifetime of having everything done for her, the tables had turned, and she had grown miserable. This was a new lease on life.

I stayed through the weekend and rode to Los Angeles with her on Monday morning. The driver was dropping me off at LAX before taking Jane to the Club; I needed to be back in Michigan for work. While stalled in traffic on the 105, waiting to get into the airport, Jane dropped her head.

"Sweetheart, I can't stand to have you go. You have no idea how much I hate being alone. My entire life, I was never alone. Our house was filled with my parents, my sisters, and all the servants, and there was always something going on. Then Dick and I worked together for thirty years—I traveled with him *all* the time, and I *ran* the showroom here—we were never apart. And then the horses! My God—twenty-three years going everywhere. I was busy all the time and always had people around. Now ... nothing. No one. I'm completely alone and I hate it. You have no idea what it's like to be alone. Do you *have* to go back to Michigan?"

I would hear that plea dozens of times in the coming years, and my answer was always some version of the one I gave that day: "Yes, I do. Things are really coming together at the company and next year is going to be big for us. Our investors have a lot of money at stake now and it looks like we're headed in the right direction. And remember, if the company is successful and gets sold, I make a lot of money. I'm only fifty-six and I couldn't think about retiring now."

"Why not? You can always quit and come live with me. I certainly have enough money."

"Well, it's not only the money; I really enjoy working. I *have* to work—it's all I've ever done—and I'd go crazy if I didn't stay busy."

"Darling, we could take trips ... to Camelback, or Europe, or Canada. I want to stay busy too. Those investors put a lot of pressure on you and Tony—wouldn't you like to get away from that?"

"Not yet—not right now. I like what I'm doing, and I want to stick this out." I would soon learn that my response had gone in one ear and out the other.

* * *

Four weeks later I was back with Jane. She had thought she would never spend Christmas and New Year's at Camelback again. She said that of all the things she would miss with Dick gone, she would miss Camelback the most. Being someone who always wants to please, I offered to take her. I said it would be an incredibly hard visit the first time—everyone would want to know what had happened to Dick—and although each conversation would be rough, once she got through each one, she would never have to have them again.

My first job was to orchestrate the loading of the plane: any bags with food or liquids went in the cabin; everything else could go in the tail. Had I not packed everything myself, I would not have believed how much luggage we needed for a two-week trip. Nothing about traveling with Jane was "simple." Tony said it reminded him of an Egyptian queen bringing all her belongings for the afterlife.

Our rental car was waiting planeside in Scottsdale and the scene from Palomar played out in reverse. I was dispatched to the reception desk when we pulled into the resort and Jane stayed in the car. When I returned, she had gotten out and was surrounded by three bellmen who knew her well. Of course, they had asked, "Where's Dick?" Jane's answer evoked hugs and warm condolences, and she was firmly implanted in the center of their attention. Although the experience was emotional, Jane craved drama, attention, and empathy, and had managed the interaction just fine. Since it had gone so well, Jane committed to memory the answer she had given the bellmen and repeated it dozens of times throughout our two-week stay.

At the end of our visit, we were having dinner at the Capital Grille in the Biltmore Plaza when Jane said, "Sweetheart, I can't thank you enough for getting me through all of this. It will be different when we come back, I promise. I could never have done this without you, but I did it, so let's plan to come back for Easter. Should we plan on two weeks?"

"I'll need to see what my travel schedule looks like for work—we've got a lot going on."

"Well, I'll go ahead and book it for the weeks before and after Easter—I want to make sure we get 558 and 559. I'm sure you can make it work. Are you going to have the lobster bisque again? I brought some of our good sherry—theirs is lousy."

And with that, we jumped into our first dinner in the next series of hundreds that would be enjoyed in booth 43 at the Biltmore Center Capital Grille.

85

Let's Take a Trip!

Only Jane Brown could make a week-long trip on a chartered yacht an unenjoyable event. I had already learned that relaxing activities—like going to the spa at Camelback for nail treatments—could become stressful events, but this yachting trip took things to a new level.

Jane had gotten to know Tony well during our many business trips to California, and she adored him. She had assigned him to find a yacht—no smaller than a hundred feet—that we could charter for the first week in July when the California Club was closed, and Jane and I would celebrate our birthdays: mine on the third and hers on the ninth. We had ruled out sailing from Vancouver to Alaska—she had already done that with her friend Jacquie Mars—and she had no interest in going someplace as foreign as Mexico, so we departed from a California port to cruise at our leisure along the coast. It took Tony several weeks, but he found the perfect vessel docked in Huntington Beach: the *Belisarius*. Just short of a hundred feet (it was ninety-one feet, ten inches, and Jane had approved) and equipped with a crew of four, it was ours for a week.

A young cabin attendant was there to satisfy our every need, along with our chef, a graduate of the Culinary Institute of America. Since Jane was unsure whether she would enjoy his style of cooking, she brought food for us. For weeks, Jane and I had cooked her favorite dishes, packed them in Seal-A-Meal bags, and then squirreled them away in the freezer. We brought home food from Tracton's and the Club and added it to the stockpile. When La Costa Limousine dropped us off at the pier, I could see the look of confusion on the chef's face when he realized half of our bags contained food. We came on board, unpacked, and Jane entertained herself by telling the crew her many, many stories.

We left the pier that afternoon and headed north, but since the captain didn't have a firm itinerary (Jane thought it would be fine to "wing it" and figure out what we wanted to do once we departed), we dropped anchor about twenty miles north of Malibu and settled in for the night. The chef prepared a gourmet meal for the crew while Jane and I dined on frozen leftovers. We had brought plenty of juice, and Kettle One, so the evening started with some melted brie and cocktails and I instructed our attendant to make sure I got extra vodka in my drinks. The tantalizing smells coming from the kitchen were torturing me—and it took everything I had, buoyed by the vodka, to pretend I was enjoying myself.

A noisy generator, powering the yacht, kept Jane awake all night. She was especially grumpy in the morning—the sound of the waves crashing on the bow had also disturbed her—and as we sipped coffee on the deck (made, of course, in the special coffee maker we had brought with us), Jane asked if we could dock somewhere with a power hookup so we wouldn't need the generator. The captain radioed Santa Barbara and reserved a slip in a prime location at the head of the harbor. Jane loved it and decided we would spend the entire trip moored there.

Except for a day trip for whale watching (we saw several whales, but Jane lost interest after seeing the first breech), we never moved. Jane emerged mid-morning in slacks, heels, and a casual top—made up and bejeweled—and lounged around the indoor dining area. The sun was too bright for her to sit outside on the deck, so she busied herself inside telling endless stories to the crew. We watched a movie after lunch, took a nap, and watched another movie after dinner. I drank a lot of vodka.

On our way back to Huntington Beach, I stared out at the ocean and thought about what had transpired over the past few years. Jane was enjoying life again after Dick's death, and I had become her escape from boredom and loneliness. I was in California at least once a month and she had gotten used to my company on the weekends at home and at the Club during the week. Before Dick died, they had secured a permanent lease on their suite at the Club, and after my first few visits, Jane took out a lease on a suite for me—a few doors down the hall from hers—to ensure I would be comfortable there and want to visit.

We planned to take a trip to Canada over Labor Day and stay at the California Club's sister, the Vancouver Club. Then Jane scheduled us to spend a week at the Amangani Resort in Jackson Hole. A two-week stay at Camelback for Christmas, another two weeks during Easter, and two more in the fall were permanently etched onto Jane's calendar. And she had suggested we spend our next birthdays at Lake Louise in Banff, Canada—a place she had always wanted to visit. A three-hour flight in a private jet, a dedicated car and driver for a week's stay, and six nights in a penthouse suite at the Fairmont Château Lake Louise, should have been something to look forward to. But I had traveled enough with

Jane to know it would be a week of indentured servitude—an endless series of minor tasks performed in service of her needs for comfort and indulgence—and my expectations did not go unfulfilled.

It felt like Jane was becoming addicted—to me. The more I was with her, the more she wanted me there. She thought I was a fabulous travel companion—able to execute all the logistics for any trip (I had no idea taking teams to the Pan American and Olympic Games had been my training ground)—and she was thrilled that I "fit in so well" at the Club.

I wondered where all this was heading. I could feel myself becoming anxious and I wondered if I had built a trap from which I would not escape. Jane demanded I phone her every day—ostensibly to make sure I was OK—and would panic if she did not hear from me. I had to give her an exact time I would call, and if I was more than three minutes late, she would phone as many times as she needed until she reached me. If she couldn't, she would phone Tony until he tracked me down and ensured I would drop what I was doing to call her. They were long calls—rarely less than an hour—and on the weekends, she would call me several times each day to ramble on about nothing. Jane was bored and lonely.

Eventually, I was in California almost every other week: spending weekends with Jane, running endless errands during the day, and going to Tracton's for dinner. Monday mornings we made the two-hour drive with La Costa Limousine to the Club, and after five days of donning a jacket and tie for meals, on Fridays we came back to the house. Throughout every car ride, I listened to the same stories about each landmark that served as a visual trigger, and acted as if I was hearing them for the first time. I wondered if her memory was failing. I had researched the symptoms of dementia, and Jane was showing many of them. Her personality was also changing.

Jane was becoming more demanding and impatient and complained nonstop about ... everything. She was in a permanent state of low-grade upset that erupted into full-blown anger with the slightest misstep by anyone: La Costa Limousine drivers (they had developed an in-house roster of all the chauffeurs who refused to drive her), cashiers, the butcher, her hairdresser, other cars on the road, and especially—anyone with the misfortune of being on the other end of the phone.

Jane was going through life with the ludicrous expectation that everything would always be perfect in her world; people would always give her exactly what she wanted when she wanted it. It was an expectation borne from a lifetime of privilege and entitlement—the only life she had ever known. Everything she wanted could be had with money, and since she felt entitled to have everything go her way, anything that did not, upset her.

The only person who could do no wrong was me; she told me so a hundred times a week. She was never short with me, never agitated by anything I said or did, and thanked me profusely for every little task that made her happy. I had learned all her likes and dislikes, her quirks, and habits, and I anticipated her needs before she voiced them. She was predictable, which made my job easy, but I felt my patience would wane, and I wondered what I would do when it ran out.

86
Can We Talk?

By the summer of 2014, things were charging full speed ahead at my company. We had long since stopped focusing exclusively on the equestrian market for our sales. Our software platform was being used by multinational equipment manufacturers, hospital networks, a global bank, and an international training company that had named us as one of its technology partners. They had an office in London where Tony and I were scheduled to meet with their management team at the end of the month, so I reconnected with my friend Mary Gober.

Mary was giving a presentation at the Institute of Directors—a membership organization that served London's elite business leaders—and invited us to attend. Her company, MGI Learning, had become a global leader in transformational development and our coaching platform was a potential fit for them.

Mary was greeting the attendees when we arrived. She made her way over to welcome me with a beaming smile and a hug so heartfelt, it almost brought me to tears. For the next two hours, I watched her in front of the room, presenting to the group of about twenty-five in a way that was familiar to me after two decades of delivering Mastery Concepts programs. Mary was the most brilliant and effective trainer I had ever met and watching her made me profoundly aware that I was no longer a trainer in the world of organizational development; I felt I had become nothing more than a salesman, and it was depressing.

We were getting a foothold in the training industry and had been successful in selling our products, but nothing was fulfilling about that; there was no opportunity to be a Catalyst for Growth in my role as a salesman and I was longing to do something as dynamic and exciting as what I was watching Mary do. Although I retained the title of Chief Operating Officer, my role had cemented itself around "business development." Tony was running the company and its operations; what it needed from me was revenues.

Tony and I enjoyed a long lunch with Mary in the club dining room and we laid out our next steps for meeting with her team. When we said goodbye, I was sad to be walking away from our inspiring day together and our rekindled friendship. I left thinking about the long slog that lay ahead in my new world as a full-time salesman, absent of any genuine sense of fulfillment but filled with the ever-growing pressure from our investors to perform.

My depression was deeper than usual after our day with Mary, and I needed to talk. I had traveled with Tony over the past five years to dozens of cities. After that much time together, we were no longer only colleagues; we had become good friends. We had adopted the practice of taking morning walks in whatever city we were visiting before heading off to our meetings. We were staying at the Doubletree Hotel on Bayswater Road, adjacent to Hyde Park, and struck off shortly after sunrise the next morning for a tour of the park. Tony is a man of few words; he will speak when spoken to—and his efficiency with words is remarkable—but if he is interested in what you have to say, he is the world's best listener. Fortunately, he cared about what I had to say.

Tony and I walked for more than an hour and I shared some stories from my past: stories about my sexual abuse from Joe; my failed relationships with Alexandra and Diane; growing up with an alcoholic father and a depressed mother; having a lifetime dream to go to the Olympics and the disappointment that followed once I had; and tales about Australia and Miguel and how my hero had fallen. Tony asked a few insightful questions, but he mostly listened— empathetically and with what seemed like a deep understanding of what my emotional struggles were.

When I got back to my room and was changing for our meetings that day, I realized I didn't have anyone else I could open up to and share my most intimate thoughts with. That's what friends are for, I thought, and no one could have a better friend than Tony. They say you only need one good friend in life, and if I was to count Tony as mine, I had all I needed.

* * *

My next trip was to give a clinic at Silver Bell Barn in California's Central Valley. Miguel had introduced me to Cindy Bell several years back and asked if I could continue to train her and her students; his calendar in the U.S. and Europe was filled and he no longer had time.

One evening after dinner, Cindy and I reminisced about the problems we had both had managing Miguel when he was drinking. She was happy to tell me

Miguel was doing much better and spending a lot of time in Portugal, teaching clinics, and sharing his classical training techniques with like-minded students of Nuno Oliveira's. Miguel's son, Joseph, often traveled with him, and they were both in Modesto that week, a short drive from Cindy's.

The number I had for Miguel from sixteen years ago was still in service and we had dinner the next night. Now in his twenties, Joseph was six when I had left Australia. I believe Latin men have a special reverence for their sons, and Miguel had always been a proud father. Their bond was deep, and I was happy they brought so much joy to each other's lives. It was good to see Miguel healthy and thriving. I was glad we could spend the evening together, not talking about the past, but rather enjoying casual conversation and sharing company. I left with a feeling of closure; we had gone through a lot together, and not all of it had been good. Miguel had made a profound impact on my life as a horseman, and I would forever be grateful for that.

About a year later, Cindy would call to let me know Miguel had died of cancer, and when his death was imminent, he had written a farewell letter to all his students and friends—a copy of which I keep inside his book. It was a privilege to have spent so many hours with Miguel, in my camping trailer, on his property, transcribing his articles for *The Horse Magazine* that became the foundation for his book. He was a remarkable man and I doubt there will ever be another Master of Classical Equitation to fill his shoes.

87

Breaking Point

Easter was a holiday I had always looked forward to—it beckoned a new spring, and its message of resurrection was uplifting. However, in April of 2017 I was with Jane at Camelback and, as much as I should have been enjoying it, the entire day depressed me. I went to bed having had too much Dom Perignon and too many *lévriers*.

I got up early and somewhere around 9 a.m. the drama next door unfolded. The living room wall separated Jane's casita from my room, and I could hear every word of her phone conversations; the walls were not especially thin—she was especially loud. She was phoning her CPA, the manager of her bank in Carlsbad, and her financial advisor at Merrill Lynch, demanding to know, immediately, exactly how much she was worth. She wanted to make some changes to her will and she wanted to know how much money she was dealing with. Her assets were divided among many accounts and their value fluctuated with the markets, so she was unable to get an immediate answer—the original source of her frustration and anger.

Next, the switch on her reading lamp seemed to be broken so she called "At Your Service" to demand an engineer be sent to her room immediately, and they had put her on hold. When she got through, she let loose her fury and then "asked" for some new towels to be brought to the room along with several boxes of Kleenex. While she took turns screaming at anybody she could get to talk to her, there was a knock at her door. Thinking it was the engineer, she called for him to come in. It was a Hispanic housekeeper who did not speak English, and since Jane had the "Do Not Disturb" sign perennially taped to the door, the housekeeper usually would not come in. Jane verbally abused the poor woman—angry screaming translates well into every language—and then returned to the phone.

I listened to the histrionics coming through the wall until I couldn't stand it anymore and headed up the hill for a workout at the spa's gym. I stopped at the bench by the front door and called Tony.

Tony and I talked every day, even if we had no business matters to discuss. Tony recognized that spending so much time with Jane had become a problem for me. Having been around her often, he understood how stressful it could be. I was falling into a deep depression, and he knew it. Tony had become adept at talking me off the ledge when the stress became overwhelming, and for a man of few words, he had done a lot of talking over the past months.

"I can't do this anymore," I vented as soon as Tony picked up. "She is driving me out of my mind, and I think I'm going to snap. I feel like screaming when this happens, and it's happening all the time. I'm stressed to the breaking point and don't know what to do."

Before Tony could answer I continued, "I'm going to crack if I don't get away from her and I see no way out. I think I need to move on—I can't stand it anymore."

Tony had mastered the art of calming me down, but this time he detected the desperation in my voice. He could tell I was serious about leaving Jane and jumped into his side job as my therapist.

"Do you honestly think you could leave her? After all these years, would you say goodbye and abandon her? She has no one else to take care of her and she would probably die; she's told you she can't imagine living without you. You are her whole world."

"I know that, but I can't see how I will make it through the rest of the week without losing it, and our flight home is always a high-stress event. There is no end in sight; this week will end, and the next trip will be right around the corner. I'm stuck, and now I'm panicking."

"Do you love her?"

"Yes, I love her."

"Would you actually abandon her, knowing it would destroy her? I know you too well—I don't think you could do that."

Admittedly, I could still enjoy being with Jane and I appreciated her friendship. I knew she was devoted to me and that she always showed her gratitude for all I was doing. I recognized Jane was lonely and she needed to know that there was someone who would look after her. I did not want to abandon her or lose her friendship.

"You're right, I couldn't. I think she would perish."

"Then try to make a game out of it. You have to disconnect—don't take it all too seriously—pretend you are watching a movie, and she is acting in it. Find the humor in it all—you've got to admit, she *can* be funny to watch."

"I know you're right. It's hard to do when I'm in the thick of it, but I'll take it day by day and somehow get through the week. When I'm back we can figure out ways I can deal with this, otherwise, my mental health is toast and you'll be putting me in the looney bin."

"I hear they serve some great butterscotch pudding there," Tony quipped.

88

The Switch

And then the stress ratcheted up another notch. I knocked on Jane's door at 11 a.m., as I always did, knowing we would head out for lunch promptly at 11:45. Although she had calmed down a bit by the time I arrived, I could tell she was still agitated. I was dreading going to lunch; there would be no end of people she could yell at there.

So, when Jane went to her bedroom to put on her earrings and lipstick, I went into the cabinet under the kitchen sink, took out the bottle of Kettle One, and slugged down a big gulp. It burned my throat and I almost heaved, but my brain told me it was the medicine I needed to get through lunch, and I believed it. Before she got back in the room, I took another gulp, and as soon as I heard the toilet flush, I took a third. The Great Deceiver had come to the rescue and the dopamine had been released. I cherished the momentary feeling of euphoria and felt fortified to face whatever dramas would play out at lunch.

When we got back, I helped Jane with her email correspondence and then wished her luck following up with her CPA, Merrill Lynch, and the bank. I hoped by the time we got together for dinner she would have the answers about her net worth. In the meantime, I had an errand to run.

I drove our rental car to AJ's Market and purchased a bottle of Kettle One. After a few sips of vodka and a long nap, I began dressing for dinner and thought: *By the time the car service gets us to Capital Grille and they bring our drinks, it will be 6:30. I'll just have a small one here and then I'll be good for whatever awaits me next door.*

Jane was wrestling with a clasp on her necklace, and she had received an email from the bank she couldn't understand, so she was agitated. Once again, when she went to her bathroom to put on her lipstick and earrings, I revisited the cabinet under the sink, swigged a big gulp of Kettle One, and settled in for the ride to dinner.

After thirty-eight years of drinking alcohol every night of my life, I changed my status from "nightly drinker and functional alcoholic" to "day drinker." I was about to spiral out of control. An addict doesn't think rationally about their substance abuse, and I now saw nothing wrong with the odd sip of vodka during the day; being with Jane warranted getting some kind of relief. I rationalized my behavior as a form of self-preservation—something I could stop as soon as I was back in Michigan and away from Jane.

The bottle I had purchased was empty by Thursday afternoon and I went back to replace it with two more—more than I needed to get through the next few days, but better to have too much than too little. I could always bring a half-filled bottle home with me and keep it in my room … in case.

That was the week my life changed forever. Alcohol can be an insidious killer and my new predator had just walked into the room and claimed me as its next victim—I was headed for three years of nonstop *sip, sip, sip.*

There is a Japanese proverb that says, "First man takes a drink, then drink takes a drink, then drink takes the man." I was under siege and would barely survive to tell the tale.

89

The Movie Ends

For twenty-five years, owning horses had been Jane's reason for getting out of bed each morning. Horses had provided access to an elite sport where she could socialize with some of the wealthiest people in the world while bringing honor to the U.S. with the medals they had won.

When Jane's last retired horse passed away, she was left with only UII. However, Jane's dementia was progressing, and her stress levels were going through the roof. Owning even one horse was proving stressful for Jane, so she sold UII to a friend's daughter for one dollar and offered to pay for a monthly shipment of California's finest hay for the rest of his life. Her life with horses had come to a close.

That was the same year my life with horses and riding ended.

My friend Anne Margaret and her husband Karl had a forty-five-acre horse farm in Madison, Georgia—about an hour east of Atlanta. Anne Margaret had earned a Bronze and Silver Medal of Achievement with the United States Dressage Federation and was working toward earning her Gold. I enjoyed working with Anne Margaret and her horses whenever I was at the farm and would check in with the progress of some of her students when I was there.

One of her students had been working through a few problems with her thoroughbred gelding with no success. On my next trip, I agreed to see if I could help. As I watched the gelding being ridden, I couldn't figure out the problems his rider was having, so I asked to get on. Apparently, the horse was having some trouble with his teeth and jaw; the vets were treating him, but the progress had been slow. I rode for about twenty minutes but I was unable to make him comfortable, so when I dismounted, I said, "You guys are doing the best you can, but this horse is hurting and probably shouldn't be ridden for a while."

I walked back to the house and thought: *How many times over the past twenty years have I been through this—investing my time and energy to fix training problems I didn't cause, getting on horses who didn't want to be ridden, and dismounting without having gained any enjoyment or satisfaction from the ride?* The answer was: thousands. Since establishing the Gil Merrick Dressage Academy in 2000, I had worked with hundreds of horses, and at some point, I had ridden most of them. The joy I had gotten from riding Pluto Alga, Alajos, Kalif, and Dancer had never been replicated. Training someone else's horse meant fixing someone else's problems, and although it could be incredibly rewarding, I needed to offset it with the pleasure of riding for enjoyment, and I hadn't since the day I sold Dancer. What I was missing was a personal relationship with a horse that belonged to me and was ridden by no one else—a horse that became my soul mate.

The next morning, under sunny skies and with a warm breeze, Anne Margaret suggested we head out on a ride around their property. She offered me her beautiful black Andalusian gelding, Onyx, for the ride—a horse I had worked with from time to time and knew well. For almost an hour we walked along the edge of the newly planted fields hearing nothing but hoofbeats and the birds in the trees. On open stretches, we would enjoy a quick gallop and then return to a brisk walk as we headed back to the stables.

It was the perfect way to bring fifty years of riding to its conclusion. I decided on that day to take off my boots for the last time, hang up my spurs, and cherish the memories of the joy horses had given me. *From Mr. Buttons to Onyx—in Fifty Years*: it sounded like a good name for a movie, and in my case, the movie had come to "The End."

90
The Chauffer's Diamonds

Over the past year, Jane had taken two falls—both while staying at the Club. The first was a slip getting out of the bathtub that landed her on its edge and cracked her rib. Jane had an extremely low tolerance for pain—combined with an extremely high penchant for drama—so for the next year, every move in or out of a chair or car, riding over the slightest bump on the road, or any movement of her upper body, produced anguished groans and yelps that seemed to have become reflexive rather than warranted by actual pain.

The second fall came when she was coming inside from inspecting the bocce ball court she had donated to the Club. She lost her balance and hit her shoulder when she fell against a brick wall. That occurred before her ribs had healed, so the combination of rib and shoulder pain became debilitating; she needed help with the simplest of tasks. I was brought into service to cut her food, squeeze lemons into her iced tea, open sugar packets, put on and remove necklaces, and lift all objects, no matter how small. She was becoming dependent on me and enjoyed the added level of service I provided.

Most valuable to her was my ability to listen patiently. She had always enjoyed telling stories about her childhood and growing up in an apartment full of servants on Park Avenue, but she was now telling those stories—along with many others—repeatedly. She shared with me the story about her wedding up to three times a day, every day, for months. Each time, the details changed, and the story no longer matched the facts. Jane asked every morning what day of the week it was, and then asked again at lunch, and again at dinner; she no longer knew what season it was. Her short-term memory was failing and her ability to remember names—whether of someone in the room with us, or someone from the past—was gone. I trained myself to listen to Jane as if hearing things for the first time and I engaged her in conversation about whatever popped into her head. It was a skill I never thought I would need, but I knew it was a valuable gift to Jane.

* * *

The Club always closed during the week of Labor Day and Jane did not want to stay at the house all week with nothing to do. She had heard that the Beverly Hills Hotel on Sunset Boulevard was under new ownership and had been completely renovated, so she booked two of their famous bungalows for a four-night stay.

She and Dick had enjoyed eating at Il Fornaio on Beverly Drive and she wanted to see if it had changed since they had last been there. To no surprise, after thirty years, it had; she hated it. The hotel sent a car to get us and when we got out, Jane looked ahead at the long, canopied walkway up to the lobby and said, "Sweetheart, I don't think I can walk that far. And our bungalows are nowhere near the lobby. I'm sorry, but I just can't do it."

The hotel swung into action and had a wheelchair at our disposal within minutes. I embarked on my first trip as Jane's wheelchair chauffeur and to my surprise, she loved it. She decided the leisure of being driven from "Point A" to "Point B" exceeded the embarrassment of being in a wheelchair and she declared it would be the perfect mode of transportation for any long distances. For the shorter ones—like getting to a table at the Club or Tracton's—holding onto my arm would be fine, but either way, I was responsible for her mobility.

The next morning, I drove us to one of Jane's long-time happy places—XIV Karats, a full floor of jewelry nirvana on South Beverly Drive. Jane had purchased her yellow diamond ring there as well as several pairs of earrings. Her contact was Cheryl—Jane's go-to person for any adjustments to her necklace or earring clasps, jewelry polishing, or heaven forbid, lost stone replacements. Our mission was to replace the clasp on a pearl necklace with one that was easier to open. Cheryl did not know about Dick's passing, so after a brief commiseration, she went about fixing Jane's necklace. When she returned from the workroom Jane said, "Cheryl, I believe you've met Gil before. Well, when I die, I am leaving all my jewelry to him, and I want you to sell it for him. Now, please promise you will only sell it to people who will treasure it like I have, and make sure you get the best price for everything; I paid a fortune for it, as *you* well know."

"I promise, Jane. But I won't plan on seeing Gil here for many years. You are a tough old broad and I'm sure you're not going anywhere soon." Jane laughed, commented on how gaudy a diamond and emerald necklace in the case was, and we were on our way.

91

Game Changer

Toward the end of March of 2019, everything changed. We were staying home on a Saturday night and while enjoying our drinks at the bar, Jane said: "Darling, I don't know what I would do without you. I'm not myself anymore. I used to be so active—able to do anything I wanted—but now I'm a mess; I can't do anything for myself. I've become dependent on you, and if I didn't have you in my life, I'd find a way to kill myself."

"Well, you *do* have me in your life, so it looks like we can take that off the list of things to worry about."

"Stop it! I'm not joking. I've asked you before—why can't you just quit that damned job of yours and move out here with me?"

"Jane, I'm with you way more than I'm ever in Michigan these days. As far as our investors are concerned, I'm still the Chief Operating Officer, and the operations are in Michigan, so I need to be there at least some of the time."

"I know. That's why I said, why don't you just quit the damned job?"

"Because I'm not even sixty-two, and although I've been able to sock away a lot of money these past years, I'm not in a position to retire yet. Besides, the company pays me well and if we eventually sell it, I stand to make a lot of money. I've got almost ten years invested in this and I'd be foolish to walk away from it now."

"Oh, for God's sake, I wish you'd stop worrying about money. Quit that job and move out here to be with me and I'll make sure you never have to think about money for the rest of your life. Would you do that for me?"

Jane had made a business proposition and demanded an answer. If I accepted her offer, I would have to resign, giving up my six-figure salary and all claims to any proceeds when the company sold. In exchange, I would be signing up for a full-time job as her companion, and based on how things were going, it would certainly include managing her healthcare.

Accepting her offer was a gamble. I would be trading one set of unknowns—

when the company might sell and for how much—for another: how much Jane would be leaving me in her will, how long she would live, and whether I had the emotional capacity to continue in what was already an almost intolerable situation. However the increased stress and lack of fulfillment in my job was also making that part of my life intolerable, so I faced a true dilemma. A side effect of alcoholism is that the sufferer can't make rational decisions, so whether mine was the right one or not, after weighing the two alternatives, I told Jane I would leave my job and move out to be with her full time.

Jane was beyond ecstatic, and true to her word, she made an appointment with her CPA, Dale, and the attorney he had recommended, Steven, to meet at the house and change her will. While Dale and Steven were assembling around the game table in the living room, they asked me to leave; since I was a beneficiary of the trust it was a conflict of interest for me to be there. Jane pushed back at their request, but I concurred and said it was the right thing to do; I went to my room and shut the door. At one point I could hear Jane raise her voice and I knew she was aggravated. After a few minutes, things calmed down and they met for another half-hour. After they left, we went to the bar, and I poured our first *lévrier*.

"I'm glad that's over with," Jane said. "They were fine with all the changes until I said that after the named bequests had been paid, I wanted the rest to go to you; along with the house, of course."

"That is incredibly generous. Are you sure?"

"Of course I'm sure; I promised I would take care of you. I told you—if I did not have you in my life, I would find a way to kill myself. You are the only thing that makes me happy."

"Wow—no pressure there," I said with a smile.

"But those jerks didn't want to do that. They said I should think about simply giving you some amount of money, like everyone else, and then leave the rest to something I cared about—like The Statue of Liberty Foundation or Niagara University."

"Well, you *do* care about them."

"Darling, I have already given them tons of money; they have enough. Dick and I have our names engraved on the pedestal of the Statue of Liberty—Lee Iacocca made sure of that—and I've told that woman from Niagara to quit emailing me and asking me to have dinner with her at the Club. I said she has all the money they're getting from me. I don't care that Dick's grandfather once saved the university from bankruptcy, they've gotten enough."

"Who won the argument?"

"What do you think? I did! The new man, Steffen, or whatever his name is, will bring by the changes next week so I can sign everything, but I want you to look at it all first; I don't know if he's any good. They were both a couple of cold fishes if you ask me."

Steven, not Steffen, dropped off the revised documents as promised. I sat at the bar and went through all the changes with Jane, and the next day we drove to her hair salon to meet Steven where Jane's stylist served as a witness and the documents were signed. As of April 2019, I was legally the "remainder" of Jane's trust and had a big job ahead of me in my official role as her full-time companion and healthcare manager. It was a role that almost killed me.

92

Time to Panic

My phone rang early one morning in June while I was preparing for my move from Michigan. I saw the call was from California and I knew it was bad news. The caller ID said it was Peter Schaub—the General Manager at the California Club—and it was 4 a.m. for him. He said an overnight guest had heard a scream in the room across the hall—Jane's room—and called the front desk. When the attendant knocked on Jane's door, she cried out and said she could not get up to open it. Using his pass key, he went in and found her lying on the living room floor and unable to move. When he told her he was going to call an ambulance, she became hysterical and threatened to get him fired if he did. All she needed was help getting back into bed; she would be fine, she told him. He phoned Peter at home and reported that Jane had fallen and needed medical attention, but she had refused to let him get it. That's when Peter called me.

"Mr. Merrick, it is Club policy that when there is any incident involving an injury, we are required to call an ambulance. Jane is being belligerent to my staff, and they don't know what to do. If she does not allow us to call for help, we will have no alternative but to terminate the lease on her suite and revoke the privilege of staying here as a resident. Can you convince her to let us call?"

I told Jane she needed to have the medics come, and the threat of being kicked out of the Club did the trick. The medics determined she had severe contusions on her left shoulder with significant bruising, but since nothing was broken, they did not need to take her to the hospital.

The immediate problem had been solved, but the more serious one came later that day in an email from Peter. He said Jane no longer appeared competent to live on her own and that she was therefore a risk to the Club. He and his staff were unwilling to go through another episode like they had that morning, and he was going to ask her to leave. She could remain a member of the Club but would no longer have residency privileges.

The thought of spending every day at home, every week, with no escape, threw me into a panic. I phoned Peter with an offer. "I know Jane has also leased the suite next to hers ..."—she had complained that the walls were paper thin and guests in the other room disturbed her, so she wanted it to always be unoccupied—"... so I could move from my suite to the smaller one next to hers and I would hear through the walls if anything ever happened to her. I am moving to California to be with Jane permanently, so I will always be at the Club if anything should happen. I would be there to help her, and your staff would not be bothered. I promise you I will not let her be a problem in the future: I'll be there."

Peter was willing to give it a try, so I moved from my large suite at the end of the hall to the tiny one next door to Jane's and accelerated the process of wrapping things up in Michigan and moving to California.

93

I'm Sick

The six months leading up to April 2019 were increasingly hard for me; I had been getting sick and I had no idea why. I complained to Tony almost daily that I had a horrible metallic taste in my mouth—like I had been sucking on old pennies all day. My sense of taste had been destroyed and I could no longer enjoy food; I was losing weight, and having been at 137 pounds for so many years, I did not need to be any thinner. I was ingesting alcohol throughout the day, and when I did manage to eat something, I could only swallow a few forkfuls before becoming nauseous. I usually finished a meal with a trip to the bathroom. I had developed a tremor that was so bad I could no longer write a check, fill out a form, or even keep food from spilling off a fork or spoon. I found myself lightheaded when I stood up and struggled to find my balance when I walked.

After nine years as my closest friend, Tony knew me better than I knew myself. He saw I was in trouble and made an appointment with his general practitioner in Michigan and came along as my health advocate. The doctor said my body was showing signs of metal toxicity and ordered a comprehensive battery of blood tests that included screening for heavy metals. The results came back and shocked us: twenty heavy metals had been detected, and my levels for mercury, nickel, lithium, and even arsenic, were off the charts.

In effect, I was being poisoned.

The internist referred me to a hepatologist and after extensive blood workups, she diagnosed a condition called hemochromatosis: a disorder that causes the blood to absorb too much iron from food and store it in the organs—especially the liver. However, this was to be a misdiagnosis. The hepatologist prescribed a series of phlebotomy treatments over the course of two months, hoping that removing a pint of blood each time would help my liver eliminate the iron. The treatments were successful in lowering the iron levels, but I felt worse, and the metallic taste did not go away. The doctors had no other answers or suggestions for treatment and said I would need to stay under observation until they came up with one. But what they did not know, was just how much I was drinking, and why.

Every time I settled into my first-class seat at LAX or San Diego, I felt a momentary sense of relief. *Finally—a break from Jane and some time to myself in Michigan.* Before the cabin door closed and I finished my first screwdriver, Jane would phone. That call followed the one I had received while passing through security, and the one after that while waiting to board. The four-hour flight ensured I could have several drinks in peace before landing because Jane's next call usually came before I could get my luggage. I was fooling myself; there was *never* a break from Jane.

Not taking a call and letting it go to voicemail would launch a torrent of follow-up calls with anguished voicemails, and ultimately, a call to Tony. It was easier to just take her calls—and Jane knew that. Whether I was traveling on business or visiting friends, I always called Jane at 7 p.m. I prepared for those calls with several drinks before dinner, and I drank glass after glass of wine during the hour we talked. Most nights at home finished with a few hits of pot to wind down and switch off.

My stays in Michigan were spent in a fog, and I was barely functional in the office during those last months before I left. I have no idea why the effects of my excessive drinking were not showing up in my bloodwork. If they had, we would have known what was poisoning me.

* * *

The poisoning intensified when Jane and I got to Camelback in October. I was drinking continually in my room, and finding every opportunity to drink more when we were together. So, one evening, when I got to Jane's casita and she left to finish getting ready, I made my customary trip to the cupboard under the sink. Jane came back to the room as I was standing up and she saw me lean into the wall, slide to the floor, and crumple on my side. I was out cold.

Surprisingly, Jane did not panic. Unaware I had passed out from alcohol, she was confused and didn't understand what was happening. She talked to me, shook me a bit, tried to get me on my back—all to no avail. She phoned Tony to ask what she should do, and he told her to give me some time to wake up. About fifteen minutes later, I came to. I told Jane I had been feeling dizzy and said I had stood up too quickly. I assured her I wasn't hurt but recommended we stay home. Jane was upset I had disrupted our plans for the evening, so I suggested she calm down with a drink, and of course, I joined her. Neither of us ate, which was fine by me; I hadn't had a normal meal in many months and knew that anything I tried to eat would come back up. My weight had already dropped below 125 and food was progressively tasting worse: the metallic taste had intensified. I had become both anorexic and bulimic.

I got through the rest of the stay without a major incident, but once back in Carlsbad, I did a repeat performance at Tracton's. After my dinner, consisting of orange slices as an appetizer and an ice cream sundae as the main course, we got up to leave for the car, and two steps from the table, I did a face plant in the crowded dining room. I did not pass out cold like at Camelback, but I blacked out when the dizziness took over. I got up right away and our regular server, Zandra, sent us home with the driver who made food deliveries; she drove Jane's car back the next morning with her husband in tow to take her home.

December was upon us, and I knew I needed to get my act together. We would take another trip to Camelback at the end of the month, and I had a Mastery Course to present there on January 6th that would require me to bring my "A-Game." I knew I was far from being able to deliver it and the stakes were high; I was about to re-enter my world as a Catalyst for Growth.

94

The Wrecking Ball

After eight years of riding in La Costa Limousine's cars, I knew a lot of the drivers. On a trip from the San Diego airport to the house in the spring of 2019—before I had completed my move to Carlsbad—I was riding with a driver I had met several times, Jeff Morris. I had been talking with Tony about a pivot we were making with the company's business strategy and when I hung up, Jeff said, "Do you mind if I ask a few questions about pivoting a business? It sounds like you know a lot about it."

"I'm pretty sure Jane will be calling soon to find out how far away we are, and when she does, I will probably be stuck talking with her the rest of the way, but until then, shoot."

Jeff was in the throes of managing his own pivot. He was an ex-marine sergeant who had spent six years as the founder and CEO of SpendSmart—an organization that provided financial literacy workshops and coaching services to underserved youth in at-risk communities. When Jeff was a young man living in Baltimore, he had been pulled from his car at a traffic light, shot, and left for dead. Rather than spend the rest of his life resenting the kind of young men who had almost taken his life for a car and some cash, he dedicated himself to coaching and mentoring those who had no skills around earning and managing money. He devoted himself to empowering disadvantaged youth to overcome their life circumstances.

He had founded a new venture, the DreamSmart Academy, and was developing an online platform where youth could connect with coaches and mentors. It would provide access to tools for enhancing their personal and professional relationships, pursuing careers, and thriving in life, regardless of the circumstances they had been born into. It was the first Black-owned behavioral science firm in the country and its mission was inspiring.

After filling me in on his background, I said, "That's an exciting mission—and you sound like an incredible guy—there might be a way we could work together." I told him about our company's technology for online coaching and Jeff thought it was a perfect fit.

We had offered to provide DreamSmart Academy with a license for our online training platform at no cost. In exchange, Jeff would help us network with peer organizations who could potentially purchase it themselves. It looked like my business development skills were still of value, but because of my commitment to live with Jane, by December of 2019, I had completed my move to California and had to resign from the company. I handed the project over to Tony.

Part of my strategy for surviving my servitude to Jane was to revive Mastery Concepts and go back to doing what I had a passion for: training and consulting in organizations like the DreamSmart Academy. Jeff and his co-founder had come to the house for several meetings. Jane was not going to be excluded from any new ventures I pursued and insisted she host the meetings at my new home office on Almaden Lane—the poolside veranda. I told them about my plans for Mastery Concepts and they invited me to become part of DreamSmart Academy's team of advisors; I was named Chief Mentor.

* * *

We scheduled January 6th for me to present my Leadership and Vision seminar to a group of Jeff's associates who were establishing a charter school in Scottsdale—one dedicated to youth empowerment. We held it at Camelback's business center. Jane sponsored the cost of the conference room, lunch, and refreshments, and in return, felt she had earned the right to serve as hostess. I sensed a disaster waiting to happen; any thoughts about leading a seminar without interruptions by her were misguided. Jane would need a babysitter, and her friend from Prescott, Patty, offered to drive down for the day and be her handler.

Jane greeted people on arrival and, with a lot of help from Patty, filled out their table name tents and made sure the catering staff were doing their jobs properly. After lunch, Jane was exhausted, and Patty rolled her back to her casita. I wrapped up late in the afternoon and went back to the casita, where Jane declared *her* day to have been a success and said she was looking forward to *our* future events.

I finished the seminar that day on a new high. I had cut back on my drinking considerably during the week leading up to it, and I was feeling somewhat alive again. That optimism was dampened by the knowledge that I would have to manage Jane every step of the way; she would be the ball and chain around my leg. I was struggling to find a way to manage my dilemma when a force bigger than anything the world could have imagined found its way into our lives and changed everything: Covid-19.

Within two months of delivering my seminar, people stopped gathering for face-to-face meetings of any kind, and my plans to revive my Mastery Courses ground to a halt. I felt like a wrecking ball had slammed into my head and knocked me off my feet. By April of 2020, the California Club had closed, as had Tracton's, and I was imprisoned in the house with Jane. It became my dungeon.

Jane spent her days in a rage. She was not used to having the things she loved most taken away from her, and she had never dealt with the word "no" before; she had *always* gotten what she wanted. She could not understand how some little virus could ruin her life, and she was angry.

My drinking became a twenty-four-hour ritual. I spent my mornings in my room—telling Jane I still needed to work on preparing course materials and handouts for future seminars—and sat in my chair, drinking vodka, and numbing myself from the inescapable pain of my situation. I was well and truly immersed in a more horrid version of *sip, sip, sip* than I had ever known.

95

The End Is Nigh

By the end of July, Tony knew I was in crisis. He had been speaking with Jane's friend, Bonnie, who knew me well, and they had been comparing notes about my health. As a retired pathologist, Bonnie knew my body was shutting down and that my demise was being accelerated by my heavy drinking.

Tony had briefed Bonnie about my medical history in Michigan and told her he phoned me throughout the day to make sure I was functional. He knew I was getting up throughout the night to have a drink. Jane had been phoning Tony, concerned about the days I stayed in bed up to sixteen hours, and reporting that I almost always ran to the bathroom in the middle of a meal to purge the food. My tremor was so bad I could hardly bring a glass to my mouth, and Jane had noticed.

Bonnie tapped into her network of medical colleagues and asked each of them one question: "If you had to see an internist, which doctor would you use?" Dr. Heidelberg at UCSD was their unanimous choice and Bonnie booked me an appointment.

Due to Covid restrictions, patients were not allowed to bring anyone into the building with them. Bonnie had phoned ahead, declaring me cognitively impaired and unable to walk unassisted. They left her name at the lobby desk so she could accompany me.

Bonnie filled out all the new patient forms, provided Dr. H with my medical history, and confirmed my symptoms. Dr. H prescribed a battery of labs and said that based on the results, he would schedule a series of appointments with the appropriate specialists; a complete diagnosis and treatment plan seemed a long way off.

I had a lot to process that night, but one thought kept me awake for hours. It had been ten years since fulfilling my dream of going to the Olympics. For thirty-seven years, every choice I had made served that dream; I always knew where I was headed, and my compass always pointed there. After leaving the USEF, I was like a cork on the ocean: bobbing along, going whichever way the current took me, with no dream as a guide, and no goals to achieve.

After all the challenges with Jane over the past two years, the opportunity to revive Mastery Concepts and partner with groups like the DreamSmart Academy had brought the hope of meaning to my life. It was all being thwarted by an insidious virus and my addiction to alcohol—neither of which was going away soon. It was only a question of which one would kill me.

96
A Matter of Life or Death

Even with the water running, I could hear Jane's scream. It wasn't her usual cry of pain from having moved the wrong way—it was a panicked shriek, followed by agonizing moans. I ran from the kitchen and saw her in front of the sofa, sprawled on her side. Jane was prone to drama, but this was no act. She had fallen after getting up and hit her left shoulder on the cocktail table.

After lunch, I had helped her over to the sofa. I had taken to giving Jane specific instructions to keep her safe—at this point, it was like managing a toddler: "Now stay there. I'll finish up the dishes and be back in a few minutes, then you can take your nap." I would then need to take her to her room—she could no longer get up the two steps from the living room to the hallway unassisted. But something had demanded her immediate attention—patience had never been her strong suit—and she tried to get up on her own.

Jane had lost all her muscle strength, and even with my assistance, she could not stand up. I knew she had hit her shoulder, but I had no idea how severe the damage was. Knowing Jane needed medical attention and hoping that with someone's help, I could at least get her off the floor, I called Bonnie. I did not need her medical expertise to tell me Jane had to go to the hospital, but the fight Jane put up confirmed my suspicion that I needed reinforcements.

"No! I will *not* go to the hospital. It's the *doctors* who killed Dick. Just get me some ice and Motrin and I'll be fine."

"No, Jane—you will *not* be fine. You *are* going to the hospital," Bonnie said.

It was October of 2020 and all UCSD's medical facilities had enacted full Covid safety protocols. Bonnie and I tested negative for the virus with a "rapid test," and we were both allowed to go into the emergency room. I was legally Jane's medical advocate and would have been the only person allowed to accompany her, but because of my own incapacities—my tremor rendered me unable to fill out patient admission forms—Bonnie was allowed in as well, but neither of us could accompany Jane into the examination and treatment rooms.

Jane had shattered her shoulder in fourteen places and needed surgery. Since neither of us could stay with her, Bonnie drove me to the house, and we planned to bring Jane home the next day. I had phoned Tony right after Jane fell. He had sprung into action and found a home care provider with the best reputation he could find. The company's owner met with Bonnie and me the afternoon Jane came home, and from that point forward, there was a caregiver 24/7. The house suddenly had a revolving door.

* * *

Bonnie had taken me to several follow-up appointments with Dr. Heidelberg, but he still did not have a diagnosis for my multiple, seemingly unrelated, symptoms. Alcohol poisoning was not yet suspected: I had been lying about how much I consumed. Dr. H declared me to be an "enigma" and ordered a more extensive battery of tests, including not only blood but urine and stool samples. The tests were scheduled for the 19th, and I realized that in four days, when my bodily fluids were sent to a lab for in-depth analysis, it would be better if they were not saturated with alcohol. Since the stakes were so high, I stopped drinking for the next four days.

My lab results confirmed what Bonnie had suspected: my organs were shutting down, I was jaundiced and suffering from malnutrition, and my brain was struggling to function properly. The clinical signs were those of a dying man.

I was admitted to the UCSD hospital on the La Jolla campus on October 22nd and did not come out until the 26th. After a series of ultrasounds, MRIs, CT scans, and endless blood work, I was released with a laundry list of prescriptions to fill and a full calendar of appointments with my new specialists: a neurologist, hepatologist, orthopedist, and psychiatrist.

My hepatologist saw me three days after I was discharged. My blood alcohol levels were five times those indicative of excessive, long-term alcohol use. He explained how my symptoms had manifested and the process by which my body was shutting down. The alcohol had created fatty deposits in my liver cells, which began to scar and die. As my liver lost healthy cells, it could no longer filter the heavy metals it was supposed to flush out. They had accumulated in my blood, which explained the metallic taste in my mouth. My liver could no longer remove the ammonia from my blood, so it had been accumulating in my frontal cortex, causing all my neurological problems. And being unable to remove the bilirubin, I had become jaundiced. Because I had stopped eating—or regurgitated anything

I had managed to get down—I was malnourished, and my immune system could no longer stop the destruction from the poisonous alcohol I had been ingesting for so long. Although I did not like hearing what it was, I was glad to have a diagnosis: hepatic steatosis and alcoholic cirrhosis. After forty-five years, treating my alcoholism had become a matter of life or death. I had to stop drinking or die.

97

Karen

The steady bouts of screaming and yelling that emanated from Jane's room were like slow water torture.

The changing of the guard was at 7 a.m., 3 p.m., and 11 p.m. I had moved from my bedroom into Dick's office so I would be able to meet each caregiver as she entered the kitchen, debrief the one coming off duty, and make sure any special instructions had been given. It didn't matter what schedule they might have been on; I would not have been able to rest.

Jane screamed whenever she was touched—or thought she was going to be—but they were not as much screams of pain as they were screams of distress; anticipation of pain was worse than the pain. She would scream as the caregivers approached to adjust her sling, pillows, or sheets.

The yelling was different: Jane hated the intrusion of the caregivers. She thought they were incompetent idiots. Jane became verbally abusive, and after threatening to hit many of them, she promised she would contact their employer and have them fired. A caretaker leaving Jane's room in tears was a regular sight and several refused to come back.

Between Jane's histrionics and the challenge of coming to terms with my own illness, I was stressed and distraught—and I now was going through detox. Tony had been talking to Bonnie and within days after my release from the hospital they called Jane's friend and CPA, Dale, to let him know what was going on. He learned Jane was incapacitated—physically and mentally—and I could no longer manage her care. Jane's medical records included "cognitive impairment" as part of her diagnosis and it was obvious her dementia was progressing rapidly. Dale and his wife, Karen, promised they would work with Jane's attorney to ensure that her care and financial affairs were taken care of while I was recovering.

The following Monday morning, November 9th, I went into Jane's room to tell her I would be gone for most of the day; I had an early appointment with an orthopedic surgeon and an afternoon appointment with a psychiatrist. As I was opening the door to leave, she asked me a question that caught me by surprise: "Do you still want the house?"

It took me a moment to understand that she was asking if I still wanted to inherit the house when she died. "Of course I do. I love this house and will always cherish it."

"I just wanted to make sure. It's yours, along with a sum of money when I die."

"Well, let's focus on getting your blasted shoulder to heal so you can stop hurting and then I'm sure you won't feel like you're going to die." She had nothing else to say and I left to meet Bonnie in the driveway to head for our first appointment.

I was quiet during the ride to UCSD, and Bonnie left me with my thoughts. I was contemplating: *What a strange thing for Jane to have asked.* It was as if, in her mind, something had changed. Why, after so many years, would I suddenly *not* want the house? And why did she feel the need to confirm she was leaving me money when she died? I didn't come up with any answers that morning, and when I got home in the afternoon, I had a whole new set of questions to answer.

As I was walking in the front door, two people I did not expect to see were coming out of Jane's room: Karen and Jane's attorney, Steven. I had met Karen many times over cocktails at the house or dinner at Tracton's with her husband, Jane's CPA. I knew Tony and Bonnie had spoken with them, but I didn't know what measures were being taken to manage Jane's affairs.

Later that week, on Friday morning, I learned that Jane was being removed as trustee of her estate, and according to the terms of her trust, Karen was the successor trustee. Karen wasted no time jumping into her new role.

I was sitting at Dick's desk the morning when Karen returned with Steven to have Jane sign the documents. After leaving Jane's room, Karen appeared at my door and said, "We've had to remove Jane as trustee of her estate, and I am now going to manage things. I need access to all her files. I also need you to give me Jane's driver's license, credit cards, checkbooks, and anything else she may have given you to keep, including her Rolodex."

I understood what Karen's new role entailed, and she was not doing anything outside of that purview, but the way she went about it disturbed me. It felt like she had been uncomfortable with my access to Jane's finances and was relieved to finally get everything out of my grasp. Did she think I was some kind of con artist who was going to bilk Jane when she died, instead of Jane's trusted friend?

I had been sober for the first month in my adult life—I had not had a drink since October 15th—and enough of my brain fog had lifted that I was cognizant of what was going on around me. I gave Karen everything she asked for and watched as she rummaged about, showing no regard for the intrusion on my personal space. One thing was certain: from then on, Karen was going to be "large and in charge."

98
Time to Die

Jane had been especially uncomfortable on the 23rd and complained about her stomach hurting. She said she did not have a "tummy ache"; her entire abdomen hurt, and I could tell she was in pain.

However, I had to leave for the hospital later in the afternoon for an MRI to determine the best procedure for neck pain and numbness I was experiencing in my arms. So, I said goodbye, asked the caregiver to check in with her every half-hour, and told Jane I would see her sometime the next day as I had to stay overnight to wait for an MRI machine to be available.

After I left, the pain became intolerable and to everyone's surprise, Jane asked for an ambulance to take her to the emergency room. It was the first time since Dick died Jane had proactively sought medical attention, and it was our clue that something serious was going on.

The next day, I got home after Jane did and Bonnie was there to explain what had happened. An ultrasound had revealed several malignant tumors on Jane's kidneys and the doctors said they needed to be removed. Jane had refused to undergo surgery and told them she just wanted to go home and die. Having refused all treatment, her condition was declared terminal, and she was prescribed home hospice as her plan of care. Jane was in her bed when I got there, ready to die.

The next day was the 25th and a physician from UCSD's hospice provider, along with Karen and Bonnie, were there to evaluate Jane and explain how her end-of-life care would be managed. Being an impatient woman, Jane said, in a frail, pleading voice, "I just want to die. Can't you give me a pill or something to kill me? Why do I have to wait? Just let me go. I want to be with Dick."

The doctor explained that under California's "death with dignity" laws, Jane was qualified to request medication that would hasten her death. Also referred to as "physician aid in dying," Jane would need to wait six weeks from the date she and her legal advocates agreed to the process, and at that point, she would have to demonstrate her capacity to make a decision and be able to ingest the medication on her own. For the last time in her life, Jane had succeeded in getting what she wanted: in six weeks, she would be on her way to joining Dick.

* * *

December dragged on forever. At first, the caregivers helped Jane go to the restroom. After a week of immobility, she had weakened to the point she could no longer stand and was bedridden. A single caregiver struggled to move Jane within the bed, and with my neck and back pain, I was unable to assist. Even if I had been physically able to, I was not mentally up to the task. Jane was in horrible pain and the morphine tablets did not seem to help much. Something triggered inside of me whenever I heard Jane scream out in pain and I couldn't bear to be in the room when she was being attended to. I would go to the den, shut the doors to the kitchen, and wait for her torment to stop. I could not escape my distress.

Every morning, after the caregivers had finished with Jane's morning routine, I would sit with her for a couple of hours. She slept most of the time, but when she was able, we would talk—about nothing in particular—but I felt it helped for her to know I was there. I checked in with her after lunch and then spent a few more hours in the evening by her side, even if she was asleep.

Zandra—Jane's friend from Tracton's—was coming to see Jane almost every day and helped take care of her most intimate needs. She respected Jane's dignity and treated her with the tenderness an underpaid caregiver would not. Although Jane seemed to know who I was, she was confused about all the people coming into her room. "Who was that tall, dark-skinned girl with the long black hair? She was nice. Those other girls are horrible," she would say, confusing Zandra with the caregivers. "And who was the little woman with the mousy-brown hair?"

"That is Karen—your CPA's wife."

"Oh—the one who took all my money," she said, remembering that weeks prior Karen had told Jane she needed to give her the checkbook Jane kept next to her bed—the last item that gave Jane any sense she had control of the most important thing in her life: her money.

As the end of December approached, it had become obvious Jane would not have the mental capacity on January 6th to make a decision about having her life ended—the day that would mark six weeks since she had asked to have a physician assist in her death. As we approached Christmas, Jane all but stopped talking. Her eyes remained shut and she was barely consuming any liquids. A doctor from UCSD came to the house to observe Jane's condition and saw that she was failing. Zandra was there and confirmed she could not get any meaningful amount of food or liquid into Jane.

The doctor got Jane to open her eyes long enough to see him when he said, "Mrs. Brown, you *must* try and eat something, or at least try to drink. If you do not, you will die." And that is all Jane Brown needed to hear. After weeks of pleading—"Please, just let me die. Why can't you just let me die *now*?"—the doctor had answered her questions. And with the resolve she had shown throughout her life to get what she wanted, when she wanted it, Jane took charge of her destiny and stopped eating and drinking. It was time to die.

99

It's Over

I was about to give away a half-million dollars. January 2nd was a Saturday, and I was sitting at my desk when Karen came in. She and Zandra had been with Jane and things had been unusually quiet. The morphine dosage had been increased and Jane was finally out of pain, but it was also causing her body to shut down. So, it surprised me when Karen put a piece of paper in front of me, handwritten by her, that she asked me to sign. "Jane said she would like to give Zandra her rings—the yellow diamond and the sapphire—and I know you believed Jane was leaving them to you, so I thought we should have something that says you are OK with that. Are you?"

I did believe Jane was leaving the rings to me, not only because of the trip we had taken to XIV Karat to plan for their sale, but also because I had read Jane's will every time she changed it and she had always bequeathed them to me. But I also knew that as the "remainder" in Jane's trust, I was going to inherit a large sum of money, and on the scale of things, a half-million dollars' worth of jewelry would not be that material. To avoid an uncomfortable situation, I said, "Sure. I guess I'm fine with that—if that's what Jane wants. Zandra has been a good friend to her."

"Are you sure? You're OK with it?"

"Yes. If that's what Jane wants, then of course I'll sign the paper."

Karen had prepared a document that removed any claims I might have had to the jewelry and any right to contest the gift. That seemed odd because Jane was still alive, so the jewelry was not part of her estate; giving it to Zandra was a personal gift and not part of an inheritance. I had to wonder how Jane had suddenly found the mental capacity to ask for Zandra to receive the rings and to sign a legal document. She had stopped talking after the hospice doctor had seen her. At the end of that day sitting with her, she had not known who Zandra or Karen were. It all seemed strange, but I let it go.

* * *

On January 6th, exactly six weeks after she was told she could die on that day with a physician's assistance, Jane died unassisted. She had once again gotten her wish.

Cindy was Jane's manicurist and had become a supportive friend to Jane and to me. Cindy had come to the house that day to see Jane for what she knew would be the last time. After an hour with Jane, she joined me in the den and spoke two words, bringing to an end a long saga: "It's over." We shared tears and a hug, and then Cindy told me about Jane's final moments.

Karen and her husband arrived an hour later, and the coroners arrived a few hours after that. Before moving Jane to a gurney for her last trip out the front door, they asked if anyone wanted to go into the bedroom to say goodbye. I went in alone and stood at the foot of the bed, looking at her deflated body, until I could bring myself to say something out loud: "I loved you, Jane. You were an incredible woman, and no one who has ever known you, will forget you. We've been good to each other and have had quite a ride together. You will always be special to me."

I stayed in the room for a few more minutes and let myself cry silently. Although I would have expected my mind to go quiet with the somberness of the moment, it flooded with questions: *What kind of a life did Jane really live? Did her privilege, indulgences, luxuries, and good times bring her happiness? Or was her life an endless series of upsets, angry moments, and nonstop frustration?* How sad, I thought, to have lived for eighty-six years and to have possibly never been at peace.

I walked behind the gurney and watched it being loaded into the hearse. As the taillights rolled out the driveway and up the hill from Almaden Lane, the reality of Jane's death hit me. Standing in front of the house, both sadness and relief welled up and my eyes filled again with tears. Something inside felt empty—like a chunk of me had been cut out. Jane had become not simply a part of my life, but a part of who I was. I had designed everything in my life in service to her and our friendship, and the realization that I was no longer needed for that, unsettled me. *What comes next?* I had known for six weeks that Jane's death was imminent, but I had never played out a scenario of what would follow. My relief seemed selfish, and feelings of guilt began taking over; Jane was the one who had died under such sad circumstances, and I was the one who was alive and on the road to recovery.

Fortunately, it did not take long for everyone to disperse, and by 9 p.m., for the first time in over a decade, I was by myself in the house.

For the past few years, Jane had followed me from room to room like a puppy, always wanting to be by my side—whether I was working on my laptop, talking on the phone, or even doing yoga on the terrace. She was terrified of being alone and I was her security blanket; and yet I was suffocating. I had only known the house to be a place where Jane and I were together; now it felt unfamiliar to me, and I was lonely.

I had gotten used to sleeping in the den and took comfort in spending that night on the sofa. After three months, there would be no rumbling of the garage door, no caregivers changing shifts, no cries of pain from Jane's room, and no more yelling. The revolving door had been removed and I was freed from my dungeon.

100

Time to Thrive

I don't know how Jane's funeral went. I chose not to go. Not because I didn't want to go, but because I got the distinct impression my presence wasn't welcomed. Those who did go felt no need to share many details with me. As far as I know, nobody on the list of people Jane wanted at her funeral in New York City went. Jane had always wanted Tony and me to manage her funeral, but Karen had taken over. I guess, in the end, there *were* some things Jane wanted she could not have.

For two days after Jane died, I phoned everyone on my long list of people I felt should know about her passing. It was heartwarming to hear their kind words, sprinkled with anecdotes about fun, and funny, times spent with Jane. Jacquie Mars had been a special friend and asked to have a photo. I sent her a copy of one of my favorites: Jane in a bright red jacket with her head thrown back in a joyous laugh. Jane's last social outing had been the night she and I went to Jacquie's home in Rancho Santa Fe for dinner, just the three of us. Jane's health was failing, but I know she reveled in the knowledge she had spent an evening with one of the wealthiest women in the world and could call her "friend."

Karen came and went during the first weeks of January and let me know I was allowed to live in the house until the estate was settled, but until then, neither the house nor its contents belonged to me, and I was to leave everything exactly as it was.

My priority was the management of my well-being, and I gave it rigorous attention. I began my day with an hour of yoga, followed by a sunrise meditation on the deck, twenty minutes of water aerobics, and a three-mile walk through the neighborhood. Three times a day I took my medications: Naltrexone to help with alcohol cravings, Lexapro to manage depression, and a whole host of other drugs to assist my brain in ridding itself of excess ammonia and help my liver to detoxify—fourteen prescriptions in total.

I was managing my alcohol addiction and depression with the help of a

UCSD psychiatrist and his licensed clinical social worker, Monique. She had started working with me shortly before Jane died and helped me get through the difficult period after her death, living in a house full of nothing but triggers, and helping me understand the diseases of addiction and depression and the costs of living with untreated trauma.

I came to understand that seven years of Joe's sexual abuse had been traumatizing—although I did not recognize it as trauma until decades after it happened. I had also not seen how traumatic the past few years with Jane had been. I learned the term "emotional kidnapping" and had to work with Monique for a while to understand that I had in fact been living as a hostage, in a situation I had enabled.

After years of Jane's relentless control, it seemed easier to quit my job and move in with her, than to continue with the ill-founded hope of getting a break from her while in Michigan. I learned that sometimes deciding to do what seems easiest is the wrong decision. It was a lot to take responsibility for, and it brought back memories of my previous therapy sessions with Dr. Macbride when all my life situations had been evaluated in the context of one question: How did I let it happen, and why?

Working with Monique was different. She provided what Dr. Macbride had not: explanations of what addiction, depression, and trauma are; how the brain processes experiences and memories; and how chemicals in the brain affect our decision-making.

I was beginning to understand the complexities of trauma. The rapes I had suffered at the hands of the Pataki brothers and Dennis were singular events— each one traumatic in its own right. My vulnerabilities had been obvious, and my abusers took advantage of them. Years of persistent sexual abuse by Joe were a different kind of trauma. I learned it is called Complex PTSD and involves betrayal by the predator over a sustained period.

I could see that allowing my vulnerabilities to be exploited through acts of violence and betrayal were partly due to my childhood fears of not fitting in and not being good enough. I wanted to please and be liked and therefore established no boundaries to protect myself from predators. I was no stranger to betrayals— in my career and in personal relationships—but I had never understood how and why they had transpired. If only I had, I may have been able to protect myself from the one that was about to be revealed.

101
Encore—Duped and Betrayed

My MRI from November showed that the surgery on my neck required an anterior cervical discectomy with fusion: ACDF. The surgeon would enter my neck from the front and remove the three arthritic discs that were putting pressure on my spinal cord and causing the pain and numbness. He would implant a plate with several titanium screws to stabilize my spine. The procedure would take close to four hours. I was scheduled for February 9th and the surgery went beautifully. I was sent home with a neck brace I would wear for several months.

Tony had flown out and helped with the first few days of my recovery as I learned how to get about and take care of myself. I was told the best physical therapy would be daily walks. I barely managed to get to the top of the driveway on the first day. Tony made sure I did not come crashing down on the pavement, took me inside, and helped me for the next couple of days until I was able to walk on my own.

Until I met Tony, I had never had a true friend who was there for me every day, no matter what, and his compassion for my struggles and his commitment to be my partner in getting well were an invaluable part of my recovery. Tony said if I felt the urge to have a drink—day or night—I should call him. I found that one good friend they say you need in life.

Cindy continued to be a friend to me. She arranged for her mother's previous caregiver, Mina, to come once a week to clean my house, do the laundry, change the bed, and cook some of my favorite dishes. Mina also began the long and arduous process of cleaning out Jane's cupboards, closets, and drawers. Cindy came by regularly and between her and Mina, I had a surrogate family looking after me.

* * *

On March 8th I was returning from my walk and stopped at the end of the driveway to get the mail. There was a large brown envelope from the law firm handling Jane's estate, and I knew what was inside: a copy of Jane's will and a letter to the beneficiaries of her estate advising them of her bequests. The document answered the questions I had asked myself in November when I had seen Karen and Jane's attorney leaving her bedroom. I finally knew what had transpired in the room.

Jane had made two amendments to her trust. I had been removed as "remainder," and instead of receiving the assets that were left after paying out her named bequests, I was given a specified sum of money. Although Jane had been generous in her bequests to others, they totaled a small percentage of her assets, and the difference between what I would have received, and what I was going to receive, was significant. The second amendment was the one that removed Jane as trustee and named Karen as the successor trustee.

I would never know how that change to my inheritance transpired, what conversations were had in private, what Jane might have thought was going on with my health, or why it was her last action as trustee of her estate. All I know is that Dale and Steven had pushed back when Jane asked them to designate me as remainder of the trust, and they had tried to get her to leave me a specific amount of money and have the remainder divided between the Statue of Liberty Foundation and Niagara University. They had won their argument because that is what had happened when they met with Jane on her deathbed.

I was still receiving the house and its belongings—minus the jewelry I had signed over to Zandra. It occurred to me that on the day Karen asked me to sign the paper saying I had no claim to that jewelry, she already knew I was not the remainder, and she also knew I had no idea what had changed. It explained why Karen needed to ensure I would not contest anything once I realized I had been duped—and that Jane's promises had been circumvented, if not broken. Although I would inherit the house and its belongings, at sixty-three, with the potential of at least another twenty years ahead of me, earning money was still going to be a concern.

When Jane asked, "Do you still want the house?"—something *had* changed. I would never know all the details. But at least I knew where I stood and I could plan for the next phase of my life, and no longer need to wonder if there were any surprises in store.

Part Five

PERSONAL BEST

Sobriety, self-discovery, and a new life

102
Shared Dreams

I had promised Jane I would live in her home and cherish it as she had. In fact, I thought I would live there for many years, and to get a fresh start, I wanted to modernize it. But when I learned about the revised will, the renovation project changed to a "staging" project: I would need to sell the house. I knew to the penny how much it cost to maintain and run it and I was no longer willing to commit to those expenses for a house that was much larger than I needed— especially since it was filled with depressing memories. I needed to go somewhere I could heal.

Tony told me he had taken several family trips to Vero Beach. It is a small town on a barrier island off the Atlantic coast, midway between Miami and Orlando. It is not an especially popular tourist destination, although it offers everything a tourist could want: beautiful beaches, a seaside town with boutique shops and great restaurants, a handful of resort hotels, an arts and theater community, an inland waterway flanked by private yacht moorings, and lots of paths for walking and biking. It has been called "The Hamptons of Florida".

Tony did not have to work hard to sell me on taking a trip to check it out. I booked a room with a balcony view of the ocean at the Costa d'Este, a resort owned by Gloria Estefan and her husband, and I flew out to see what life there would be like.

I arrived in the evening, opened the doors to my balcony, and took in the scent of the ocean. Lulled to sleep by the sound of the waves, it was one of the best night's sleep I had ever had. After coffee on the balcony, I took a long walk on the beach, looking at the homes and condominiums that hugged the dunes, imagining what it would be like to step outside my door every day and take the same walk I was enjoying.

Tony had made an appointment for me at the Sotheby's office in town and my realtor spent the day showing me a dozen condos in gated communities with direct access to the beach. By the end of the tour, I had seen several that I loved and confirmed my budget would allow me to buy something similar. I went back to the resort to phone Tony and thanked him for, once again, being right: Vero Beach would make the perfect home for my new life.

* * *

On the morning I was to check out of the Costa d'Este, I was looking at my online newsfeed and came across an article about the 2020 Tokyo Olympics. Due to COVID-19, the Games shifted to July 2021, and they were beginning in three days. I still checked in from time to time with the world of international dressage, and I knew Heather had become an active supporter of dressage in the U.S. and owned some of the top horses in the country. The U.S. won team silver in 2018 at the World Equestrian Games, and in 2019 at the Pan American Games. Heather had owned a horse on each team and her top stallion was now on the 2021 Olympic team.

I brewed another cup of coffee as I looked out on the ocean and reflected. Heather and I had known each other since we were twelve years old. When we were fourteen, we had both been inspired by Joe's assertion that with hard work, a goal to achieve perfection, and the discipline to train rigorously, the dream of one day going to the Olympics could become a reality. That was the night he had invited Heather and me to stay at his house, and that was the night Heather and I dedicated ourselves to fulfilling that dream.

After the upcoming Games in Tokyo, we both would have traveled down the same path: from a World Equestrian Games to the Pan American Games, and then to the Olympics. From the day we embraced our dream, life had presented us with different circumstances, and we had each made choices in the face of them that led us down that path. We had started with the belief we would go to the Olympics as athletes and compete, and we both ended up going, but in different roles than we had imagined. The power of dreams is amazing.

Heather was an active rider, competing at the international level, and she owned some of the world's top dressage horses. She served on multiple boards of directors in service to promoting and sustaining the sport of dressage and was respected throughout the horse world. She had achieved success at a level that would enable her to go to as many Olympic Games as she wanted.

I had left the USEF and given up the life that had gotten me there. I stopped riding and walked away from a sport that had fueled every passion in my life. That morning, on the balcony, sipping coffee and contemplating my new life in

Vero Beach, I became painfully aware I had spent the last decade without a dream to live into. I was still that cork on the ocean, going wherever the tide carried me, falling prey to the destructive forces of my depression and addictions.

But that morning, I was in a mood to celebrate the victories we both had achieved and to see them as confirmation that dreams can be the most powerful force in our lives. It was time for me to create my next dream and invent a future that would lead to new victories.

103
Closure

Escrow on Jane's estate closed at the beginning of August and the house was finally mine. I hit the "go" button for its sale and within three days of its listing, it sold.

Mina had spent months preparing everything for a final clean-out. Dick and Jane had thrown nothing out in the forty years they lived there. Every drawer, shelf, and cupboard had been stuffed with a life's worth of odds and ends, none of which had any value, emotional or otherwise. I gave many photos and pieces of horse memorabilia to friends who said they would cherish them and sent the rest home with Mina, who promised to display them as proudly as Jane had. Clothing was donated to Goodwill, the furniture and artwork were put into consignment for sale, and I set aside a few of Jane's *objets d'art* to take with me. PODS delivered their smallest container to the house and within an hour Mina and her son had it loaded with the few things I was taking with me, and it was on its way to Florida.

I had contacted my realtor in Vero Beach and told her I was ready to find my dream home. She sent a link to a listing on Zillow, and I knew immediately it was the place where I wanted to live. I had seen properties in the condo's neighborhood and there were three dozen photos to review. I trusted my gut and made an offer at the asking price. By the end of the next day, the condo was mine.

I spent my last day on Almaden Lane reflecting on the past years. After yoga and meditation by the pool, I took my customary three-mile walk around the neighborhood and enjoyed the hilltop views of La Costa Resort. I imagined the days when Dick and Jane had played golf there and decided to buy an acre of land and build their home for weekend escapes from Los Angeles, never imagining it would be their permanent residence for forty years.

I went into each room and marveled at the transformation it had undergone with the staging. I was glad I would leave with new images to help replace the nightmarish ones from the last year in the house. My bedroom would become the guest suite for the new owners' grandchildren when they came to visit, and Jane's room would be a brightly lit master suite with a welcoming sitting area and direct access to the pool and gardens. And I realized that my decision to sell the house and move as far away as possible was the right one, regardless of my financial situation. With too many painful memories in that house, no amount of remodeling or renovation work would have erased them.

I didn't sleep well during my last night there—my brain was too busy reflecting on the past and planning for the future—but a single thought told me everything was going to be for the best: for the first time in my adult life, I was sober.

104

Reconciliation

The Eagle has Landed—I've finally arrived in my version of paradise. Those were my thoughts pulling into the gate at the Palm Beach International Airport on the evening of September 2nd. The documents for the purchase of my condo were signed before noon on September 3rd, and I moved right in.

I had a Sleep Number bed delivered that afternoon, but otherwise, the only furniture I had was a canvas beach chair with a fold-out side table the previous owner had left behind. My PODS container would not arrive for another week, and the new furniture I had picked out would arrive in dribs and drabs after that. Tony had offered to help with the interior design, and I gave him one theme to direct the whole project: bright, modern, and cheerful. Marie Kondo would have been pleased to hear me say, "Everything in my home is going to spark joy; if it doesn't, I don't want it there."

I left home for eight weeks while renovations were underway and spent most of the time with my brother, Doug, in Ohio. While staying there, something about New York called to me and I wanted to visit the city again. When I moved away in 1989, my life had derailed: my business failed and I was bankrupt; the only healthy relationship I had ever known had ended there; I was also deeply in debt, homeless, and unemployed. I had always loved New York and had revisited many times since 1989, but this time I wanted to go with the sole purpose of bringing closure to my past so I would be able to enjoy the city in the future.

I stayed at the Ritz-Carlton on Central Park South and got a room with a view of Central Park. I went by Dick and Jane's apartment buildings on Park Avenue and then visited my old apartment on 86th Street. I passed the Frank E. Campbell Chapel on Madison Avenue and the Carlyle Hotel, where Jane had held court before Dick's burial. I walked my old commute down Park Avenue to the office building at 57th Street and went through Times Square for a stroll through the garment center and to see the home of the embroidery business.

I took the ferry to Liberty Island to visit the statue that had meant so much to

Dick and Jane. Inside the museum entrance was the large display of major donors to the Statue of Liberty Foundation. The plaque dedicated to members of *The Pedestal Club* held the inscription for "Richard H. Brown & Jane S. Brown"—the place of honor they had received decades prior for their generous donations to the Foundation. I had to wonder, because of the major bequest coming the Foundation's way, if the Browns' name might eventually be moved up a level to *The Crown Club*. Jane had been happy with their place in *The Pedestal Club* and felt no need to donate more money, but in the end, whether she intended to or not, she did.

I spent an entire day walking through Central Park reminiscing about the hundreds of hours I had spent there. When I walked past The Ramble, I paused to give some thought to the voyeuristic acts I had engaged in there forty years before.

Most of my sexual experiences—consensual and non-consensual—had been with men. I had only had heterosexual experiences with two women: Alexandra and Diane. Following the many years of Joe's sexual abuse, and while in my relationship with Dennis, I came out as gay, convinced that I must be. Yet, when I met Alexandra, I experienced a depth of emotional and sexual connection that I had never experienced with a man. I wanted to hold her and kiss her and share my body with her. I longed to be with her if only to gaze at her. I had never felt that way about Joe, or Dennis, or Mark. With Alexandra, I came to understand why intimate sex with a man had always been impossible for me—I was straight. After my experience with the Pataki brothers, even with women, having oral sex performed on me was out of the question. I could never break through the psychological barrier my trauma had built.

When my relationship with Alexandra ended, I returned to my old habits of seeking voyeuristic and anonymous encounters with men. Perhaps the need to feel sexually attractive in the face of my failed relationship had me return to places where that kind of attention was familiar—behind shower curtains in the gym, or within the bushes of The Ramble. I also came to realize that my boyhood explorations, compounded by the years of sexual abuse by a pedophile, normalized homosexual experiences for me, and enabled me to embrace the gay community and its lifestyle. As my friend Loren had once so clearly said to me, "You are not gay, that was only a phase." I had to agree. Being gay was never what I was, it was what I became; encounters with men were the sexual experiences with which I was most familiar.

Admittedly, I liked to admire and touch lean, well-built men. Yet, my attraction was always to their athleticism and the image of what I wanted for myself. I enjoyed being able to touch an athlete's body and appreciate it—like someone attracted to a beautifully sculpted marble statue might be. But even before the rapes, I never craved physical intimacy with men, regardless of the sexual acts involved.

Once I left New York, all that behavior ended. Now it was time to put my past behind me and open up to the possibility of one day having a healthy, intimate relationship. I needed to turn off the little voice in my head telling me I wasn't worthy of a woman's love and that I was somehow lacking. Alexandra had given lie to those thoughts, and after thirty-four years, it was time to discard them.

105

Thriving

It was off to the races with my new full-time job: managing my well-being.

I had done extensive research about cirrhosis and the immune system's ability to regenerate healthy liver cells. I already knew a lot about nutrition, yoga, meditation, cardiovascular exercise, strength training, and sleep management—I had been rigorous about managing them throughout my life as an athlete and trainer. But I wanted to up my game and challenge myself with a new level of discipline. From now on, every action I took would be in service of fulfilling my commitment to thrive.

There was a wealth of information on YouTube, and from time to time I would come across a testimonial from someone who had been diagnosed with advanced cirrhosis and had been successful in restoring their liver to normal health. I came up with my own theory based on those testimonials: if the immune system were functioning as efficiently as possible, it should be able to slowly dissolve the dead cells in the liver and eliminate them through the bloodstream. It would be a long process, and since the science seemed to prove cirrhosis was irreversible, I was playing against the odds. But I loved the challenge.

There was certainly no downside to strengthening my immune system. I would commit all my time and energy to my healing, using all the tools from my Mastery Courses with new rigor and a level of discipline I had not known before. It was time to live my life masterfully again, and for the first time, I would live true to my teachings while sober.

When I returned home to Vero Beach in August, I continued to do exhaustive research—this time on nutrition, especially as it related to supporting a healthy liver. I made major changes to my diet. I committed to a program of daily intermittent fasting: dinner at 6 p.m., breakfast sixteen hours later at 10, and lunch four hours after that at 2—with no snacking in between. I ate only whole foods and cooked everything myself. I put an end to eating rice, bread, pasta, potatoes, and most dairy. Nothing came out of a can, nothing had ever been frozen, and nothing contained sugar or additives of any kind.

Breakfast was no-fat Greek yogurt with a cup of organic blueberries, lunch was a large green salad with either avocado or apple slices, dinner was usually a legume dish with some version of roasted or sautéed vegetables, and dessert was a piece of dark chocolate, or maybe some pears with honey if my sweet tooth kicked in. I started each day with the juice of two lemons squeezed into a glass of iced green sun tea and drank nothing but water throughout the day. And every morning featured coffee made with freshly ground organic beans.

My research showed that by adhering to my new nutrition plan, I should be able to reduce inflammation in my joints and soft tissue. I had experienced some arthritic pain in my hands and knees, but I wrote it off as a normal part of aging. My stomach had always felt slightly bloated, due to my previous two nemeses: sweets and salty snacks. After a year on my modified diet, all the inflammation left my body. I experienced a new vibrancy in my entire being, and the pain left my joints; in fact, I was 100 percent pain-free.

My sleep pattern had been erratic throughout my life, and for the first time, I had complete control of my sleeping habits. I read about the importance of having a routine for going to bed and training my mind and body on how to sleep. The last half-hour of the day was spent reading and I was in bed by eleven. I had a "starting position" on my back when I got into bed where I allowed myself to replay the movie of my day, then a "second position" on my left side where I listened to the surf and focused on my breathing, and a "final position" on my right side where I told myself it was time to go to sleep. After a few months, my brain figured it out, and I fell asleep before going into the "final position."

I always set my alarm for 5:45 and went right to a one-hour yoga routine in front of the open sliding door—drinking a bottle of water and listening to the surf—followed by a twenty-one-minute meditation in the lotus position.

My next activity was twenty minutes of water aerobics, and every day at low tide, I took a three-mile walk on the beach. Everything I had read, every YouTube video I had seen, and every doctor I had spoken to, concurred: walking every day was the best exercise anyone could get. I had been walking three miles a day, every day, for the past two years, and I had never felt better.

Three times a week I went to Vero Fitness. I signed up for three months with a personal trainer who designed a program that developed my strength while protecting my spine. It was the best gym I had ever belonged to. With expansive, open spaces, state-of-the-art equipment, a large cardio area, an outdoor lap pool, and a clientele that was fit, energetic, and serious about improving their health, it was my go-to place for immersion in an environment dedicated to well-being.

The Cleveland Clinic was my new healthcare network and my internist had access to all my medical records from UCSD. After reviewing my new blood panels and conducting a full physical, he declared me to be in great shape. He referred me to Dr. Burke, a hepatologist at the liver center on their main campus near Palm Beach, and in May I had my first appointment with him.

Dr. Burke said my bloodwork looked "good" and I was doing "well," but before my follow-up visit in six months, he wanted me to have a Fibro scan: a type of ultrasound that specifically analyses the amount of scar tissue and fatty deposits in the liver. He wanted to know how much of my liver was damaged and what my monitoring and treatment protocols would be going forward. Cirrhosis also predisposes the liver to cancer, and I was at high risk.

I knew of nothing else I could do to manage my physical well-being and I was enjoying every part of my new lifestyle: it required structure, planning, and discipline—things that I craved. I woke up every morning well-rested, energized, pain-free, and ready to take on the day—I was thriving.

106
The Simple Things

From the day I drove down the wooded lane to meet Rosemarie Springer at *Gestüt Halloh,* I continued a journey that had me interact with—and in many cases, befriend—some of the wealthiest people in the world. I enjoyed visiting their homes and estates, eating at exclusive clubs and five-star restaurants, and flying in private jets to stay at luxurious resorts. I managed an elite equestrian sport with a group of athletes, horse owners, and sponsors who lived lives most people only see portrayed in movies.

But I was always aware of how unhappy and unfulfilled so many of those people were—like Jane, with nothing ever being enough or to her liking—always wanting more, despite all they had. Many had dysfunctional relationships with their partners and families. Many were tormented by their own life traumas. Many were overcoming, or lost in, the grief of losing spouses, friends, and family. Many struggled with addictions to alcohol, drugs, or both. Just like everyone else, regardless of their wealth and apparent successes in life.

I had lived the past two decades embedded in social circles where alcohol took center stage—nightly parties in private homes, fundraising galas and award ceremonies, celebrations for victories—but until I lost my way with Jane, I had stayed highly functional, even with the nightly drinking. It's no accident I designed my life to be included in those social circles, but in the end, it almost killed me. It certainly brought the message home that money does not buy happiness.

My new lifestyle in Vero Beach revealed the incredible sense of fulfillment I got from the simplest of things. Whether going through my morning yoga routine, sitting in meditation, walking on the beach, doing water aerobics, working out at the gym, planning and preparing meals, or practicing mindful eating—everything was an opportunity to be present in the moment and enjoy the experience. I was no longer driven by the unrelenting need to quickly wrap up whatever I was doing so I could jump ahead to the next activity, knowing that as soon as I began that one, my mind would be racing off to the next. In two years, I had escaped from imminent death to now embrace a life filled with joy.

After my hepatologist told me it was alcohol that was killing me, I was in a state of disbelief. I could accept my medical condition—I understood what was happening to my body and why—so I was not in denial. But I could not comprehend how I had let the events in my life transpire to the point that I was killing myself. I was a well-educated, conscientious, and disciplined man who had spent decades teaching others the principles for living life masterfully, using my life as my training ground. I simply could not believe I had been blind to my alcohol addiction and ignorant of the damage it was wreaking on my mind and body. I needed to understand how it had gotten to that.

I committed to managing my mental health with the same rigor I brought to my physical well-being. I already had a fantastic support structure in place. Tony phoned, without fail, every day. His compassion, understanding, and sage advice were something I could count on. My last drink approach had been on October 15, 2020, and on the fifteenth of every month for the next year, the mailman delivered a small brown envelope from Tony with a half-dollar-sized token celebrating another month of sobriety. The front of each bore the inscription: "To Thine Own Self Be True," and on the back was the Serenity Prayer. Tony never spent a day wondering how I was doing or whether I would get through twenty-four more hours without a drink; he knew. He was walking with me on my path to sobriety, one day at a time.

In 2017, Mary Gober felt it was time to leave London and move back to her home in New York. Four decades after starting her own business and empowering thousands of people throughout the world to transform the service culture in their organizations, she handed off her legacy to her team in London.

Our visits to London had allowed us to catch up on major events in our lives, but they were relatively quick and followed by long periods where we did not talk. After her return to New York, we spoke regularly, and she coached me through my struggles in California. After Jane died, we had calls every week that usually lasted for longer than an hour. Mary was the most gracious person I had ever known, and every call became her celebration of my successes. I cherished them. She also agreed to take on a very special role: she became one of my writing coaches.

I had been told by my therapist that one of the best ways to gain a deeper understanding about our lives was to write about them. Writing the story of our life, for ourselves, was proven to be a therapeutic process for bringing closure to past events and our experience of them. Telling my story honestly—without judgement or blame, acknowledging the failures, and celebrating the successes—would be a powerful way to answer my questions and free me up to invent a new dream. I had never been healthier, and I was sober, so it was time to figure out where my journey would take me next. Writing was a perfect form of therapy, and I had all the time I needed to do it.

I spent the first few months in my new home creating an outline of my life. Always a fan of Excel, I put together a spreadsheet with a chronology of where I had lived and what I had been doing there. The process was harder than I thought it would be. Remembering the dates of key events in my life posed its own set of challenges. Visualizing being there, understanding how I experienced everything, and seeing what impact it had on my choices going forward, was even more difficult. Tony had heard most of my life stories during the hundreds of hours we had traveled together, on our morning walks, or talking on the phone in his role as friend and therapist. His input to the project was objective and insightful and helped me tremendously.

In writing my stories, I could see how the circumstances of my life—from the day I was born—had shaped who I became. At every turn, I faced new circumstances—some that I created myself, and others that life had simply thrown in my path. I could see how each choice led me to the next, and how I made each choice in service to fulfilling my dream to become an extraordinary horseman and go to the Olympics. When those dreams had been fulfilled, I embarked on the next decade without a commitment to anything other than earning enough money to retire comfortably. Mary and I both saw that minus any passionate dream to call me forward, I had floundered and made choices based on what was in front of me in that moment, without regard to a grander purpose.

By November of 2022, I had been sober for two years, and I had spent a year writing my story. During these two years, I had been competing against myself—like a rider executing a dressage test—and I had finally achieved a "personal best" that lay beyond what I had ever imagined. But I knew it was not going to be the pinnacle. I would raise the bar and strive for my next personal best. And after that? Raise the bar again.

107

Like Father, Like Son?

I scored my next personal best with my health outcomes.

In May, I made it through the rush hour traffic on I-95 and arrived early at the Cleveland Clinic liver center in Palm Beach. I was scheduled at 9:30 for a Fibro scan—an ultrasound procedure that would tell my hepatologist how much of my liver was healthy and functioning properly. The procedure was quick and simple and ten minutes later I was in Dr. Burke's office.

He switched on his monitor to review the imaging and said, "This is really interesting. Your steatosis grade is zero—which means you have essentially no fat in your liver. And what's even more remarkable is your Fibrosis score; it's F0-F1, which means there is no scarring. Mr. Merrick, you have a perfectly healthy liver. You have no cirrhosis."

Hardly able to believe what he was seeing, Dr. Burke went back to the screen to reconfirm the efficacy of the Fibro scan and the validity of the results. He questioned whether I had perhaps been misdiagnosed at UCSD. He accessed my records there and reviewed the lab results and notes from my doctor. He then asked me to confirm my original symptoms. There was no question my symptoms had been consistent with cirrhosis.

Dr. Burke appeared to be at a loss of what to do next; he hadn't treated a patient before who had reversed their cirrhosis. I helped him out by explaining how I had spent two years devoting all my time to managing my well-being.

"How did you stop drinking?" he asked.

"I wanted to live. It seemed like a binary choice: keep drinking and destroy my liver for good, or get the help I needed to stop drinking and stand a chance at living a long life. I got help."

"Well, that's amazing. Given your results today, there is nothing for me to treat. Let's keep you on a program of biannual abdominal ultrasounds—to be safe—and we can have a Telehealth call to follow up after each one if that works for you."

I floated out of his office and made my way to my car.

I phoned Tony from my hands-free as soon as I got onto the freeway and gave him the news. About three minutes into the call, an eighteen-wheeler in the right lane pulled in front of me with no warning, leaving less than five feet between us. Had I not braked when I did, the truck would have clipped the front of my car, and at sixty miles per hour, the crash could have been fatal. After screaming a stream of obscenities at the driver and apologizing to Tony for blasting his eardrums, I calmed down enough to say, "Well now, that would have been the kicker. Sixty-five years old with a clean bill of health for the first time in my life, and it all could have come to an end because of one idiot in a truck."

Tony told me to get over it and celebrate my win.

* * *

On the heels of a full recovery, it was certainly time to celebrate my victories and personal bests. But something was keeping me from embracing them fully and being able to declare a victory on all fronts. There were still some internal forces putting a negative cast on what should have been an unbridled celebration of my new life.

I would get up every morning and look out at the red hues from the sun rising over the ocean horizon, palm trees waving in the breeze, and pelicans passing by my third-floor balcony. But as soon as I felt the joy of living in my version of paradise, destructive thoughts would take over. I became anxious that it was too good to be true, afraid that something would cause it all to go away, worried that someone I loved would deliver news that they or their loved ones were sick, or injured, or had been dealt a bad blow.

I would stand on the deck leading across the dunes and gaze in both directions, excited to begin my walk on the seemingly endless stretches of sand, in disbelief they would be available to me every day, anytime I felt like enjoying the solitude of a walk in the surf. But disempowering thoughts were always there: persistent feelings of inadequacy, lurking in my subconscious like a ghost in the attic—haunting me. *Maybe I'm not worthy of having this. Maybe I'm flawed and undeserving.* Those were the thoughts of someone who as a child felt he didn't measure up to the other children, thoughts of being less than he should be, thoughts of being unlovable. That would explain my lifelong quest to be perfect in everything I did, to always strive to do more, to be the best, and to disprove what others might think about my shortcomings; my need to be liked and accepted—to belong.

I knew they were the unsettling and omnipresent thoughts that were harbored in the mind of the traumatized. These thoughts kept me from the one thing I had been searching for my entire life: peace with myself, and peace with the world around me.

Like the character Brick in *Cat on a Hot Tin Roof,* I had been drinking since my twenties in search of that elusive *click:* hoping the switch in my brain would have flicked on when it was numb from alcohol, bringing me peace—but it never did. I was successfully managing my addiction to drugs and alcohol, and my sobriety was a victory to celebrate, but my depression and PTSD had not been treated with psychotherapy since I left California, and their ongoing presence haunted me. I knew that until they were treated, I would always be at risk of having that one bad day—just one distressing event—that could cause me to take my first sip and send me right back down the path to drinking. Or just as frightening, as happened with Miguel in Lisbon, I could become elated with a new experience and turn to alcohol to celebrate, wrongly thinking I could handle "just a few drinks." I knew alcoholism was a disease that cannot be cured; it can only be managed. I found myself haunted by the fears of a relapse and the knowledge that my recent victories could vanish in a heartbeat.

Even in those low moments, I never stopped telling myself there was nothing "wrong" with me. Looking back, I could see that what happened, had simply "happened"—because I was there when the circumstances appeared. Sometimes I created them, and other times they were thrown in my path. But things didn't happen to me because I was flawed, or lacking, or unworthy. In every situation, I made the choices that moved me forward to the next situation, and the next set of choices. Like everyone does in the face of their circumstances, I did the best I could with what I had at the time.

I had been thinking a lot about my father. I didn't know him well during the first ten years of my life—he had always been away from home, in a bar—but he had been sober for the seven years before he died, and I finally got to know him then. I remember watching him around horses when we went riding together or loading and unloading the car on our family ski trips, driving fourteen hours to Sandbridge for summer vacations, or skating along the rinks and coaching Doug's hockey team. He had always been calm and patient—full of humor and joy. A tranquility surrounded him, and he seemed at peace with himself, and the world. I learned after attending his Alcoholics Anonymous meetings that he was a man of faith. He began every day on his bed, reading from *A Day at a Time*—a collection of daily reflections based on the spiritual foundations of AA—and a copy of the Holy Bible was always on his nightstand.

My father found peace in his life, sourced in his belief in a Higher Power. He had been a vivid example of the power of faith—right in my home. I couldn't recognize his peace and tranquility for what it was because my depression and anxieties had driven me out of the house and into the stables—a place where I felt safe and could thrive. I had needed to get away from the sadness of being at home with our emotionally unavailable mother and to escape from the fear of being bullied at home and at school and the pain of not fitting in. Those choices led me straight into the grips of Joe and his sexual abuse—trauma I had never treated. My father had self-medicated with alcohol after World War II to treat his PTSD, and I had done the same—like father, like son.

But I knew there was no power in playing the role of a victim: regretting events from the past, blaming others for my misfortunes, or lamenting what could have been. All the power in life comes from taking responsibility for the way things are, accepting the way things have been, and inventing our future, day by day, based on our passions and dreams. I had all the tools at my disposal to live a fulfilling life and celebrate new victories along the way. And for the first time, I was ready to ask for help from a power I had yet to invite into my life—it was time to believe in miracles and pray.

> *God grant me the serenity to accept the things I cannot change,*
> *Courage to change the things I can,*
> *And wisdom to know the difference.*

> — Alcoholics Anonymous—and my father

THE END

Epilogue

As soon as I told my friends and family I was going to publish a memoir, many of them asked: "Aren't you afraid to make yourself vulnerable to the opinions of others?" They reminded me we all have parts of our lives we are embarrassed about, or even ashamed of—things we regret having done and wish no one knew about. "Aren't you worried people will judge you?"

I told them all, *no*—that was exactly why I wrote my story and why I wanted to share it. There are eight billion people on this planet, and I'm only one of them. But there are certain things about how we live our lives that every one of us has in common; they are the things that make us human. There is nothing shameful or embarrassing about being part of humanity.

Some of us will have a dream that inspires us, and we will be fortunate enough to have access to the resources that can help us fulfill them—others won't. Many would call that luck, or fate, but I don't believe in those. I believe every human being can dream and invent a future that wasn't obvious to us after we were dealt our hand of cards. And no matter how awful our circumstances may be—whether we created them or had them thrown at us—we *always* have a choice about what to do with them. Even Holocaust survivors, prisoners of war, hostages, and victims of natural disasters had choices to make in the face of life's most horrific circumstances. Each of them will tell us the dreams that empowered them to endure, move forward, and survive.

I believe living life masterfully is an art. It requires being brutally honest about the facts in our life at any given moment—being able to say "what's so" without attaching any meaning to it or judging ourselves negatively: "It is what it is—I've done what I've done. Where do I go from here?"

From that place, we can invent dreams, and realizing them will require more from us than is available at the time we create them: new tools, teachers who will show us how to use them, coaches who will inspire us to achieve more than we think we can, and mentors who can guide us along the way. It becomes our job to search for those resources, and if we don't know where to find them, ask for help.

When we do, our success will be accelerated by our willingness to trust our teachers, coaches, and mentors fully—to surrender ourselves to their methods—

and never lose sight of the passion and commitment they have for our success. And if we are fortunate enough to encounter a true master—someone who isn't *doing* something that inspires us but is *being* that thing—we are well served to make the choices that enable us to be in their presence as much as they will allow. A mentor who takes us under their wing is one of life's greatest treasures.

Living life masterfully does not require money—it requires human connections: finding people who believe in us and are willing to help us along the way. But if we don't tell them where we are headed, they can't help us get there. Our responsibility is to invent a dream and declare our commitment to realizing it to those who can help us. Doing that is a matter of choice, not money. I have always believed that anyone can live their life masterfully, but it takes an act of heroism to do so.

> *A hero is an ordinary human being*
> *with an extraordinary commitment to empowering themselves.*

We can all be heroes, because each of us is an ordinary human being, and we need not be held back from fulfilling our dreams by events from our past or stories we tell ourselves that limit our ability to have what we want in the future. We all have our own stuff—the cruelties we have suffered, the mistakes we have made, the harm we have done. But I have come to see there is nothing wrong with any of us—everyone is doing the best they can with what they have at any given moment. Believing that allows me to embrace humanity and my part in it.

I wrote my memoir for anyone who is dealing with depression, addiction, or trauma—either their own, or that of someone they love. Telling my story is done out of a commitment to share my insights and thereby empower others to grow as they make their way through life. I would consider it a privilege if I could be a catalyst for that growth; it is a cause worth dedicating myself to, and a dream worth fulfilling.

I wish everyone a successful journey and say thank you for letting me be a part of it.

> *If I don't manage to fly, someone else will.*
> *The spirit wants only that there be flying,*
> *As for who happens to do it,*
> *In that he has only a passing interest.*

> — Rainer Maria Rilke

Acknowledgments

In 1997, while sipping a vente mocha at Starbucks, I shared with Linda Wetzel my love for writing and my aspiration to one day be published. Being a professional writer, Linda shared many of her insights, but one resonated for the decades that followed: "The biggest challenge for most writers is 'finding their voice.' Start working on that now, and it will serve you well." She was right. Thank you, Linda, for your inspiration and friendship.

Twenty-three years later, I began a course of therapy to heal from a lifetime of addictions. Monique was the therapist who helped me through my biggest challenges. Monique encouraged me to write my story as a way of healing. I spent a year chronicling the events of my life and revealed the connections between my circumstances, the choices I had made in the face of them, and the reasons for my actions. I was ready to pull out the major themes and thread them together as a story. The healing had begun.

Mary Gober has been my dearest friend since the day we met in 2002, in Sydney, Australia. After decades of living on different continents, Mary and I reconnected in 2017. She was there for me every step of the way as I broke the bonds of my addictions and found my way to recovery. When I was ready to begin writing, she asked the most important question any memoirist can ask themselves: "Why do you want to write your story?" Mary helped me rediscover my passion for teaching and showed me how sharing my story could help others understand the complexities of trauma. Thank you, Mary, for the gift you are in my life.

After twelve months of writing, I knew it was time to turn my story into a memoir. I began doing extensive research that included reading *The Memoir Project* by Marion Roach Smith and *The Art of Memoir* by Mary Karr. I watched hours of YouTube videos that delved into the craft of being a successful memoirist. On the day I found Brenda Smit-James's channel, I knew I had found my book coach. I received an email from her with "The 7 Key Ingredients to Writing a Great Memoir," and Brenda invited me to join her writing group. Within weeks, I engaged her to be my book coach. She taught me that unless I were a celebrity, nobody would really care about my story, no matter how well the scenes were written. She showed me how to turn my autobiography into a memoir that would give something of value to its readers. Brenda guided me through multiple drafts of the memoir, providing insights that were critical to making it a meaningful story. Her compassionate coaching kept me "doing the work that needed to be done"—regardless of how long it took to get it right. Without Brenda's coaching, there would be no memoir.

Halfway through the project, Brenda suggested we engage the help of her colleague, Melody Ann Owen, the founder of Author Nation. Melody joined our team as a developmental editor and brought a fresh set of eyes to the manuscript. She shared her expertise in crafting a story that focuses entirely on the reader's experience and ensured the memoir fulfilled its promise of being rewarding to the reader. At every turn, Melody's input made this a better book.

Early in the writing process, I came across a man I've never met, but who has helped me tremendously: Jerry Jenkins. Jerry is the *New York Times* best-selling author of over two hundred books. He is dedicated to helping people who are passionate about achieving their full potential as a writer. After watching several of his YouTube videos, I joined his online Writers Guild and learned an immense amount about story writing—especially when it comes to editing. His advice is to "self-edit aggressively," and he showed me how. His input has been an invaluable contribution to my education as a writer, and I apologize ~~to him~~ for every unnecessary word or phrase in the manuscript. ~~I did my best.~~

And special thanks to the man who has stuck with me through everything for the past fourteen years: Tony. With all I have put him through, he is still willing to pick up the phone every day and continue with me on my journey. His words of advice over the two years writing this book—when I would overthink my story and fret about the details—provided the kick I needed to power on: "Just shut up and write your damned story." I hope he had as much fun during that time as I did; I know all the other years were a real picnic.

www.ingramcontent.com/pod-product-compliance
Lightning Source LLC
Chambersburg PA
CBHW042137140626
46547CB00038B/745